D0811053

The Listener's Companion

Series Editor: Gregg Akkerman

This series is devoted to giving readers a deeper understanding of music by teaching them how to listen to key works by major musical artists and composers from recognized musical genres.

Titles in the Series

Experiencing Stravinsky: A Listener's Companion, by Robin Maconie

EXPERIENCING STRAVINSKY

A Listener's Companion

Robin Maconie

THE SCARECROW PRESS, INC.
Lanham • Toronto • Plymouth, UK
2013

Published by Scarecrow Press, Inc.
A wholly owned subsidiary of The Rowman & Littlefield Publishing Group, Inc.
4501 Forbes Boulevard, Suite 200, Lanham, Maryland 20706
www.rowman.com

10 Thornbury Road, Plymouth PL6 7PP, United Kingdom

British Library Cataloguing in Publication Information Available

Library of Congress Cataloging-in-Publication Data

Maconie, Robin.
Experiencing Stravinsky : a listener's companion / by Robin Maconie.
p. cm. — (Scarecrow's listener's companion series)
Includes bibliographical references and index.
ISBN 978-0-8108-8430-4 (cloth : alk. paper) — ISBN 978-0-8108-8431-1 (ebook)
1. Stravinsky, Igor, 1882–1971—Criticism and interpretation. I. Title.
ML410.S932M26 2013
780.92—dc23
2012038525

™ The paper used in this publication meets the minimum requirements of American National Standard for Information Sciences Permanence of Paper for Printed Library Materials, ANSI/NISO Z39.48-1992.

Printed in the United States of America

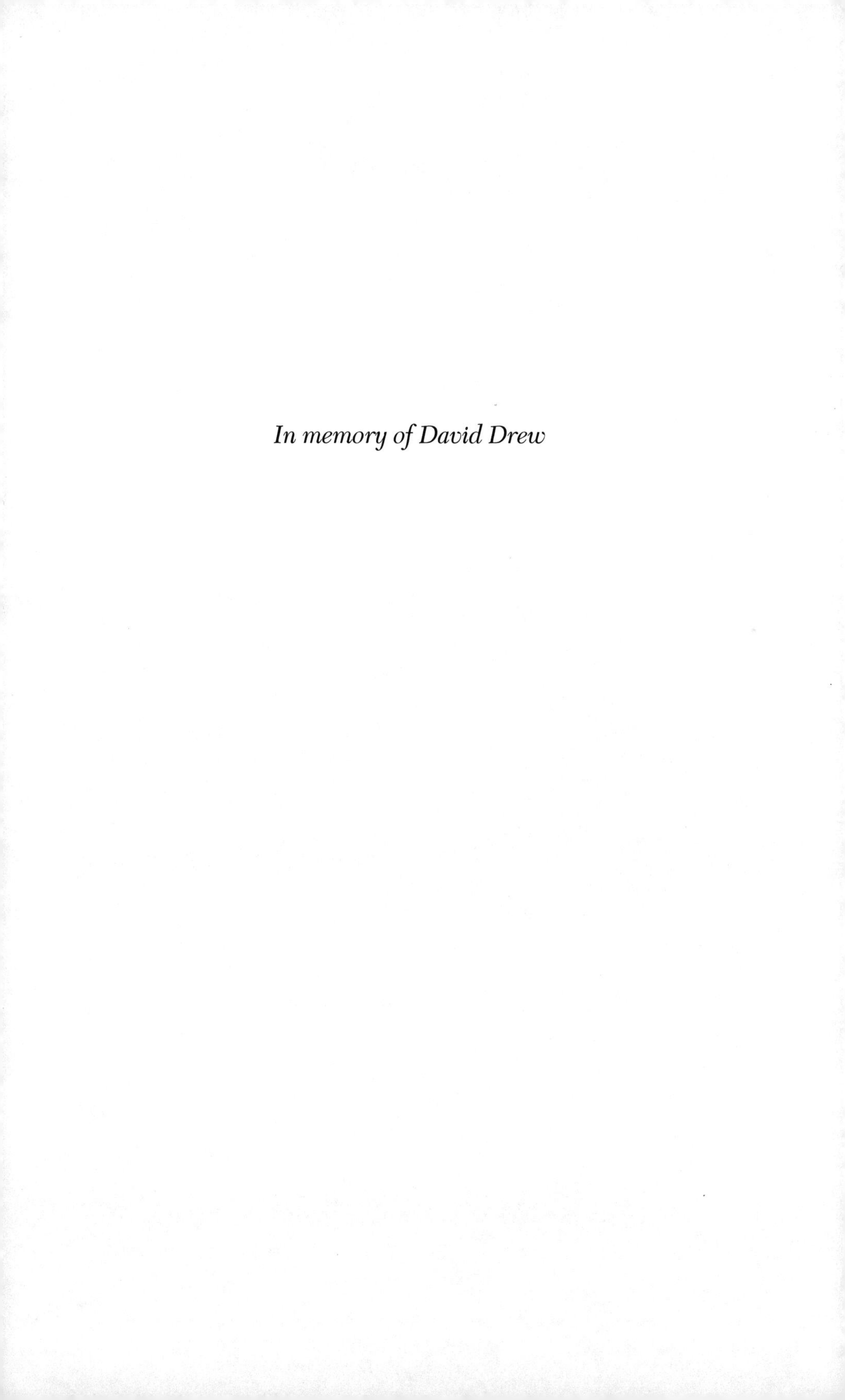

In memory of David Drew

CONTENTS

SERIES FOREWORD

The Listener's Companion is a series devoted to giving readers a deeper understanding of key musical genres and the work of major artists and composers. It does so by describing in lay terms the structures and historical contexts that serve as the ground for our experience when we listen to representative examples. By placing the reader in the real or supposed environment of the music's creation, a deeper enjoyment and appreciation of the art form are laid open. Authors within the series, drawing on their own expertise as performers and scholars, offer readers a broad understanding of major musical genres and the achievements of artists within those genres as a lived listening experience.

With these goals in mind, no better subject could be offered to launch this series than the work of Igor Stravinsky, without whom no thorough discussion of posttonal music is possible. Stravinsky is one of the world's most revered twentieth-century composers and designated one of the one hundred most influential people of the century by *Time* magazine. Even after his death, honors continued to crown his achievements, including a Grammy for lifetime achievement in 1987. During his lengthy career, Stravinsky was at the forefront of compositional movements that included primitivism, neoclassicism, atonalism, and serialism. What better example could be found of a composer who embraced the disparate genres of his lifetime to create work of such consistent brilliance and relevance? From his childhood years hearing his father sing in the opera to his waning years as an Americanized mentor,

Stravinsky steeped himself in music across cultures, wars, academic divides, and rapidly changing societal tastes in art.

With the rapid onset of technological advances during the opening decades of the twentieth century, music found itself, with other art forms, dragged into the postindustrial age, leaving many composers of these transitional years unable to convincingly bridge the gap. Not so Stravinsky. From his early successes with the Ballet Russe in the form of *L'oiseau de feu*, *Petrushka*, and *Le sacre du printemps* to his dalliances with American jazz to his experiments with the posttonal compositional styles of the midtwentieth century, Stravinsky made music that begs to be listened to with an informed ear. Although sometimes accessible to the music hobbyist, much of Stravinsky's music benefits from studied guidance—a helpful soul willing to offer the occasional traffic sign and map coordinates.

Robin Maconie is uniquely qualified to serve as that guide. His past writing accomplishments, which include four books for Scarecrow Press, demonstrate his remarkable ability to condense so broad a musical life into a series of cohesive topics. Throughout, Maconie challenges us to recognize that Stravinsky's music is the reflection of an age and its temperament at a level one rarely sees in any artist for so long a period. To learn how to listen to the music of Stravinsky is to better understand all art music of the twentieth century and ultimately pull into focus larger elements of our recent history. With his vast knowledge of Stravinsky and his milieus, Maconie delivers what is truly a first-of-its-kind complete guide to an informed musical appreciation of Stravinsky's works. As the title of this work advertises, Maconie opens wide the door to listeners truly interested in *Experiencing Stravinsky*.

—Gregg Akkerman

PREFACE

In the part of the world where I live, the most memorable art event of 2009 was a television commercial for Fresh'n Fruity yogurt ("Wrecking Balls," by Colenso BBDO, which can be seen on the Internet). It purported to show what happens when plain yogurt and fruit flavors collide, in slow motion, against an appropriately alien background of Wassoulou traditional female song from southern Mali (or something very like it). The visual experience brought together an art of slow-motion science film with the action painting of Jackson Pollock (e.g., *Number 23, 1948*, a souvenir postcard from the Tate Gallery, London) and African traditional music, all in the service of a product selling good taste, fresh flavors, natural goodness, and a healthy lifestyle. Anybody encountering that television advertisement would know in a minute what the art of Jackson Pollock was about, without having to know any art history—or if one did know the artist, in a way one was unlikely to have known him before. Best of all, the viewer would understand the beauty of it: that the message of Pollock's action painting is not all about destruction and chaos in the aftermath of war but nature in the instant—patterns of energy at a fundamental level, at that zone in the mind where art calligraphy meets the Large Hadron Collider.

To the point, Jackson Pollock died in 1956. Eadweard Muybridge and Etienne-Jules Marey—pioneers of stop-motion photography for the scientific study of time and motion in the natural world—completed their work, published their discoveries, and died the same year, 1904. Their discoveries inspired Picasso to cubism, Marcel Duchamp to paint

Nude Descending a Staircase, the Italian futurist art of Carrà and Boccioni, the animations of Walt Disney, and the science films of Mary Field and Percy Smith, makers of the *Secrets of Nature* series and codevelopers of the art of slow and accelerated motion (now cliché) featuring bullets passing through apples and drops from a milk bowl rising in a perfect circle like a crown. All of these artists are long gone. Even the advertiser's use of African traditional music is a reference to the impact of African traditional art on the twentieth-century European sensibilities of Picasso, Modigliani, Klee, Brancusi, and other greats. In other words, the success of a television commercial in 2009 is predicated on awakening and bringing together cultural memories that have been lying dormant in the Western psyche for sixty to a hundred years. If anything, it is a stark indication of how long it takes for new ideas—in this case, a climate of new ideas associated with European modernism between 1900 and 1950—to be assimilated into the consciousness of a media-aware general public. Even today, despite the impact of their discoveries, a reader may look in vain in a majority of dictionaries of the arts for any mention of Marey or the science movies of Field and Smith, let alone Wassoulou.

You might wonder why it should take a lifetime or more for the penny to drop. Think of modern art and most people still think of Picasso, and in music, Stravinsky. The informal definition of modernism is any art of the twentieth century that challenges the perceptions and values of nineteenth-century art. The idea that art is entitled to advise or instruct the taste of the majority is still seen as socially divisive and therefore intrinsically unsafe, and that is the problem, especially in the case of a classical music that is supposed to be all about social equivalence and group identity. Public acknowledgment of the status of a Picasso or a Stravinsky, despite their art remaining controversial, may have less to do with understanding their aesthetics than native respect for an older generation—a generation that, born in the late romantic era, has become part of history and survived into the cybernetic age, along with the vague intuition that, if we only knew how, their artistic development could be explained in relation to a lifetime of dramatic and rapid technological change.

Igor Stravinsky grew up in a world just beginning to come to terms with the telegraph and the telephone: a Sherlock Holmes era of mystery, bicycles, newspapers, intrigue, and hansom cabs; of trains and boats but, as yet, no cars or planes; before the information deluge of electrical power, sound recordings, radio, and movies. And he would survive into the age of television, IBM computing, Richard Nixon, and the first men on the moon. No lifetime before or since has witnessed revolutionary change on quite such a scale. So the question is not whether art endures over a lifetime with its aesthetic principles intact but how it may be possible to "read" Stravinsky's music and its many changes of style in relation to so turbulent a history and to emerge from the experience with a sense of the composer's artistic integrity still in one piece.

Books about Stravinsky are not thin on the ground. Most are literary or polemical or both. Studies of the historical record typically reflect the preferences of the scholarly community. In his earlier *Autobiography* and Harvard lectures (gathered together in *The Poetics of Music*), along with the later books of interviews and conversations with Robert Craft, published in the last decade of his life (and which form a critical addition to his musical legacy), the composer goes to deliberate lengths to distance himself from the views of orthodox scholarship to defend and endorse the music of his contemporaries and juniors—Schoenberg, Varèse, Webern, Boulez—against prevailing currents, even in the 1960s, of media and academic disbelief. This sin against the canon rendered Stravinsky an object of suspicion in conservative musicological circles. As a result, in a number of recent and ostensibly exhaustive scholarly surveys of the composer's life and bank statements, his personal reputation along with aspects of his music has been critically undermined. Part of the difficulty for scholars is that Stravinsky has a lively and mischievous wit and a talent to mislead. The composer has little patience, indeed shows no mercy, toward those who take themselves too seriously and who, musically speaking, do not get it. At the same time, his critics should take his views more seriously and to realize that behind the grin is the mind of a thinker, a rare philosopher in a musical world dominated by nonthinkers.

Learned analysis and criticism of Stravinsky's moral character—accompanied by accusations of a conspiracy of ventriloquism and astute self-promotion on the part of his junior colleague and amanuensis—have become a minor industry since the composer's death, with the effect, perhaps intended, of diverting public attention from strictly musical considerations. Needless to say, the composer's wit and tone of voice to which exception is taken are utterly consistent with his public and private views, dating from times long before Craft was born, as we now know from an abundance of correspondence and other material published after his death in memoirs to which the present guide will refer from time to time.

The more helpful issue is not arguing over whether Stravinsky's views are his own or who else's they might have been but discovering what the composer may have intended by them and how seriously they should be taken, since he forgave offenses as readily as he criticized and since he was scrupulous in distinguishing the opinion or object of reproach from the person expressing it, in the same way as a conductor corrects a false note in rehearsal without condemning the person making it—a necessary virtue in one whose orchestral scores and hire parts were not infrequently disfigured by former borrowers or copyist errors or subject to last-minute changes from the podium.

History is a funny thing. It is true that those who do not learn from the past are condemned to repeat it, though that is just another way of saying that we continue to live in the present with many of the same issues that engaged the best minds of former times, even though outward circumstances and the tools for dealing with the same issues may have altered dramatically. We are taught that history is about the past and that the past is another place, beyond our cognitive reach, when in reality there is no past but only people who move on. As St. Augustine declared and Stravinsky repeated, "Time does not pass. *We pass*." His music remains contemporary as long as the issues addressed in his music remain unrecognized and, in the case of his late serial music, unresolved.

Overstate the power of time's onward march to erase the past and its controversies, and you are likely to encounter history unexpectedly repeating itself. Philip Glass, Steve Reich, and John Adams are three leading US composers in a modern classical idiom widely, if imperfectly, recognized as American minimalism. In strictly procedural terms, minimalism belongs to the same organizational category as European baroque music, applying essentially the same techniques and strategies to attain much the same philosophical and organizational goals as the music of Vivaldi, J. S. Bach, Handel, and others from the first half of the eighteenth century, a genre of classical music that is, needless to say, still widely appreciated by the record-buying public in the twenty-first century.

The combination of features adopted by US minimalism in the mid-twentieth century is designed to reassure American audiences and make them feel comfortable with the onward march of time, and it is attuned to the restless dynamic of industrial progress, a combination of emotional objectives that in the seventies, an observer notes, is already some decades out of date, reflecting a wartime Movietone view of the world from when these composers were at junior school. The new minimalist aesthetic amounts in a functional sense to a staged revival of a baroque idiom dating from the time of the pilgrim settlers, ironically a progressive trend to escape which many first families may well have decided to leave Europe and settle in America in the first place. A time, in the early eighteenth century, when the British, a nation and world power of bankers, in newly expansive mood imported the German Handel to be royal composer in residence, to provide the imperial cause with morale-boosting music in the latest style. Distinctive features of the baroque aesthetic include a sense of abundant energy, an accelerated pace of life, and an attention to teamwork; a focus on keyboard-related programming skills, software design, and literacy; stressing the importance of time and motion planning, organized by the clock, and depicting images of growth and change by means of repetitive formulae inexorably modified over time.

In such fundamental terms, there is little to distinguish the aesthetic intention of a Philip Glass (or a British Michael Nyman) from the art of a Brandenburg concerto by J. S. Bach, equally based on motoric rhythms, multitasking, impersonal clock time, and production line values. A potential source of irony is that while eighteenth-century Europeans and twentieth-century moderns alike recognize such a way of organizing corporate music as an expression of contemporary values, for the European generation of Bach and Handel it represents a new style of people management, whereas for US minimalists the same combination of ingredients is open to interpretation as a subtle repudiation, rather late in the day, of traditional American values of freedom of action and self-expression. As exercises in the rhetoric of national identity and international relations, there is relatively little to distinguish the musical language and intention of Handel's "Zadok the priest" (from the oratorio *Messiah*) from John Adams's *Nixon in China*, both works on themes of kingship and international relations. Or the message of Adams's opera *Klinghoffer*—whose scheduling at the time of September 11 attracted press criticism on the ground of political insensitivity—from the equivalent aesthetic and human message of Bach's *St Matthew Passion*, also on the subject of the death of an innocent man at the hands of religious zealots. To make the comparison is not to condemn one at the expense of the other but merely to observe that a composer's choice of idiom and subject matter may also be tapping into universal cultural messages at a different level from personal taste and timely subject matter, along with the thought that public appreciation in the particular case may be influenced as much by cultural memory as persuaded by individual talent.

A mind-set that characterizes the music of Adams, Glass, Reich, and others as contemporary, because these composers happen to be alive, may be disposed to dismiss the music of a Schoenberg or a Stravinsky as passé or less relevant, simply because these great European geniuses and former Hollywood exiles are no longer living. All the same, the inherent paradox of attempting to dispose of still-problematic geniuses of the twentieth century by substituting present-day imitators of eighteenth-century manners may not totally be lost on fashionistas of the *New York Review of Books*, who continue to live emotionally and intellectually in the eighteenth century of Mozart and Franklin and decorate their literary-political opinions with period illustrations in the spirit and style of William Hogarth.

"The linguine, on the other hand, are quite delicious and not at all didactic." Woody Allen's postmodernist riposte[1] gets it about right: what matters is how the music tastes, and the taste of Stravinsky's music, whatever one might say about the composer, remains as fresh, piquant, and appetizing as ever.

INTRODUCTION

A book about listening, on the face of it, appears paradoxical. Books are for reading; records are for listening. What could be simpler? The musical legacy of Igor Stravinsky (1882–1971) evokes the trip of an extraordinary lifetime, extending from the tsarist Russia of Tolstoy and Tchaikovsky to Hollywood in the era of the computer and the first astronauts on the moon.

Most music books are written by specialists for specialists, not for the general reader, and tend to focus on one work at a time, in search for clues to the kind of person he was, not so much on the message he intends to deliver. Stravinsky's music is admired and feared in equal measure for its volatile mix of stylistic and rhythmic unpredictability, raw aggression, strident dissonances, plaintive high-alcohol emotion bordering on kitsch (or indeed, *kirsch*), exotic tone colors, intricate precision of gesture, dry wit, and a chameleon-like ability to adapt and blend in to any change in the prevailing cultural environment. Small forests have fallen in attempts to explain the composer's many outward inconsistencies as just another symptom of a twentieth-century musical culture in disarray, climaxing with an unexpected and aesthetically alarming conversion, after Schoenberg's death in 1951, to a personal version of the Austrian master's controversial "method of composing with twelve tones."

For an author, as for a reader and listener, the challenge is to find purpose and unity in a lifetime's creative legacy that, even a century after the premiere of *The Rite of Spring*, is perceived as disjointed and lacking in direction. The critic looks for consistencies in the music as evidence of artistic and, indeed, *moral* integrity: values at least of good citizenship, if not of great art. Stravinsky is an especially interesting case because it is only gradually becoming apparent that the consistency to which his music adheres is not where a scholar is likely to look, in textbooks of traditional aesthetics, but rather in the art of mechanically reproduced music.

Kandinsky's criticism of Matisse, that "his paintings are *pictures*," objected that the French artist was content to imitate how a painting should look, rather than inquire into the nature of the thing seen. In the same spirit one is able to identify Stravinsky's defining characteristics, building on the skills and techniques of his teacher Rimsky-Korsakov, as the exquisite and exacting imitation, in live instrumental terms, of the distinctive shaky rhythms, rustic sonorities, and artificially broken textures of the antique musical box, orchestrion, and pianola.

Why should we be surprised to encounter a music that is designed to sound like a luxury musical box, and does it matter? The idea of a machine aesthetic is clearly problematic for many listeners on the deeply philosophical ground that such music is incapable of having a soul. If the world of painting is supposed to instruct others in how to see the world and is having to face the challenge of photography in order to survive, surely it is fair and reasonable for artists such as Cézanne, Gauguin, or Seurat, let alone a Marcel Duchamp, to report in their own terms on the impact of technology on how the world is seen. Kandinsky himself was inspired to give up a career in music and become an artist after a dazzling epiphany of Monet's *Haystack* seen at a Moscow exhibition in 1895. Was the impressionable Russian consciously aware at the time that Monet's painting amounted to a study of the image-forming process and cultivated assessment of the visual impact of a Pathé color photograph, intuitively conveying the photographer's uncanny sense of detached wonder, as well as communicating the aura of light and shimmering texture newly revealed in chromophotograph technology? I hardly think so. It would be interesting to know what a Kandinsky (or indeed, a Duchamp) would make of Roy Lichtenstein's version, a century later, of the same Monet *Haystack* reinvented as a playful exercise in how to read an artist's representation—reduced to the exaggerated halftone and deliberately synthetic three-color print of a souvenir postcard—of a work of art *about* a photographic image of an actual reality.

Since ample evidence of an ongoing affair with a machine aesthetic is clearly, even indecently, exposed in the sound design of Stravinsky's music and expressed with considerable finality in the composer's recorded legacy and, most of all, because the mechanical analogy fits with the composer's public persona and is easy to identify, it is possible for a casual listener in the age of the Internet to approach Stravinsky's music without intimidation as a portfolio of exercises in the art of musical animation, artistic simulation in live performance terms of a music conceived and executed in the strident colors, flat planes, and jerky rhythms of domestic mass media.

That art can be about technology, about a world experienced through the lens of a mechanical device, remains a morally challenging concept for many people. Painter David Hockney insists that artists of the classical canon, great names of the caliber of Vermeer, Canaletto, and Holbein, along with their descendants Cézanne and Degas, have freely employed the *camera obscura*, prism, mirror, or photography as imaging and drafting aids. Purists pale, but nobody can deny that cubism and futurism in the early twentieth century are genres playing with the subjective sensation of a movie representation of reality. The garish screen portraits of Andy Warhol invite the viewer to see the exaggerations of the print medium as ironic comment on celebrity preserved in the limited and transitory vision of the camera and news media. From such examples, it is easy to defend the view that ways of seeing and hearing are what art can legitimately be about.

That Stravinsky was one artist among many conscious of growing to maturity at a time of culture imitating technology imitating life should come as no surprise, given the frequency of mechanical processes appearing in works of his as different as *The Nightingale*, *Petrushka*, *The Soldier's Tale*, and *Rag-Time*, through to *Agon* and *Requiem Canticles*, along with numerous expressions of devotion to mechanical processes scattered throughout his career, to the end of his life. For the composer of *The Nightingale* to declare that he much prefers a musical box to a nightingale (*Retrospectives* 34)—volunteered after enduring an avalanche of birdsong transcribed from nature by Olivier Messiaen, enough to inspire a sequel to Alfred Hitchcock's 1963 movie *The Birds*—may read like reverse psychology. However, such a declaration is more than consistent with the composer's lifelong disavowal of attachment to sentiment. As he says in *The Poetics of Music*, "it is not art that rains down upon us in the song of a bird; but the simplest modulation correctly executed is already art" (*Poetics* 23–24).

In reviewing Stravinsky's life and opinions, Robert Craft, the composer's Boswell and advocate, is at times driven to exasperation at the composer's outwardly absurd devotion to obsolete technologies.

> The reader's heart sinks at Stravinsky's statement to the press on arriving in New York in 1925: "I will not compose while in America; that requires too much concentration. Instead, I am making entirely new versions of my work for your mechanical reproducing instruments, forty-four pieces in all. Not a 'photograph of my playing,' as Paderewski has made of his, through recordings, . . . but rather a 'lithograph,' a full and permanent record of tone combinations that are beyond my ten poor fingers to perform; in effect a new orchestration for the whole piano keyboard." (*Documents* 165–66)

Craft adds: "Needless to say, whatever the technical interest in these arrangements, all of them together are not worth the briefest original composition." Possibly sensitive to European condescension, he appears unwilling to concede that by avoiding talk of high culture and focusing on what at the time was high technology, the composer is not just being true to himself (since the enthusiasm is genuine) but making a calculated appeal to a cosmopolitan New York readership that he guessed would be more interested in hearing him talk up the value of a technically savvy modern music to industry than talk down to American readers from the perspective of a particular brand of old-world aesthetics.

Take a moment to consider what Craft is objecting to and Stravinsky is defending in the citation above. Craft is implying among other things that Stravinsky's interest in a technology designed for the less-than-perfect—indeed, distorted—replication of art music is a betrayal of art. That being the case, if art is about the imitation of nature, the mechanical imitation of art is twice removed from nature. But Stravinsky is quite clear about his intentions, describing the planned recordings as "lithographs," that is, as reproductions in the sense of reproduced artworks in the eighteenth-century world of Hogarth. Furthermore, he is intending to use piano-roll technology as a consciously artificial medium, for multitracking, not as a vehicle for himself playing like a Paderewski, to reproduce the inflections of a live performer. That does not interest him. In the sense that a lithograph reproduction of an oil painting is a mass-produced article for sale to the general public, a piano-roll edition of Stravinsky (he is assuring his public) will be a uniquely customized creation—"a new orchestration"—for the medium and not a pale imitation of the real thing or of a live performance. The composer is making a marketing decision in favor of mechanical reproduction in an age when cylinder and disc-recording media are acoustically and logistically far from perfect reproducers of music, electrical recording has yet to make an appearance, radio is only just beginning to make an impact, and movies remain largely silent. At a time when Irving Berlin and George Gershwin are investing in machine technology—Berlin in a transposing piano, Gershwin in a state of the art reproducing piano—here is a leading European art house composer making a pitch for piano-roll technology he knows and has worked with, from Aeolian Duo-Art in London to Pleyela in Paris, for over a decade.

Such a labor of love or expression of loyalty to the machine makes more sense if the original compositions have already been conceived and orchestrated in imitation of the peculiar sonorities, and timing traits and constraints, of mechanical reproduction. If the reader is persuaded that the composer's distinctive art of broken rhythms, rippling arpeggios, and breezy rustic sonorities is based not on the imitation of life but of mechanical reproduction, with all of its characteristic imperfections, then for the composer to create piano-roll editions of the same works is simply to acknowledge their status as mechanical inventions, as well as allowing purchasers the luxury of hearing them reproduced in a domestic setting as original compositions for machine, rather than as cheap imitations of live performances.

To the objection that music predesigned for mechanical reproduction and brought to life by living performers is missing the point of composing for machines in the first place, the composer responds that live performers are only too ready to breathe their own life into music at the expense of the life that is already there and that it is the intention of his music to instruct performers (and conductors) in how to suppress their unwelcome instincts for self-preservation in the interest of coming to terms with what the music itself, and through it, the composer, is actually intending to say. By composing in the style of a machine, Stravinsky not only raises his expectations of the physically possible but forces the performing artist to respect his intentions as a real person.

His works are "portraits of machines," in the sense he observes of Chopin's waltzes, that "they are portraits of dance, not the dance itself."

ABBREVIATIONS

Autobiography — Igor Stravinsky, *An Autobiography (1903–1934)* (London: Gollancz, 1936), English translation of *Chroniques de ma Vie* (1935), written with the assistance of Walter Nouvel; reprint with corrections and an introduction by Eric Walter White (London: Calder and Boyars, 1975); new edition (London: Boyars, 1990).

Chronicle — Robert Craft, *Stravinsky: The Chronicle of a Friendship 1948–1971* (London: Gollancz, 1972).

Conclusions — Igor Stravinsky, *Themes and Conclusions*, rev. and exp. Robert Craft, UK edition of US *Themes and Episodes* and *Retrospectives and Conclusions* (London: Faber & Faber, 1972).

Conversations — Igor Stravinsky and Robert Craft, *Conversations with Igor Stravinsky* (London: Faber & Faber, 1959).

Dialogues — Igor Stravinsky and Robert Craft, *Dialogues*, originally *Dialogues and a Diary* (1968); reissued in abridged form, omitting extracts from the diary of Robert Craft, which are republished separately in *Chronicle* (London: Faber & Faber, 1982).

Documents	Vera Stravinsky and Robert Craft, *Stravinsky in Pictures and Documents* (London: Hutchinson, 1979).
EWW	Eric Walter White, *Stravinsky: The Composer and His Works* (1966), 2nd ed. (London: Faber & Faber, 1979).
Expositions	Igor Stravinsky and Robert Craft, *Expositions and Developments* (London: Faber & Faber, 1962).
Grove II	J. A. Fuller Maitland, ed., *Grove's Dictionary of Music and Musicians*, new ed., 5 vols. (London: Macmillan, 1910).
Memories	Igor Stravinsky and Robert Craft, *Memories and Commentaries*, UK ed. (London: Faber & Faber, 1960), US ed. (New York: Doubleday, 1960).
Poetics	Igor Stravinsky, *Poetics of Music in the Form of Six Lessons* (Charles Eliot Norton Lectures 1939–1940), tr. Arthur Knodel and Ingolf Dahl (New York: Vintage Books, 1956).
Retrospectives	Igor Stravinsky and Robert Craft, *Retrospectives and Conclusions* (New York: Knopf, 1969).
Taruskin	Richard Taruskin, *Stravinsky and the Russian Traditions: A Biography of the Works through Mavra*, 2 vols. (Oxford: Oxford University Press, 1996).
Themes	Igor Stravinsky and Robert Craft, *Themes and Episodes* (New York: Knopf, 1966).
Works	*Works of Igor Stravinsky*, complete works, twenty-two CDs (Sony Classical, 88697103112; 2007).

TIMELINE

1882 Igor Fyodorovich Stravinsky is born 17 June (new style) in Oranienbaum near the family home in St. Petersburg, to Fyodor Stravinsky, a bass specializing in character roles with the Imperial Opera, and Anna née Kholodovsky, a talented pianist.

1885 Early signs of a musical ear and gift for mimicry of gipsy and street music; lives in fear and awe of his father; is teased by older brothers.

1887 Discovers a liking for peasant songs and fairground mechanical music.

1890 Introduced to ballet with Tchaikovsky's *Sleeping Beauty*.

1891 Begins piano studies; improvises; attends opera, ballet.

1892 Pursues interest in folk origins of melody.

1897 Practices piano arranging to improve technical skills.

1901 Directed to study law and philosophy at St. Petersburg University; through fellow student Vladimir, the composer's son, meets with Nikolai Rimsky-Korsakov, who encourages him to continue private tuition in harmony and orchestration.

1902 Fyodor Stravinsky dies, leaving son free to pursue art and music interests.

1904 First sight of motion pictures, a Pathé short.

1905 Law studies interrupted by a street uprising (the "Bloody Sunday" massacre); begins lessons with Rimsky-Korsakov; is engaged to cousin Catherine Nossenko.

1906 Marries Catherine Nossenko.

1907 Sees Mahler conduct his Fifth Symphony in St. Petersburg.

1909 After success of *Fireworks* and *Scherzo Fantastique* in St. Petersburg, Diaghilev commissions *Firebird* for the Ballet Russes, to premiere in 1910.

1910 Travels to Paris for *Firebird* premiere; is introduced to Debussy, Ravel, Falla.

1911 Premiere of *Petrushka*, incorporating multiple barrel organ simulations.

1912 Composes *The Rite of Spring* on Russian and primeval motifs using movie based and piano-roll techniques; piano-roll transcriptions are required for rehearsals.

1913 Last visit to St. Petersburg to collect folk material for *Les Noces*; in Paris, cements friendship with Cocteau and Satie; public uproar at premiere of *The Rite of Spring*.

1914 War declared; takes up residence in France, later in Switzerland; consults Aeolian Company in London and hears piano-roll editions of his works; composes numerous short works on folk and childhood themes; continues to develop precision timing techniques and explore New Orleans jazz–inspired combinations.

1915 Befriends Ernest Ansermet; obtains a Hungarian cimbalom; composes *Renard*.

1917 Sketches version of *Les Noces* for large orchestra; Russian Revolution creates personal financial crisis; puts paid to extravagance of the former tsarist era.

1918 Death of Debussy; war ends; composes *The Soldier's Tale* for touring players, including narrator, in jazz-influenced style including a suite of drums.

1919 Parts of *Les Noces* recomposed for impractical ensemble of solo voices, pianola, two cimbaloms, harmonium, and percussion; Diaghilev commissions retrostyle *Pulcinella* based on Neapolitan baroque material, décor by Picasso.

1922 Obtains a retainer and workspace with Paris firm Pleyela to make piano-roll editions of his music; is introduced to Vera Sudekeina by Diaghilev.

1923 Protesting Nazi gunfire in Vienna forces Otto Klemperer to abandon a rehearsal of Stravinsky's *Song of the Nightingale*; Stravinsky is targeted by the Nazis as a Jew and gipsy sympathizer.

1925 Arriving in New York, Stravinsky announces plans to arrange his works in multitrack style suitable only for mechanical reproduction; records *Serenade in A* for piano solo, using the newly announced electrical method, a work composed in four movements each timed to fit on one side of a record.

1927 Composes *Oedipus Rex* to a politically auspicious libretto after Sophocles by Cocteau, done into Latin, presented in static, radio-adapted style with male narrator.

1928 *Apollo*, a US ballet commission for string orchestra in markedly melodious, tonal idiom suitable for radio transmission, choreographed by a young George Balanchine; arrival of the "talkies" with Al Jolson and Disney's *Silly Symphonies*.

1929 Continues to tinker with issues of balance of orchestra for radio and studio recording; replaces string orchestra with massed voices in *Symphony of Psalms*, another US commission; takes on more engagements as piano soloist and conductor.

1931 Teams up with violinist Samuel Dushkin, in part to improve his knowledge of violin technique; composes *Concerto in D* and *Duo concertant* for Dushkin; an uncooperative orchestra at the German premiere is rebuked by Hindemith.

1933 Collaborates with André Gide on *Persephone*, presented once again in static radio style, this time in French with dedicatee Ida Rubenstein as narrator.

1934 Becomes a French citizen.

1935 Publishes *Autobiography*, in which he declares that "music is powerless to express anything at all."

1938 Death of daughter Ludmila in a tuberculosis sanatorium; the following year wife Catherine and mother also die of the disease; is himself out of action for five months.

1939 Meeting in Hollywood with Stokowski and Walt Disney to agree terms for use of *The Rite of Spring* as accompaniment for a sequence in the animated movie *Fantasia*, to be recorded in a novel form of optical surround sound.

1940 Marries Vera Sudeikina and settles in Hollywood among exile community, including Charlie Chaplin, Otto Klemperer, Schoenberg, Eisler, Ernst Krenek, Thomas Mann, Christopher Isherwood, Aldous Huxley; completes *Symphony in C*; continues to collaborate with Balanchine.

1942 Composes *Circus Polka* for dancing elephants; *Four Norwegian Moods* is declined by Columbia as incidental music for movie *Commandos Strike at Dawn* on the ground that the movie had not been filmed.

1944 Participates in Nathaniel Shilkret's *Genesis Suite* project, a collaboration of exiled composers, including Schoenberg and Milhaud; continues to experiment with jazz and "musical animation."

1945 Becomes a US citizen; war ends; relief expressed in powerful *Symphony in Three Movements* and sardonic *Ebony Concerto* for jazz band and vanishing clarinetist, composed for Woody Herman.

1946 In *Concerto in D* for Paul Sacher and *Orpheus* for Balanchine, discovers the dark side; consulted by neighbor Thomas Mann for the novel *Doktor Faustus*, is ashamed at the author's covert attack on the composer of *A Survivor from Warsaw*.

1947 Signs with publisher Boosey & Hawkes, who commission a libretto for *The Rake's Progress*; Auden is engaged; differences emerge when Auden unilaterally co-opts his friend Chester Kallman as colibrettist.

1948 Schoenberg disciple and advocate Robert Craft is engaged, then adopted as permanent assistant; he encourages Stravinsky's curiosity toward twelve-tone composition and renaissance counterpoint, key ingredients of his later serial style.

1949 A disastrous but amusing encounter with Evelyn Waugh, from whom advice is sought on English manners and social customs for a new opera.

1951 After three years of continuous work, *The Rake's Progress*, an *opera buffa* reworking of Mozart's *Don Giovanni* as a moral fable after Hogarth's series of satirical engravings, premieres to great acclaim but mixed reviews.

1952 Continued fascination with counterpoint and the English language on display in *Cantata* and *Three Shakespeare Songs*; assists Craft and Los Angeles concert scene by recomposing earlier songs and short pieces for serially inspired instrumental combinations; donates recording time for Craft's complete Webern project.

1953 Schoenberg and Webern influences on show for the first time in the playful *Septet*; Pierre Suvchinsky relays news of the new French school of Messiaen and Boulez; is attentive toward electronic music and *musique concrète*.

1954 A planned opera collaboration with Dylan Thomas comes to grief with the poet's sudden death; Stravinsky composes an *In Memoriam* to Thomas's lyric in an austere blend of twelve-tone canonic and Italian baroque idioms; is impressed by Varese's *Deserts* for orchestra and tape.

1955 *Canticum Sacrum* premieres, an ebullient commission for St. Mark's Basilica, Venice, its centerpiece the astonishing "Surge, aquilo" from the *Song of Songs*; contributes a dedication in Webern's memory to *Die Reihe* 2, a new music periodical edited by Herbert Eimert and Karlheinz Stockhausen.

1957 *Agon* premiered by Balanchine in New York, a suite of dances on old French models, set in a kaleidoscope of styles from high baroque modal to Webern serialism; the periodical *Encounter* publishes "Answers to 34 Questions" assembled by Craft to mark the composer's seventy-fifth birthday, later issued in book form as *Conversations*.

1958 Differences over the premiere of *Threni*, a setting of lamentations recognized by Christian and Jewish faiths, lead to a rift with an unapologetic Boulez.

1959 With *Movements*, a piano concerto, Stravinsky feels personally vindicated and predicts even stricter applications of serialism in the future.

1960 Adopts features of Messiaen's theory and aesthetic, with the exception of birdsong.

1962 Composed for television after the story of Noah, *The Flood* injects the humor of *Mavra* into the twelve-tone era, drawing on Hollywood skills in musical animation; a long-awaited return visit to Soviet Russia and meeting with Khrushchev attract world media attention.

1964 With declining health, his serial language becomes thinner in outline and more concentrated from *Variations* through to *Requiem Canticles*, in which the peasant idioms and abrasive contrasts of his childhood remain detectable.

1968 Is reconciled to German and Spanish traditions of his youth, arranging two songs by Hugo Wolf for mezzo-soprano and alternating quintets of winds and solo strings.

1971 Dies on 7 April in New York; is buried at San Michele, Venice, alongside Diaghilev.

I

GHOST IN THE MACHINE

Stravinsky is a uniquely compelling figure in the history of classical music. A ballet specialist and genius, he is responsible for some of the most complex and rhythmically dislocated compositions in the history of Western music. In particular, his *The Rite of Spring* is famous not only for the heart-stopping arrhythmia of the solo Sacrificial Dance but equally for the first and perhaps only example of pogo dance in the classical repertoire, in which a portion of the music is reduced to the seemingly endless up-and-down repetition of a single dense chord played with brutal, pistonlike force by multiple strings (violins, violas, cellos, bass viols) and intermittently reinforced by a blasting eight-horn chorus, all sounding like a manic express train driven at full speed. It is an image of steam power to compare with Arthur Honegger's *Pacific 231*, the musical portrait of a real express engine premiered ten years later in 1923 (Erato 3984-213340-2).

Stravinsky is routinely accused of fatal inconsistencies of style, of switching allegiance at will to meet changes in current fashion, from late romantic decadence to futurist bruitism to art deco neoclassical to eclectic modern—in other words, of being an opportunist always ready to sell out to the latest fashion, however unpopular it may be. The composer's uncanny knack of staying one step ahead of aesthetic opinion is also linked, incongruously, to an alleged miserliness in money matters, a respect for financial security apparently difficult for comfortably tenured academics to reconcile with the responsibilities and uncertainties of a self-employed creative life. In the final decades of a brilliant career, Stravinsky turned away from neoclassical irony to embrace a synthesis of late renaissance polyphony and abstract twelve-tone music, a hybrid idiom doubly denounced by outraged opinion makers as barren and out of touch. Even so, Stravinsky still managed to compose a cluster of difficult works of vibrant energy and invention in that idiom, works that even today remain controversial and, to many commentators, aesthetically inexplicable. His artistic philosophy—summarized in a series of acutely opinionated dialogues with associate Robert Craft and aimed directly at a younger generation of listeners—is clearly intended as a personal and cultural manifesto defending musical modernism and attacking conservative attitudes in academic life and the musical press.

The Swiss-born architect Le Corbusier famously described his vision of a properly designed modern home as a *machine à habiter*—a machine for living. Among French speakers, the term for a typewriter is a *machine à écrire*—a machine for writing. In the same spirit, Stravinsky's music, designed at a piano keyboard, deserves to be recognized as the aesthetic of a manufactured product: a *machine à musique*, a machine for music. We do not ask a machine to have feelings but simply to work. "A nose is a nose," the composer once said. "So too is my art." ("Long live your nose!" responded a friend.) All his life Stravinsky defended his music-making as a natural function, in opposition to the traditional view of music and the arts as mysterious products of divine inspiration. Such a view deserves respect as serious and grounded in the skeptical realist tradition of Voltaire and Rousseau (and their descendants Debussy's Monsieur Croche and Erik Satie), in resolute opposition to the beguiling fuzzy logic of German romanticism, from Herder and Hegel in the late eighteenth and early nineteenth centuries to descendants of Adorno in the twentieth and twenty-first.

Forced to rely on the printed score—in the absence of free access to the actual sound of any number of live or studio recorded performances—past generations of music specialists and students (myself included) were easily lured into believing anecdotal accounts of a composer's character and personality, solemnly represented as artistic traits, that the reader was invited to hear confirmed in the music itself. Such tactics remain all too common in the textbook world. But for a new generation of genuine amateurs with no emotional axes to grind, there is no point in being told what to listen for or what to expect, since the proof is in the listening and ready access to the composer's authentic personality, as conveyed in musical terms, is now freely available.

A redirection of focus from the printed word to the actual sound of music—from reading about music to hearing it for oneself—introduces a previously marginalized range of contextual issues, relating to performance and interpretation, as well as considerations of audio quality, into the assessment process. Such criteria of a technical nature are real and familiar enough in the arcane world of audiophile and record review but are rarely encountered or discussed in the scholarly literature, perhaps out of indifference or, in some cases, willful neglect. Stravinsky's musical development is intimately related to patterns of growth and change within the music industry and for that reason alone deserves to be evaluated in the terms and context of evolving pressures and constraints within the market. During his lifetime, the world of music faced a succession of new technologies of production and reproduction, manufactured alternatives to live performance from which a young composer might plan to make a living. From childhood, he was exposed to the musical box, pianola, barrel organ, and orchestrion, instruments programmed by pin cylinder, paper roll, or perforated metal disk—reproducers of music routinely encountered in the street, marketplace, and fairground, as well as in upper-class homes. As a junior member of a relatively well-to-do household, he may have encountered new cable entertainment services, music and theater performances delivered by telephone line to subscribers equipped with multiple headsets on turned wooden handles with dual earpieces. By 1900, the scratchy sounds of commercial acoustic cylinder and disc recordings were coming to town, hopes of a potential market for classical music dramatically confirmed with Fred Gaisberg's pioneer recordings of Enrico Caruso in 1903. In direct competition for the home entertainment market, the piano industry launched the orchestrelle, a paper-roll-programmed harmonium, and advanced professional piano-roll technology capable of recording the personal features of a live performance and designed to allow the private listener, in the comforts of home, to audition not just any rendition of a musical score but the authentic and particular artistry of a chosen virtuoso performer.

Stravinsky recalled seeing his first movie in 1904. "A woman stood by a table pouring hot chocolate into a cup, and a child then swallowed the contents of the cup. That was all. The whole performance lasted no longer than a bagatelle by Webern, and the cup and the liquid trembled terribly" (*Memories* UK 109, US 103). The arrival of silent movies initiated a futurist aesthetic of unprecedented and surreal concoctions of popular themes and sound effects, improvised or compiled to follow the action on screen. Imitating the fractured continuity of silent movie music would be key to Stravinsky's breakthrough to public notoriety with the ballets *Petrushka* and *The Rite of Spring*. With piano-roll technology came the sounds of New Orleans hot jazz, the mechanical rhythms of ragtime, displacing Fritz Kreisler's soft Viennese violin and stridently celebrating the impersonal aesthetic of a new machine age. In 1922, amid the cultural aftershock of the Great War, public radio emerged to challenge opera as the voice of national identity, a new and powerful information and entertainment medium capable of bringing classical music to vast new audiences. In 1926 the genteel spirit world of acoustic recording was laid to rest with the advent of a music of bright, new, hard-edged, raw, abrasive textures of amplified electrical recording. In 1928 Al Jolson launched the talkies, heralding a change of movie culture from historical romance to the documentary idiom and urban gangster aesthetic of Hollywood and German *Neue Sachlichkeit* (new realism). The tide of innovation continued with metal tape recording, optical sound on film, television, rapid advances thereafter in hi-fi and surround sound by the early 1940s and after the end of World War II, the launch by Columbia in 1948 of the vinyl long-playing disc, and the arrival of domestic stereo, along with pioneer essays in electronic and computer art music in the fifties and sixties.

The conventional view that Western music is somehow separate from mechanical ingenuity and that developments in musical aesthetics across the ages are entirely willful, are random, and have nothing to do with science and engineering, however comforting to a majority of professionals, is sadly mistaken. Progress in musical thought is inseparable from advances in musical design and instrumentation, from the medieval pipe organ and mechanical chiming clock of renaissance times to applications of music software in the present era. The generation of Mozart and Haydn was happy to adapt to the challenge of new tuning systems, touch-sensitive keyboards, and the vagaries of mechanical reproduction, but few composers of any age have faced so many changes in music-related technologies as Stravinsky's generation, and among them, only a handful took care to acquire the technical expertise to accommodate them.

In the scholarly literature, the mutual influence of mechanical design and music has been largely ignored or regarded as taboo. In *Rhythm and Tempo*, Curt Sachs's magisterial survey of musical time management published in 1953, the author/ethnomusicologist discourses at length on notated examples of mechanically geared music from the middle ages to the midtwentieth century of Stravinsky and John Cage, without once referring to the role of self-playing instruments. Specimen measures from the nineteenth century alone range from seven against six in Beethoven's "Emperor" concerto to the same device in Richard Strauss's tone poem *Till Eulenspiegel*; examples of rhythmic layering in operas by Auber and Berlioz and throughout the solo piano literature of Chopin, Schubert, and Schumann; and adoption of irregular rhythms, often in the guise of folk idioms, by a host of Stravinsky's direct antecedents and influences, including Berlioz, Cui, Dvorák, Glinka, Tchaikovsky, Mussorgsky, Brahms, Rimsky-Korsakov, Pierné, and Debussy (Sachs 325–59).

Stravinsky is one of a small but significant minority of composers from the early to midtwentieth century—a group including Fritz Kreisler, Maurice Ravel, George Gershwin, and Benjamin Britten—to have left permanent legacies of their compositions in personally supervised recordings. The present guide is a meaningful enterprise largely because, with occasional exceptions and additions, virtually the entire repertory is referenced to a single budget-price box edition of 22 CDs (*Works of Igor Stravinsky*; Sony Classical, 88697103112; hereafter, *Works*), all performed to the composer's specifications and nearly all under his personal direction. The advantages of a unified collection of reference can be summarized positively as a guarantee of authentic and consistent interpretation and negatively as avoiding stylistic and personal mannerisms to which the composer would object.

Among the earliest memories that Stravinsky recalls—in his conversation books as in his compositions—are gipsy melodies, barrel organs, and children's songs to nonsense words, vivid memories of a sharpness and indiscretion perhaps surprising in the child of an upper-class household and distinguished bass-baritone father. At the piano the small boy fingered a scale note by note, skipping one note on the way up and another on the way down, and was reprimanded for not playing correctly. "I don't care," he thought. "I invented it, it is my composition" (EWW 555–56). His gift for mimicry impressed his parents, but his choice of material—animal-like syllables accompanied by loud armpit noises—was cause for despair. At table he was the butt of family jokes. Asked out of the blue what he had learned of French that day, the boy reddened, blurted out "Parqwa" (*Pourquoi*), and burst into tears (*Expositions* 38–39). On music his father had definite views. Song was the oldest and highest form of music because song has words and words have meaning, even (wink) when they are sung in a foreign language. In turn, opera was the highest form of song because, whereas art song conveys personal feelings, opera expresses the ideals and sensibility of an entire race. Great music is the servant of words because its role is to draw out and enhance the message of the drama. Nursery rhymes and nonsense lyrics are trivial child's play, meaningless and of no account. Good diction is the key to good character. And so on.

"But Father, what about ballet?" the boy interrupts. "Surely ballet has meaning, even though nobody is singing?" Silence.

As a young man growing up in St. Petersburg, he was exposed to a vibrant musical culture, receiving piano lessons from a strict lady teacher who interestingly refused to let him use the sustaining pedal, forcing him to rely on his two hands. From an early age he was taken to the opera to see his father perform and to be impressed by intimations of an awakening nationalism in Glinka, exotic Spanish-influenced rituals of courtship and death in Bizet and Rimsky-Korsakov, and the social realism of Mussorgsky's *Boris Godunov.* He was especially drawn to the dynamic visual complexities of Russian ballet, choreographed patterns of movement aligned but not exactly synchronized to an accompanying music, and enchanted by the delicate choreography of Tchaikovsky's *Nutcracker*, in which inanimate toys are brought magically to life by the power of musical suggestion. Smoldering resentment at being constantly put down by members of his family may have contributed to the boy's decision to become a composer, since as a composer, he would be treated with more respect: roles would be reversed, with his father and brothers obliged to sing to his tune and acknowledge the emotions that the youngster was going through.

Tsarist Russia in the late nineteenth century was becoming a major influence in European literary and intellectual life. Despite historic ties to sophisticated Paris and Vienna, Moscow and St. Petersburg were regarded in the decadent west of Europe literally as the primitive east end of civilization, gateway to an exotic and mysterious orient. The assertion of cultural identity through the promotion of performance arts of music and ballet was an important ingredient of imperial Russia's emergence as a European power in turbulent times. During the nineteenth century, classical music was officially promoted as a medium of international gamesmanship to demonstrate leadership, national pride, social harmony—and military preparedness. Among patrons and leaders of industry, classical music was recognized as the supreme art of people management, competence in performing complex tasks laid out in symbolic code, good teamwork, aptitude for service, and a high level of literacy among the workforce. In their joint pursuit of national identity, Russian composers—many of them from the military—sought inspiration in imagery of primeval human nature, the uninhibited and volatile emotions of Italian opera, and an invented nostalgia toward ancient musical traditions of Moorish Spain. In contrast to poets and novelists, who were free to engage with intimate and controversial subject matter, state composers were expected to attend to politically approved themes of heroic sacrifice, leadership, human destiny, and social and tribal loyalties. As cultural propaganda, the operas of Verdi and Wagner and the concert music of Paganini and Liszt played to officially sanctioned norms of extravagantly rhetorical leadership and identity politics.

Ballet was different. In Russia at least, ballet was about cooperation. It was benign. It offered an alternative program to the operatic worldview and empty rhetoric of contemporary politics. To the young Russian, ballet represented an authentic alternative world of magic realism, collective responsibility, personal transformation, humor, and freedom of expression. Advised to prepare for a career in law, the student composer to be was moved to reflect that behind the glamorous façade of a people's artist, his father's professional status and role amounted to little more than the responsibilities of a civil servant playing to a script. The uninhibited freedom of expression that the son was looking for lay elsewhere, among the oral traditions of despised minorities and in the impersonal, motiveless play of programmed mechanical devices.

His own early and visceral attraction to the music of rustic peasant and gipsy traditions, sung by cracked voices in ancient, incomprehensible words, to the sound of wheezy popular tunes of fairground organs, happened to coincide with a newly fashionable interest in the science of ethnomusicology among emerging composers of the post-1890s, a group including Bartók and Kodály in Hungary and Vaughan Williams in England. The new generation was attracted to the task of preserving authentic native folk idioms in their natural state by the arrival of new Edison technology of portable wax cylinder recording. The phonograph stimulated public consciousness of elusive oral music traditions by providing a means of transcribing and studying cultural relics profoundly implicated in the popular assertion of national and cultural identity. In the fine arts, Kasimir Malevich and Wassily Kandinsky were similarly engaged in retrieving signs and symbols from oral tradition to be used as raw material for a new artistic vision.

In academia even today Stravinsky is routinely stigmatized as a brazen recycler of other people's idioms rather than an "original." It is a criticism to which he is rightly sensitive, one repudiated in his maturity with vigorous irritation in the Harvard Charles Eliot Norton lectures published as *Poetics of Music.* In his massive, albeit incomplete, two-volume compendium *Stravinsky and the Russian Traditions* (1996), Richard Taruskin goes to great lengths to prove that the young composer plagiarized relentlessly, though omitting to mention—perhaps out of innocence, as he is not a composer—that to do so in 1900 was perfectly normal; it was apprentice work: one copied to compare and, from comparing, to learn. To copy others is to learn and also to criticize. From early in his career, Debussy was an obvious and persistent target, the music for strings introducing act I of Stravinsky's *The Nightingale* (1908–1909) an obvious riff on the cooler woodwinds of the French composer's *Nuages* (from *Nocturnes*, 1897–1899) and the strangled cry of the solo bassoon opening of *The Rite of Spring* (1911–1912) a calculatedly primitive response to the languid *art nouveau* nonchalance of the opening flute melody of Debussy's *L'Après-Midi d'un Faune* (1894). Appropriating the music of others was a practice widespread before the advent of copyright law and destined to survive in the low art of noncopyright music in the world of commercial movie, radio, and music theater to the present day. Stravinsky's creative manipulation of musical "found objects" would become a lifelong habit and ingredient of a deliberately cultivated machine aesthetic, wholly consistent with the composer's view that music is powerless to express anything other than itself.

To the art of instrumentation, Stravinsky brought an ear finely attuned to the peculiar traits, tonal qualities, and rhythms of mechanically reproduced music programmed by perforated paper roll, clearly audible in the marvelously simulated mechanical bird of *The Nightingale* and the street organs of *Petrushka*. To compose like a machine, one has to be able to think like a machine, which for a composer at the keyboard is to think of the piano as a machine and of staff notation as a programming language. Imagining the piano as a machine for making music was far from being a new idea. In purely functional terms, as a programmable code for describing movement in space and time, the development of five-line staff notation, as long ago as the fourteenth century, was the primary conceptual breakthrough enabling the manufacture of chiming clocks and associated mechanical automata. Staff notation is about clock time, whereas a musical performance is inevitably about organic, physical time. The composer's role is to reconcile the two. Clock time is precisely measured, objective time. It lends itself to the mechanical simulation of natural actions in the same way as successive frames of a movie can be used as templates for cartoon animations. The interior of a clock is called a *movement*, just as a segment of a classical symphony is called a *movement*, in respect of the dynamic integration of its various components.

For a mechanical performance of music to deliver an impression of natural motion, something more is required than a simple reproduction of the time values on the printed page. As the beat of a metronome lacks rhythm, so a piano roll that is cut directly from the score will appear to lack fluency and personality, unless the composer has a very good sense of timing (Plato, Benjamin Franklin, inventor of the glass *armonica*, and the late Milton Babbitt among others representing the opposing view that music should always aspire to the disembodied purity of a musical box). For Stravinsky, who insisted that his music was sufficient in itself, it was vital to identify an idiom and incorporate into the score all the cues necessary for a mechanical reproduction to give a realistic impression of a live performance. The pursuit of realism led him to conclude that to sound convincingly like a human performer, a mechanical notation should incorporate natural inequalities of play. Stravinsky's notorious changes of time signature, tempo, and accent, as well as broken textures, hesitations, and stuttering repeats, are among a range of features and strategies imported into a musical text specifically to emulate live performance traits of indecision, real-time improvisation, memory lapse, and problems of technique.

Stravinsky's cultural and musical origins were Polish, like Chopin's, grounded in the eighteenth-century pianism of Mozart and Clementi, an aesthetic technically and emotionally aligned to the romance tradition of Chopin, Hummel, Mendelssohn, Saint-Saëns, Grieg, and Granados, through to Debussy and Ravel, representing values of precision and emotional restraint. Its characteristic virtues of detachment, elegance, and lightness of touch are very different from the heavier, hands-on rhetoric of the more northern German school of Beethoven and Czerny. Both schools of pianism were well established in Poland and Russia in Stravinsky's youth, the German school represented by the great teacher Leschetizky, and virtuosos Moszkowski, Paderewski, Moiseiwitsch, Scriabin, and Busoni. In the 1920s, when the time came for Stravinsky to embark on a solo piano and conducting career, he consciously turned to the school of Czerny to beef up his piano technique and develop confidence through adopting the musical rhetoric of the more physical German performance tradition.

The precedent for creating a deliberately "distressed" mechanical performance—as a way of masking naturally occurring mechanical defects in a piano-roll or pin-cylinder storage device—dates back to the eighteenth century, its purpose analogous in visual terms to Charlie Chaplin's adoption of an exaggerated style of walking in his early silent movies. Under conditions of mechanical reproduction, the use of controlled, idiosyncratic motion is a device for holding the attention but with the secondary aim of preventing an audience's sense of continuity of movement being eroded by a flickering and unpredictable machine action. In theater and the movies, exaggerated or formalized behavior traits also acknowledge the reality that human nature and individual personality are more readily conveyed through consistent aberrations or defects in performance—for example, in timing or accentuation—than through their absence. Anonymity or absence of personality is what we expect of a newsreader, and it has its place. A performance with personality is naturally imperfect but consistently so, unlike a machine.

In the era of Haydn, Mozart, and Beethoven, the art of transferring music from an original piano score to the paper roll or pin cylinder of a mechanical reproducer involved two processes. First, the musical content had to be reduced to conform to the limited note range of the player; second, the scatter of notes was rearranged to reduce the quantity playing at any one time to a manageable number, to regulate the flow of air pressure to the keyboard so that the notes played evenly. Specialist Arthur W. J. G. Ord-Hume observes,

> No mechanical instrument . . . can be expected to perform with the nuance of a manual performer although it can undoubtedly exceed his capabilities in areas of precision, accuracy, and fluency of repeated performances.[1] (103)

Added "dither" was apt to disguise unresolved imperfections in programming while simulating an appearance of natural liveliness. Let me explain. Since piano music can be pictured as a stream of notes of varying density, with each note requiring a puff of air to sound, it will be apparent that an original music of greatly fluctuating density—for example, the first movement of Beethoven's "Waldstein" sonata, Op. 53, of 1804—runs a serious risk of lumpiness and inconsistency of speed in piano-roll performance. To ensure clarity of attack, a score was rearranged to detach the melody line rhythmically from the accompaniment and to ensure a natural continuity of flow to break up solid chords into rippling arpeggios. Stravinsky's art of controlled approximation and broken texture builds on classical practice and is consistent with a motivation to create an original style and repertoire preadapted for domestic mechanical reproduction.

The eighteenth-century art of mechanical "dither" is derived in turn from earlier baroque practice. We tend to forget that domestic keyboard instruments—including the organ, clavecin, hurdy-gurdy, and harpsichord—were originally designed for evenness of touch, specifically to eliminate inequalities in finger action and ensure a desirable consistency of tone: a quality associated with the art of a highly trained (and expensive) guitarist or lute player. The message of perfect tonal control becoming available to an amateur of limited strength or education was typically advertised, in more prejudiced times, in images of a young female member of the household at the keyboard—with famous examples including the engraved cover of *Parthenia Inviolata*, an English collection of pieces for keyboard dating from 1613, and Jan Vermeer's better-known oils from the 1660s and 1670s of a pretty young lady standing or seated at the virginals. In the smooth German idiom exemplified by the Preludes and Fugues of J. S. Bach, multiple parts are woven in textures of more or less constant density in the interests of maintaining a mechanically even flow, an image of divine impersonality that the arrogant French opted to disturb into life by the liberal application of grace notes, set piece ornamental figures corresponding to speech accents and exclamation marks freely inserted into a plain musical text as a substitute for natural expression. The convention of incorporating "French baroque" expression marks—as a means of adapting touch-sensitive keyboard music of the late classical period to the even-toned self-playing instruments of the Clementi era—is clearly audible in the popular "Rondo alla Turca" of Mozart's 1783 Piano Sonata in A (K.331) for piano (Ord-Hume 104–5).

In a humorous portfolio of caricatures of famous conductors by Gerard Hoffnung (*The Hoffnung Music Festival*), Malcolm Sargent is portrayed as a preening hair stylist in front of a mirror, while on another page a taciturn Stravinsky is imagined hand on hip, holding up a ticking metronome for the orchestra to follow—a characterization endorsed by the composer in a tale of Dutch conductor Willem Mengelberg having to be reminded at rehearsal of the correct tempo of *Capriccio*, an entertaining work for piano and orchestra in which the composer was appearing as soloist.

> Greatly flustered, [Mengelberg] embarked on a self-justifying oration: "Gentlemen, after fifty years as a conductor I think I may claim to be able to recognize the proper *tempo* of a piece of music. Monsieur Stravinsky, however, would like us to play like this: tick, tick, tick, tick." And he cocked his forefinger in mockery of Mälzel's very useful invention. (*Themes* 150; *Conclusions* 226–27)

Interestingly, it is Stravinsky's only allusion to the inventor of the metronome in all his published conversations with Robert Craft. Resistance to the expressive intentions of others does not necessarily imply absence of feeling on the composer's part, though for Stravinsky in Tsarist Russia, as for Shostakovich under Stalin (not to mention the John Cage of "Lecture on Nothing" in Joe McCarthy's America), feigning absence of intention to express anything in particular was arguably a prudent line for the composer to take. For a youthful aspiring "machine composer," St. Petersburg had interesting historical associations with leading composers of late-eighteenth-century Vienna and London, centers in the manufacture of mechanical musical devices. Among distinguished former St. Petersburg citizens are counted the Danish-born Christian Gottlieb Kratzenstein, inventor in 1779 of a set of five organ pipes configured to produce the vowel sounds a–e–i–o–u, originally for use in the manufacture of androids capable of speech. Another was Daniel Steibelt (1765–1823), a prolific composer of German origin associated with Beethoven in demonstrations of the Maelzel Panharmonicon, in later life a St. Petersburg resident whose piano studies with idiosyncratic changes of key continued to circulate among the piano teaching profession in Stravinsky's youth. Beethoven was connected to St. Petersburg through Count Razumovsky, dedicatee of the Op. 59 string quartets, and as Maelzel's collaborator in arranging existing works and composing a new work, *Wellingtons Sieg*, for the Panharmonicon, a mechanical organ deployed to advertise a series of fund-raisers in celebration of the 1813 victory over Napoleon at the battle of Vittoria. A subtler influence was Beethoven's rival Muzio Clementi, a Mozart disciple whose piano exercises in touch and technique formed an essential part of Stravinsky's musical upbringing. In his day a successful businessman and solo artist, Clementi entered into partnership with the London firm of Collard for the manufacture of self-playing pianos, in doing so establishing the principle of a light, mechanical touch as a desirable goal for human executants.[2]

Popular fascination with mechanical automata is widespread in music and literature. E. T. A. Hoffmann's tale *Coppélia*, set to music by Delibes, is the story of a mechanical ballerina, a subject prefiguring *Petrushka*; Tchaikovsky's ballet *The Nutcracker* premiered when Stravinsky was ten years old, yet another fairy tale of dolls brought to life by a music composed partly in imitation of a musical box. The theme of manufactured objects imitating life is familiar from Mary Shelley's *Frankenstein*, Hans Andersen's *The Nightingale*, and the story of Pinocchio—a thread continued in Frank Baum's *The Wizard of Oz*, Colette's fairy tale *L'Enfant et les Sortilèges*, set to music by Ravel, through to today's world of Transformers and movies of the *Terminator* genre—the subtext even of Alan Turing's "Imitation Game" in modern robotics. All of which beg the age-old question of whether human beings are machines in the Cartesian sense—how human nature is defined—and in political terms, whether a majority of working-class citizens (including women) are worthy or capable of exercising freedom of identity and action. In times of political uncertainty, such ideas have serious implications. For a composer and artist to court controversy in the musical treatment of potentially sensitive themes of national and cultural identity—in works as outwardly innocent as *Firebird*, *Les Noces*, or *Oedipus Rex*—is evidence of moral courage as well as political and artistic integrity.

Composing for ballet is an art of motion dynamics, of mechanically geared rhythms expressible as eloquent and graceful gesture. In contrast to song, which is identifiable with a text of relatively fixed meaning, music for dance is composed of infinitely malleable units of rhythm predicated on the realities of physical gesture, an art of gracefully managed instability. Words are static, but dance involves a presumption of movement. A conductor beats time, but a dancer moves to the melody, counting the notes. A beautiful example is the familiar musical box melody for celesta and glockenspiel of Tchaikovsky's "Dance of the Sugar-Plum Fairy" from *The Nutcracker*. Stravinsky would easily find this out for himself. Over a simple four-by-four pulse, Tchaikovsky positions a descending melody phrased in groups counted in *fives*: five short beats followed by five long beats—delicate rhythmic sophistication of a kind more robustly expressed in the piano rag music of Scott Joplin, in such classic "elite syncopations" as *Maple Leaf Rag* (1899) and *The Entertainer* (1902).[3]

In numerous works throughout his career, including sketches for the austere *Symphonies of Wind Instruments* in memory of Debussy, the *Piano-Rag Music*, *Etude for Pianola*, *Duo Concertant*, and elsewhere, Stravinsky follows the lead of Erik Satie in dispensing with barlines on the page. This has the effect of first eliminating the conventional pattern of strong downbeat, weak upbeat, to give every note equal status and, second, creating an impression of music as a ribbon-like continuum or stream of events in the terms of a punched paper roll, the same conceit adopted at different times by Debussy, Satie, Ravel, Ravel's pupil Vaughan Williams, and Pierre Boulez (who in a BBC interview defined *tempo* in terms of a conveyor belt as "simply a quality of speed in the passing of time").[4] To create and perform a music without a regular beat requires a different approach to timing and a new way of thinking about movement in general, a looseness not always compatible with instinctive physical gesture. Such a sense of free association had become a permanent feature of Stravinsky's aesthetic by the 1920s: a sleight of hand responsible not only for the innocent-looking multivoice counterpoints in *Threni* that took an embarrassed Boulez by surprise in 1958 but also the simple but teasing to-and-fro of the composer's farewell setting of Edward Lear's nonsense verse *The Owl and the Pussy-Cat* as late as 1966. Of the role of the pianola in a discarded version of *Les Noces*, Stravinsky confessed,

> The pianola part was not intended for human hands but for direct translation into the punch-card language of the automated poltergeist [a reference to Gilbert Ryle's "ghost in the machine"]. (*Retrospectives*: 119; *Conclusions*: 199)

It was intended to bolster the impression of an impersonal, abstracted ritual: "alienated" or "factual" in keeping with the age of the machine, a concept of externally programmed motivation adopted and identified in theater with the Bertolt Brecht of *Mahagonny*. As guest of honor at a celebration in Paris in June 1965, the composer was alarmed to witness a staged performance of *Les Noces* choreographed by Maurice Béjart and conducted by Boulez, in which the plain peasant wedding ceremony was violated by the added presence of nude body doubles. As Craft explained,

> the gratuitous psychological dimension dilutes, or sells short, the severity of the musical emotion, which, at the end anyway, is tragic emotion of a rarefied kind. . . . *Les Noces* is musically mechanized ritual . . . [expressing] the thoughts, feelings, visions of people who are not individuals in the first place, but types. (*Retrospectives*: 213; *Chronicle*: 282–83)

From this, it should be obvious that absence of emotion is an aesthetic choice, not a void; likewise, a ramshackle tonal quality is an aesthetic choice, not an act of carelessness; and the wish to reproduce a ritual executed with the plain automatism of cultural memory is also an aesthetic *and philosophical* choice, as well as an acknowledgment of cultural reality. The composer's clear message is "Don't meddle with aesthetic choices or try to cover their nakedness by substituting gratuitous nakedness of your own devising. Failure to understand that is not just a failure of nerve but a failure of conscience." A machine aesthetic is not to be dismissed, in T. S. Eliot's phrase, as "the emotional equivalent of thought": it is the thought itself.

In Stravinsky's music, time and motion are primary whereas the musical idea is secondary—hence, his love of the pure verbal music of nonsense verse and approval of Stéphane Mallarmé's riposte to Degas, "It is not with ideas that one makes sonnets, but with words" (*Autobiography* 117): apt advice for a composer already showing promise as a naturally gifted photographer, as testified in *Documents* in splendid portraits of Debussy, Ravel and Ravel's mother, the dancer Vaclav Nijinsky, and other personalities from the Diaghilev era. A photographer does not complain of lacking subject matter, since subject matter is all around; what is required is a good eye and the skills to select, focus, and turn reality into art. For a composer of music, he implies that the task is the same: a time to fill, a service to provide, and choices to make: after that, sheer hard graft, as any Hollywood composer will agree. Through his apprenticeship with Diaghilev, Stravinsky acquired the habits of working at pressure to extreme deadlines, creating music measured to the exact second, along with the value of retaining total control over the process. Working to strict deadlines was yet another motive for not having to rely on fickle inspiration as a precondition for composing, instead imitating, borrowing, and adapting materials overheard or obtained in the public domain as necessary. Academic and intellectual objection to Stravinsky's use of preexisting thematic material is missing the point that the words assembled by a Mallarmé are available to be used by anyone else.

Wail, *hug*, *sneeze*, *fidget*, *squirm*, and *cough* are characteristic gestures of Stravinsky's music, from the earliest student works to the serial compositions of his final years. The *wail* is associated with the lullaby or comfort music, in the ballet *Firebird*, in the tearful first movement of *Ode* in memory of Natalie Koussevitsky, and elsewhere in some of the most moving and beautiful slow movements in all music. The extended wail is the subject and content of *Threni*, a setting of the Lamentations of Jeremiah, a searing elegy from the composer's portfolio of twelve-tone compositions. Tears are frequent in the composer's emotional makeup: tears of loss, anger, joy, as well as tears of intoxicated merriment (naturally, in a Russian).

The *hug* is a gesture of arrested movement by powerful forces, a useful corrective for a composer whose themes often tend to motor along under their own steam until brought into line. Stravinsky recalled,

> One day in my eleventh or twelfth year, while waiting my turn before the confessional screen, I began to fumble impatiently with my belt buckle. . . . Suddenly a priest came from behind the screen, took my arms, and pushed them to my sides. His action was not reproving; indeed, he was so gentle and full of Grace that I was for a moment overcome with a sense of what [poet] Henry Vaughan called the "deep, but dazzling darkness." (*Expositions* 74)

Hugs have an emotional significance in his music; they are the tall, anchoring columns in the *Symphonies of Wind Instruments*, harmonic pylons between which flute and clarinet melodies are strung out like wires, chattering past one another like urgent telephone conversations, the horizontals and verticals together forming a cross.

A *skip* in Stravinsky is a Buster Keaton attempt to march alongside a regiment parading down the street and getting out of step: a running gag in *The Soldier's Tale* and *Renard*, revisited in the ballet *Agon* in the tongue-in-cheek castanet accompaniment of the Bransle Gay (fond reminiscence, perhaps, of a tapdancing Fred Astaire). The broken rhythms of the Danse Sacrale from *The Rite of Spring*, another solo for female dancer, perfectly capture the agitation of a beating heart in the final stages of tachycardiac arrest. How Stravinsky in 1912, the age of acoustic recording, could have been able to reproduce so accurate and compelling a representation of a beating heart in the process of collapse remains a complete mystery.[5]

Physical signs are a constant presence. A *sneeze* is an explosive gesture for beginning a new work, say the *Capriccio* for piano and orchestra or the *Symphony in Three Movements*. The composer's daily sneezing fits, noted by Craft, were wont to occur at mealtimes: volcanic interludes highly anticipated and quickly forgotten. An opening sneeze may be a sign of anger, as at the start of the *Violin Concerto*, or good humor, like an exploding cigar at a party, as with the *Circus Polka*, a dance for elephants (pity the poor pachyderms); violent sneezes punctuate the *Concertino* for string quartet, and a sashay of snuffling saxophones initiates the *Ebony Concerto*, composed for Woody Herman's band. The habit persists into the austere serial world of *Agon*, *Movements* for piano and orchestra, and the 1964 *Symphonic Variations*. An exception to the pattern is the violent sneezing fit detonated at the end, rather than the beginning, of the first movement of the *Symphony in C*.

A *cough* is quieter, a polite "Ahem" to signal that a movement has rolled to a stop. Examples include the off-switch clicks at the end of *Octet*, the one-act opera *Mavra*, the "Building of the Ark" sequence in *The Flood*, and the door-closing full stop of *Canticum Sacrum*—works choosing to end, in T. S. Eliot's phrase, "not with a bang but a whimper." All such gestures are real and emphatic tokens of a tangible and physical musical sensibility explaining why the composer continued to maintain, against opinion to the contrary, that he was not an intellectual. (When asked if the bass clarinet's repeated note at the end of the first movement of the *Symphony in Three Movements* was a representation of "laughter," the composer did not exactly deny it.)

For Stravinsky, a notation is not an index of motion in itself but rather a mechanism for initiating movement in the performer (dancer or musician), through whose actions a sense of movement may be triggered in the listener. In contrast to Matisse—accused by Kandinsky of painting what he imagined a picture should look like rather than striving to represent nature—we might characterize Stravinsky as an artist concerned to "awaken a sensation of motion" rather than "imitate things in motion." The difference is subtle but critical. What the same Kandinsky identified and admired in Monet's painting of a haystack was that the artist's true subject matter was vision and light, expressed in terms of an anonymous feature in the landscape: the haystack. For his part and for exactly the same reason, Van Gogh painted a pair of worn-out boots. The choice of deliberately unheroic, even despised, subject matter was the artists' way of making a statement that it didn't matter what you were looking at; it was the quality of looking that mattered. (René Magritte, who did not get the point, painted a pair of boots morphing into bare feet.) Stravinsky's musical "found objects," of borrowed and folk material, make precisely the same point that what you are listening to is ultimately less important than how well you listen.

2

SORCERER'S APPRENTICE

"Was it right always to compose at the piano?" he asked. His teacher Rimsky-Korsakov replied, "Some compose at the piano, and some without a piano. As for you, you will compose at the piano." Stravinsky adds, "I think it is a thousand times better to compose in direct contact with the physical medium of sound than to work in the abstract medium produced by one's imagination" (*Autobiography* 5). In between bouts of practice, the young man improvised. Nineteenth-century pianism invented keyboard exercises, graded studies, up and down scales, and broken chords, in parallel and contrary motion, designed to strengthen the fingers, cultivate an upright back posture, and develop relaxed hand and arm maneuverability over the keyboard—all in the interests of an "even touch" in which every note would sound with precisely the same pressure and a right-hand melody would flow as seamlessly as a mechanical instrument. It was the price pianists had to pay for following Mozart in accepting the touch-sensitive *fortepiano*. Older keyboards had been deliberately designed for evenness of touch, so a performer did not have to worry about finger pressure, only about timing and the graceful gesture. After Mozart and Haydn, it all went pear shaped; small industries sprang up to manufacture self-playing pianos capable of producing an even tone on a touch-sensitive keyboard, while composers pushed ahead in the opposite direction, creating sonatas in which dynamic contrasts continued to proliferate: loud against soft, fast against slow, clockwork march versus free-flowing arabesque, taking the art of pianism to a level of incoherence barely comprehensible by the domestic performer, all in the name of truth to the artistic impulse. A strange reversal of fortune for a keyboard instrument originally designed to make the planning and execution of musical ideas simple and functional.

So now the piano had turned from a practical measuring device of even tone into a performing device sensitive to the least inequality of touch, and in response, the nineteenth-century teaching profession had created an industry to train human beings to perform like robots. It was not fair. And what exercises! A culture of mindless, repetitive, emotionally empty gestures, up and down, up and down, like a mouse in a treadmill, day in, day out—and for what? To make the musician a better person? Unbelievable.

And yet the meaningless, total artificiality of scales and broken chords—repeated endlessly up and down the full extent of the keyboard and transposed by degrees up and down the scale—generated its own fascination. Although there was absolutely no *musical* significance to a diagonal sequence of notes—no nobility of purpose or excess of subjective emotion, just constant, relentless, machine-like, empty routine—as a last resort, such exercises did trigger a sensitivity to the *potential* grace and intensity of pure gesture and provoke the young musician to look for the seeds of a personal language in an aesthetic built not on sentimental rhetoric but on the power and immediacy of an exotic practice of musical calligraphy: like the Japanese, a culture for whom meaning and artistry lay more in the act of inspiration expressed in the gesture than in the content of the gesture itself. The art of calligraphy is using the act of writing to communicate an enduring mark of the physical person at the instant of writing, an act in which the thought written, while deliberately chosen, becomes secondary: a "found object." The young man improvised his way at the keyboard toward an art of musical gesture to be applied to familiar found objects in the musical environment.

* * *

Scherzo for piano (1902); *Piano Sonata* in F sharp minor (1903–1904; Naxos, 8.570377); *Symphony in E flat* (1905–1907; *Works* 8:1–4); *Faun and Shepherdess* (1907; *Works* 15:1–3); *Pasto-*

rale for vocalise and piano (1907), arranged in 1923 for muted violin and chamber orchestra (*Works* 12:11).

The earliest works to survive, though not great music and not included in the complete edition, are of interest because they are by Stravinsky and because they show that the relatively late starter (a twenty-year-old law student by the time the *Scherzo* was composed) had acquired a useful technique, if limited vocabulary of gestures. The brief *Scherzo* has about as much emotional interest as winding up a clockwork toy, but at the very end, the piece takes off, as though set loose on the polished floor and left to race and hide under the sofa. In four movements, the twenty-eight-minute long *Sonata in F sharp minor* furnishes a catalogue of technical effects and priorities applied to a medley of piano styles drawn from the piano literature. Beethoven is alleged as an influence, but I don't hear it; a lot of Liszt in I, "Pomp and Circumstance" by Elgar, a touch of Scriabin here and there. This is music eager to impress and music as performance (gesture) rather than as content (argument), a sign of a natural disposition to compose for the ballet.

In every movement, the composer appears to be locked in a struggle with an opening flourish, giving the performance the appearance of a physical workout in the gym, as though the point of the exercise were to escape, and what is uplifting is that at the end of each movement, it is as though the maneuver succeeds: the ending of the first movement, descending to low G and F sharp, is the same pair of notes that, half a century later, marks the end of *Movements*. II is a restless Scherzo, revisiting the 1902 piece of the same name but technically more versatile and looking ahead to the impressionism of *Fireworks*. In III are hints of Frederick Delius in pastoral mode, but the Andante flow cannot be sustained, and the fingers wander off into coarse, Brahmsian filigree; the final movement is possibly an attempt at humor, melding flights of pianistic fancy after Rachmaninov with a signature theme sounding suspiciously like "Mademoiselle from Armentières." In sum, this is music about broken textures, drawing on Romantic conventions of the virtuoso piano reduction of the orchestral repertoire; it shows a restless spirit, a constant search for transitions, for making connections, deliberate cultivation of polyrhythms, a confidence in using the entire sweep of the piano keyboard, and from time to time, a willingness to venture into atonal or enharmonic no-man's-land—seeds of the colorful tonal and gestural language of *Firebird*.

Stravinsky declared himself not unashamed at the revival of the *Symphony*, his Opus 1 and first major length composition, a symphony in four movements. He would be listening technically rather than globally to how specific problems of instrumental balance, continuity, and statement were originated and adapted from other sources and how they were fitted together. This is manifestly a set piece, an academy piece after Raphael's *School of Athens* or a classical landscape by Fragonard in which the viewer's game is "spot the celebrity"—or, in the case of a Fragonard or Poussin, spot the tree, since features of a classical landscape were also stereotypes to be borrowed and knowingly inserted into an artist's work to show familiarity and breadth of knowledge. The point was not to demonstrate originality but skill and certainly not "realism." For a musical expert, the game is spotting the cameos: a Wagner fanfare to bring movement to a stop and the audience to attention at critical moments (very German, very functional), segueing to a smoother ride after the style of Schubert and Tchaikovsky, rather like a ride on an electric tram. In movie terms, this young composer likes tracking shots and rapid "camera movements" or changes of scene; in an emergency, all one has to do is pull the cord, and Wagner rings out again, to apply the brakes and bring matters to a temporary stop. This is a music crafted like a first movie, and the way to enjoy it is to imagine it as a movie stitched from apprentice footage of reasonable quality and considerable technical variety. From time to time, the music dithers over a change of key, giving the impression of pausing at the curb to look left and right. Looking back, Stravinsky would be well satisfied at the craftsmanship and selection of images on display and the knowing way in which one style is offset (and sometimes shrewdly undermined) by the next in line. The whole work is a conversation piece put together in the manner of a hostess organizing her guests at table to ensure a lively current of conversation, precisely because those sitting together will not always agree and that is the point.

Though Stravinsky likes to use changes in tempo as an expressive device, the underlying pace of travel in this first movement is relatively uniform. At around 6:05, a brawl breaks out in the horns—thereafter, a promenade passing shop windows, noticing fashions: Brahms at 8:00, followed by a glimpse of Debussy, a touch of Elgar at 9:00, then Dvořák at 10:00, followed by a lovely four-part chorus of muted horns. The end of the first movement is full in sound but also transparent, an effect that takes skill and is destined to become a hallmark of his mature style.

Mendelssohn in fluttery *moto perpetuo* style—a typically Leipzig staccato style adopted by Arthur Sullivan of Gilbert and Sullivan fame—introduces the second movement, a light-footed dance for flutes and plucked strings in a style to be revived in the ballet *The Fairy's Kiss*. Once again, the layout of the movement is foursquare, the composer relying on divisions within the frame segment to add variety, among which are some wonderful mixture changes of instrumental color. Skillful handling of instrumental color leads at 2:00 into a passage reminiscent of Frederick Delius, more Dvořák at 3:00, including a tiny glimpse of Rimsky-Korsakov at 4:30 (a single chord from his orchestration of Mussorgsky's *Night on the Bare Mountain*). The movement ends abruptly, as if a door closes.

Low strings in opposing thirds, slow and solemn, set a deliberately Russian tone for the more expansive third movement, acknowledging the Russian nationalist school and laying claim to a typically Russian trudging motif to be reinvested with interest in the ballets *Firebird* and *Petrushka*. A strongly hieratic, ceremonial quality, distinctively different from the conventional Wagner formulae, introduces a new sense of identity with the musical action, distinct from the somewhat detached, onlooker spirit of earlier movements. The action builds at 2:00 to another "Great Gate of Kiev" moment, neatly dissolved into a charming piccolo and cello duo, very Tchaikovskian and lyrical. A brass and timpani climax, though formulaic, is beautifully managed and quite Mussorgskian, succeeded at 3:45 by a new and strident assertiveness, lurching away from Tchaikovsky toward Scriabin, in a sudden switch of loyalties from rhythmic management to the darker resources of harmonic suggestion. One can quite easily follow the composer's changes of mind and growing confidence in musical direction finding in real time. Growing self-assurance is indicated at 7:00, a climax of repeated brass into horns, strings, and timpani that, instead of grinding the movement to a halt, suddenly and dramatically dissolves leaving a solo bassoon alone in the dark. This light and shade movement is more complex and involved than anything before, Brahmsian in density but more sumptuously varied in color in a quite un-German way, and developing a new and striking sensuality relating to instruments not just as colors but as characters, voices, and personalities. Russian keynote thirds return at 10:00 in a passage of accumulating layers, a piano-roll additive technique of overprinting one pattern on another of which Stravinsky is already a master, to become a mainstay structural resource of the ballets *Petrushka* and *The Rite of Spring*. At 11:30 in a sudden blast of tonal eau de cologne, Scriabin suddenly returns in an "air of other planets" moment of chromatic uncertainty that also leads a listener to wonder if Stravinsky is signaling an acquaintance with Schoenberg's *Verklaerte Nacht* at a St. Petersburg new music concert.[1]

The fourth movement, a *Presto*, bristles with nervous energy: Tchaikovsky, Mussorgsky, a touch of Sousa, then, out of the blue, an unexpected foretaste of Leonard Bernstein's overture to *Candide* (don't ask). This is Stravinsky in businesslike mode, creating music "about being busy" and setting up structures like trapezes and high wires on which solo instruments are let loose to teeter dangerously and swing recklessly between punctuation points solidly anchored by the full orchestra. The symphony ends with a foursquare peroration in an overripe Russian style to be spirited away by the Chinese after the Russian Revolution, eventually to resurface in the era of Chairman Mao as stylized accompaniment to the song and circus of Revolutionary Red Chinese opera.

Stravinsky's Op. 2 is dedicated to his first wife, Catherine. There is no suggestion of self-portraiture by the composer, though the possibility has to be a consideration that the work is intended as a kind of formal portrait in classical style. Nor does the composer admit any significant influence (a bit of Tchaikovsky's *Romeo and Juliet*, a smidgen of Wagner). It is, however, a style of word setting that, despite the text being Russian, is French influenced, syllabic, and speechlike: a style newly identified in 1902 with Debussy's opera *Pelléas et Mélisande*. When the two composers eventually met, Debussy invited him to a performance of his opera, which Stravinsky recalled not enjoying. One can understand why: first, an irritating habit by the French of expressing words in the style of a sewing machine, syllable by syllable, with a glazed expression oblivious to meaning, and, second, a natural languor in accompaniment that appears designed to send a listener to sleep rather than encourage any sort of critical or emotional response to what is being said. Cuteness in Debussy is all very well, but for Stravinsky it would not be enough. Against that standard, it is not hard to appreciate Stravinsky's more consciously artful word setting, which flows with a natural buoyancy and grace as if one were talking to a real person. At times, too, the accompaniment appears to be playing coquettishly with the mezzo voice, a steadying influence, a charming and revealing touch.

For a composer used to creating by a process of montage, of cut and splice, the setting of a relatively long and continuous text brings its own challenges. In this case, the music appears to "digest" the verses as they are declaimed in real time; so, unlike act I of *The Nightingale*, whose word setting it at times resembles, here one is conscious of an attempt to deliver the text smoothly and eloquently rather than attempting to "interpret" it. As such, even at this early stage in his career, Stravinsky is resisting the idea of imposing a superfluous layer of interpretation on a text considered to be sufficiently explicit on its own terms. The final effect is a sweet, lingering poignancy, a *groundedness* reminiscent of Erik Satie but also conveying a sense of gravity.

The first movement is gestural in a manner anticipating the *Three Japanese Lyrics*; the second comes across as a preliminary sketch for *Petrushka*; and the third, a curious combination of hot and cold emotion, focused on shivering (or perhaps shimmering) strings and pre-*Firebird* heroics, nicely orchestrated. In I and III, octave leaps by the voice send mixed messages of ecstasy and fear, a flourish to recur, rather less successfully, in *Fireworks*. In II at 0:48 and III at 2:58, a listener may hear fleeting allusions to the folk song "The Keel Row," a musical found object more usually associated with Debussy's *Gigues* for orchestra, composed in 1912.

Irreverently identifiable as Stravinsky's "Surrey with the Fringe on Top," the delightful *Pastorale* is music for a ride in the country, gently evocative of country music based on the drone of a *musette*, or simple country pipes over which weaves a sinuous, introspective melody phrased in lines of a faintly Arabic character, each line beginning with an ornamental flourish. I hear hints closer to home, of life on Stravinsky's country estate on the Polish border, a hurdy-gurdy among the trees, an image that, if referenced to Debussy's *L'Après-midi d'un Faune*, strikes the ear as unaffectedly appealing, less precious and more resinous, and smelling of the soil than the conventional French stereotype of pastoral Grecian myth.

The deliberately ornamental style is a giveaway *truc*, or feature of older mechanical instruments, a world of barrel organs and wheezing calliopes encountered at the fairground, whose authentic roots are among the rural peasant community. Bagpipes are a feature of Pieter Bruegel the Elder's *Peasants' Wedding Feast* and *Peasant Dance*: a music of outdoor country life typically expressed in sharp, penetrating, reedy timbres of constant loudness and tremulous finger ornamentation. There is enough authentic quality in *Pastorale* for a listener to suspect a knowing response to folk music researches elsewhere. The work after all coincides with Bartók's first transcriptions of Hungarian folk idioms, to which Stravinsky's message in a piece of deliberately modern tuning replies that cultural identity is not achieved by assigning modern chords to authentic melody figures but reproducing a particular tonality and quality of sound. Perhaps this is the first hint of an attraction to subject matter that would lead after many years to *Les Noces*, a testament to peasant marriage ritual that involved the composer in a succession of massive artistic and moral crises and redrafts, to make the transition from a costume drama of *Firebird*-style luxury emulating a Russian Fragonard to an authentically plain style divested of superfluous decoration.

One detects a tremulous, slightly ramshackle quality in *Pastorale* reminiscent of an old musical box, blending nicely with the Arabica of Le Café from Tchaikovsky's *Nutcracker*. A wonderful Hungaroton CD from 1987, *Musica Curiosa*, offers a taste of the pastoral tradition to which Stravinsky seems to be referring. The recording comprises *Peasant Wedding* and *Sinfonia Pastorella* by Leopold Mozart, father of Wolfgang, and a rowdy *Partita for Rustic Instruments*, by Georg Druschetsky (1745–1819). The music is joyful, abrasive, strident, and vital and features such concert rarities as bagpipe, hurdy-gurdy, dulcimer, alphorn, and *tromba marina*.[2] There is enough in this traditional music and in Stravinsky's *Pastorale* to suggest that the composer is making a quiet but deliberate statement about his personal and national roots as a composer, in extending a hand to a tradition of real music despised and rejected by leaders of musical fashion, especially since the work could also be interpreted as a love song without words, about "tying the knot." The distinctive attack flourishes of country music eventually reappear to dramatic effect in the slow movement of the *Piano Concerto*, in the answering trumpets of the first movement of the *Violin Concerto* (a chicken-clucking effect delivered in reverse by the trumpets at the start of *Agon*), and with a hint of menace in the mock Arabic cor anglais solo of the Ancestors' Ritual Action in part II of *The Rite of Spring*. The soprano saxophone is a happy choice of solo timbre in a compilation CD by Branford Marsalis.[3]

Above all, this is work in which, perhaps for the first time, one senses real contentment. It is all of a piece.

* * *

Scherzo Fantastique (1907–1908, revised in 1930) for large orchestra (*Works* 1:24); *Fireworks* (1908) for large orchestra (*Works* 1:25); *Four Studies* for piano (1908; MusicMasters, 01612-67110-2).

An orchestral interlude of decent length, somewhat aimless, *Scherzo Fantastique* resembles a discarded intermission from *Firebird*: full of interesting special effects but empty of drama. Stravinsky is beginning to use the orchestra as a character as well as a color resource, extending control of melodic gesture to take account of the tonal quality of the instrument as well. It is not altogether original, because we have heard it before, in Berlioz and Dukas, but rather a tactic indicative of greater confidence in instrumentation and adding an extra dimension of vivid Fauvist color contrast to an already sophisticated handling of texture.

All so-called minor works deserve attention because, however minor, they are still personal and they all have a reason to be composed, usually technical. In this case, Stravinsky is moving on from the *Symphony in E flat* to create a showpiece without an academic program, in which to deploy a greater range of skills and greater technical refinement, notably in writing for strings and clarinets (including the bass clarinet) but also in the use of exotic sounds of multiple harps and celesta.

Rimsky-Korsakov's "Flight of the Bumble-Bee" from *Tsar Saltan* (1900) is a useful point of comparison, in the way that the elder composer is able to conjure an entire movement out of a single idea of an insect in flight in which the airborne melody is not in the notes but in a sustained, textured line passing back and forth between flute and violins, at the same time effectively conveying an impression of a real insect darting about in real space. Here is a banal subject elevated to high art in which instruments are transformed into characters. In *Scherzo Fantastique* (the very title is a giveaway), Stravinsky uses similar techniques to similar effect, including a "bumble-bee" episode at 6:50

and a startling "breeze" effect for muted strings at 7:30. At times the movement resembles Mendelssohn on speed (a Russian *Midsummer Night's Dream*).

Stravinsky commented that the work "owes much more to Mendelssohn by way of Tchaikovsky than to Rimsky-Korsakov" (*Conversations* 41n)—fair enough, in respect of his handling of the string orchestra, both as a resource and in relation to the winds. But another significant innovation, for which his old teacher deserves some credit, is a newfound freedom to prolong a characteristic motif indefinitely, without losing momentum but at the same time not having to go anywhere. This is a very useful skill to have to hand, especially for a composer destined for a life in ballet, since it allows the composer to spin out a scene or figure of speech as long as may be dramatically or structurally necessary, without losing the thread or the audience and without having to submit to the internal direction of whatever melody motif is in play. It is an early glimpse of a technique fully exposed to view in *Petrushka* and *The Rite of Spring*, transformed into a kind of Gertrude Stein stutter in which, like a novice politician, continuity of musical speech is delivered as broken phrases constantly modified, as though the composer were making it up on the spur of the moment.

Fireworks could be described as an impressionistic tone poem presented as a series of connected hinged panels, like a Japanese screen. As such a title suggests, this is music about bright, spinning, and floating objects high in the air, an evocation of light and space consistent with the artist James McNeill Whistler's *Nocturnes*, in particular the *Nocturne in Black and Gold* of 1877, in which a falling rocket and other fireworks are suggested by what looks like a random flick of the brush. If Stravinsky did indeed have Whistler in mind, he would deliberately be setting out to court a response from critics, of a kind similar to Ruskin's accusation against Whistler, that his art was "throwing a pot of paint in the public's face." (Whistler sued and won, and Ruskin was fined one penny in damages.) That is quite a bold challenge for a young composer to make, signifying a sense of confidence in the medium equivalent to Whistler or indeed to a master calligrapher, which is the other connection (Japanese art was an equal influence on Whistler's avant-garde aesthetic). This is a music of deliberately exotic effects playing on a sense of constant tension between dark and light, earth and sky, weight and buoyancy, gravity and flight.

The opening is dramatic: an oscillating flute motif against whizzing streaks of high violin. The music simply appears: up there, in the distance, its rich but spare and lightweight combination of motifs suggesting a minimalist arrangement of brush marks on a Japanese screen. Such an entrée is a direct challenge straight away to the bucolic world of Debussy's *L'Après-midi d'un faune*, to the languid flute of which the Russian opposes the musical image of an insolent fire siren and violin figures as unintelligible graffiti against the night sky. Stravinsky's music appears out of nowhere in midair, but unlike Debussy's, it does not need to go anywhere, a daring conceit given that there is nowhere for it to go: no framework or landscape to which these gestures can relate, only a listener's powers of association of such sounds with objects floating high in the air. The opening gesture repeats, and the musical landscape fills out, as though the listener's eyes were adjusting to the dark. The opening panel ends with an orchestra flourish of cymbals and piano evoking an ascending rocket.

A moment of suspense, and we are into panel 2, a vision of an aurora borealis in high string harmonies: a shimmering, translucent, gently descending lullaby in exotic Scriabinesque chromatics against ascending arpeggios of stylized pyrotechnics suddenly and fortuitously interrupted by trombone fanfares. These I can well imagine the composer originally intending as a three-voice upward *glissando* in imitation of Schoenberg, then deciding not to risk it.[4] The pace stiffens; then the world comes to life, turns on the lights, and springs to attention with yet more trumpets and drums fanfare, provoking a series of ecstatic bursts of melody and accompanying dazzle, quite possibly erotic in implication, an exhibition brought to an end by a remarkable modulation of drumroll and jumping jacks (or automatic rifle fire) on the entire orchestra, ending with a bang.

The work is strongly visual and dazzlingly orchestrated but in other respects cartoonlike (Katzenjammer Kids), wayward, and inconsistent. It is the music of a composer with a keen tactile sense but one not quite sure of what he is reaching for and easily distracted—understandable, perhaps, in an onlooker at a fireworks display. What is deservedly impressive, however, is the music's unprecedented density of information, a skill in impressionist texture creation taken to an extreme point where the distraction itself becomes the subject matter, like a widescreen movie in such high definition that the observer is visually saturated and cannot decide where to look. Once again, short repeating motifs are compiled into larger gestures that ultimately are simply about chord changes: a style of musical animation very much in keeping with pianola broken chord technique.

The *Four Studies* for piano are of interest as a resumption of interest in layered timescales, conducted at a level of neutrality and persistence suggesting that they were composed as a higher level of digital expertise, in the spirit of Clementi. The attraction of multiple tempi is directly related to piano-roll technology, as later taken up by the American composer Conlon Nancarrow, from whom the style passed to Elliott Carter. The *Etudes* show that Stravinsky's endorsement of Stockhausen's *Gruppen* (1957) and MS citation of the score as a title-page epigraph to the US edition of *Memories and Commentaries* (1960) were genuine gestures of recognition.

After the "portraits" of mechanical and rustic instruments (hurdy-gurdy, harmonium) in *Pastorale*—which were bucolic and atmospheric in intention, capturing the charm of antique, somewhat wheezy mechanisms—these four piano studies are very specific "white" exercises in moiré-related extended pattern recognition (to be regarded perhaps as the aural equivalent, somewhat before the fact, of the op art of Bridget Riley or Victor Vasarely). An interest in flicker effects is not unexpected at a time when artistic interest in the movies and optical illusion was high and the shutter speed of the movies somewhat slower than 24 frames a second, leading to interference with the moving image, such as wheels appearing to rotate backward. Layered metrical tempi is a different sensation from layered accentual tempi (as in *The Soldier's Tale*). The idea of pushing mechanically geared metrical combinations to excess becomes a distinctive feature of Stravinsky's dynamism in a few places in *The Rite of Spring* (e.g., Cortège du Sage) through to the *Symphony in Three Movements* and making a final appearance as late as the prelude of *Requiem Canticles.* Pianola expert and virtuoso Rex Lawson has identified a hand-punched piano-roll edition of the *Piano Etudes* as the composer's first public association with the medium, a four-roll set published by the London-based Orchestrelle Company in late 1914, along with a second, private set commissioned by British composer Philip Heseltine, better known as Peter Warlock, also including piano transcriptions of the *Scherzo Fantastique* and *Fireworks*.[5]

Individually, étude I is a brief, Scriabinesque concoction that runs out of breath before a minute is up, then finds second wind. Étude II engages in *Firebird*-like chromatic flourishes and rhythmic combinations, chromatic expansions in improvisatory mode garnishing plain harmonic sequences in the German style. Étude III is a Schumann-inspired lullaby with the melody line in the left hand and broken chords in the right. The very fast étude IV—one wonders if Prokofiev knew and was influenced by it—exploits upward scales in pre-*Firebird* flickering surges very effectively imagined for the self-playing piano and yet another indication of the composer's attraction to gliding effects.

* * *

Firebird: Ballet in Two Scenes (1909–1910; *Works* 1:1–22).

First there was Rimsky-Korsakov, then there was Catherine, then there was Diaghilev. Rimsky-Korsakov recognized an unorthodox talent, trusted the young composer, and helped give him the skills necessary to succeed in his art while recognizing that the artistic direction that Stravinsky wanted to follow was beyond the imaginative vision of the academy. That he did is a measure of Rimsky's culture as well as his humanity. Stravinsky's wife Catherine brought love, stability, trust, and emotional acknowledgment within his own family. In a sign of true devotion, she also became a trusted copyist of his music, her neat, authoritative hand virtually indistinguishable from Stravinsky's own finished manuscripts. To a young artist of growing professional skill and emotional confidence, Serge Diaghilev brought a national culture, recognition, and career prospects. A St. Petersburg resident and distant relative of Stravinsky on his father's mother's side, Diaghilev had trained in music with the intention of becoming a composer, sought Rimsky's advice, then, deciding that he did not have the talent, instead set himself to become an impresario, fixer, and promoter of Russian modern and heritage art throughout Europe at a time when a decadent European culture was in serious need of new energy and fresh ideas.

As a complete art connoisseur, Diaghilev lived in a very different cultural space. Composers in general are timid, conservative creatures who stay indoors, bluster, and do as they are told. There was a Russian music to present to the world. What he was looking for was a Russian musical imagination to compete with the young radicals of Paris: the Debussys, the Ravels, whose effortless and airy pastel-colored impressionism was wasted, as he saw it, on vapid classical and medieval legend. He listened to *Pastorale* and saw the peasant world of Van Gogh and Millet; he listened to *Fireworks* and *Scherzo Fantastique* and heard sounds of a vigor and directness that reminded him straight away of Kandinsky's improvisations: a musical art not only richly seductive and dazzling on its own terms but an art intelligent enough to offer subversive and witty comment on the contemporary art scene. The young man was offered an impossible temptation: to replace Liadov as composer of a sumptuous, full-length ballet, *The Firebird*, to be presented in Paris, all to a very tight deadline.

For Stravinsky it was a vote of confidence and an opportunity to apply his skills to a feature-length programmed dance narrative to be worked out in consultation with Diaghilev and a choreographer. Creating ballet then was something like the movie industry today. Diaghliev had powerful backers. Russian realism was perceived as a primal force of nature, with a mission to reform and revivify a diseased and war-ravaged European consciousness. Underpinning the cultural messages lay a substructure of trade, diplomacy, and political oneupmanship. For Diaghilev, ballet was key, a visual spectacle of superior physical beauty and skill, a vivid exhibition and social event of movable and wearable art, exceptional music, and high cultural symbolism. The Russians under Petipa had transformed the art of ballet from a species of decorative interlude between acts of opera or drama, a minor art of costume gymnastics, into a major performance spectacle of newly appreciated abstract formal beauty and symmetry to compete with the grandiose but plodding rhetoric of Wagnerian opera and opera in general. Since Mozart's time, opera had declined from a witty action spectacle to a wordy, interminable theater of overweight people shouting at one another. In ballet you had lights, action, physical beauty, an orchestra, and no need to wait for words to be squeezed out, like toothpaste from a tube.

Firebird is Stravinsky's first major-length dramatic work. To call it "dramatic" is a bit of a stretch: more like a "themed" formulaic compilation of set-piece dance actions. For a composer, the challenge was to make the formula work, not only for a paying audience, but for the players. To take a familiar example from the 1820s, Schubert's *Rosamunde* ballet music—composed as dance interludes to a play of the same name—is tactically engineered to achieve three things: (1) to accompany the dance moves, setting the pace and mood; (2) to control changes of pace within the dance from slow to fast; and (3) to act as a musical cue sheet for the dancers to know when to make their moves, when to enter and exit. The character and atmosphere of a dance and its sense of movement and continuity are carried by melody and rhythm—the role of timing by mechanically geared transitions and divisions of an easily counted constant pulse, as well as cues and divisions within the action, which in classical ballet tend to follow standard routines by repeats of musical phrases and gestures and by repeats within phrases, distinguished by changes of instrumental color, a melody motif passing (say) from flute to clarinet, repeated by oboes, then violins (Maconie, *Second Sense* 208–12). (In creating music for silent movies, the process worked the other way: the accompaniment was bound to follow the action, and changes in the music, invariably late, reacted to changes of viewpoint and scene as they appeared on the screen.)

Outwardly, the story of *Firebird* is an exaggerated formality, a fairy tale of set-piece actions exhibiting physical prowess in a choreography of varied moves and combinations of dancers at different degrees of pace corresponding to emotional states. While there is no singing, it is interesting to note that Stravinsky's approach here is anchored by set pieces corresponding to songs without words on recognizable Russian melodies identifiable as "hug moments" or lullabies, linked by transitions of tempo and mood that, for Hollywood composers, would come to represent a new and wonderfully pliable language of musical gesture for movie applications.

A ballet has a program, and for a composer that means working to someone else's script and timetable. For Stravinsky the challenge is not "to think himself into the role" but rather to fill dance modules of specific length with musical activity of suitable pace and energy level and to manage entrances, exits, and transitions with elegance and grace. What he brings to the task are qualities designed to dazzle and impress, to show who is in command. Anna Pavlova resisted, as did others, the demands of a music that tested her ability to follow the beat of a music of kaleidoscopic texture and brilliance, like a dazzling casket of jewels, reviewed at high speed. It was an experience of challenging the corps de ballet to cope with a movielike continuum of flickering images, extreme contrasts of movement, and irregular rhythms of five and seven beats, weird syncopations, deliberately misaligned and out-of-step ensembles, and jazzy, off-the-beat entries. In the midst of all of this elegant, brilliantly costumed industry, there also lurk expressions of subversive humor, moments in which the female corps de ballet in delicate jitters are slyly portrayed as headless chickens with male leads as posturing farm animals: ox, ass, pigs, ducks. Below the ultrarefined surface of Stravinsky's animation is a view of life under the tsars as a combination of rococo pastoral and panic attack, an edgy, executive nervousness to last the composer's entire life.

The unprecedented aural complexity of *Firebird* arises from a deliberate application of "dither," applying texturing and layering techniques to a tonal framework of relatively simple chord progressions. When four-by-four formalism is a personal issue, as we hear in the *Symphony in E flat*, the simple answer is "to apply to music the techniques of the movies," as Debussy recommends, and turn your art into a species of faceted fragmentation.[6] To hold the music together, however, and prevent an art of fragmentation from turning into a music of chaos and dissipation, Stravinsky intuitively borrows from another technology, the phonograph, to control an audience's perception of the music's speed of motion in a global sense. By gearing the tempo of music to its instrumentation and tonal quality, instead of arbitrary fluctuations of pace, audiences would register that slow and heavy music was associated with the bass register and that fast, elated musical spirits were associated with high-pitched instruments and fluttering textures. It would be as though the music—and the story—were a gramophone recording subject to speed alteration, beginning in the murky bass, gradually winding up to maximum speed, and, at the finale, broadening out like a decelerating train coming hissing and squealing into a terminus. Such ideas were in the air, visually in the diverting trick anamorphisms of moviemaker Georges Meliès and musically in Ravel's 1906 piano sketches for *La Valse*, an inebriated parody of Viennese waltz finally put to bed in 1920.[7]

The device is anchored in this case by the simplest of motifs: an undulating melody corresponding to a circular motion. It starts the music off in the bass, slowly and deliberately, accelerates to a peak with the Dance of the Firebird, and serves as a linking motif throughout the entire action. It is a technical device among a composite of technical devices brought to bear on a narrative that is frankly rather stale and anachronistic. The most interesting and impressive features of the ballet score—and the reason why *Firebird* remains so instructive to movie composers and successful as a concert item for orchestras—are not the set pieces but the transitions. Ultimately, the work is a concerto for conductor and orchestra rather than a fairy-tale ballet. With an eye to commercial success, Stravinsky immediately redacted the full score into the 1910 concert suite, preserving the set pieces (the wail and the hug) and eliminating the finale and transitions, along with a few Scriabinesque figures of musical speech that he may have felt were potential liabilities. A more balanced suite was created in 1919, restoring some earlier cuts and the popular Great Gate of Kiev ending, an overlong signature Russian anthem that had become politically charged by the events of 1917. (Rimsky-Korsakov had composed an opera, *Kashchei the Immortal*, as recently as 1902 and toward the end of his life been harassed by the imperial censors demanding cuts in texts regarded as critical of the tsar. It is possible to interpret the climax of *Firebird*, when the egg containing Kashchei's power is shattered, as a symbolic act of destruction of a Fabergé egg representing the power of a failing imperial Russian régime.) That the pompous ending continued to raise issues for the composer can be seen from his 1947 revision of the score, in which the music's sense of grinding to a stop, like a movie slowing down until each frame becomes isolated and distinct (quite a neat and interesting idea), is reinterpreted as a musical box slowing down, the chords transformed into hammer or guillotine blows in a succession of staccato downbeats separated by gaps of increasing length, in direct contradiction to the message of the final blazing statement of the cyclical motif.

To appreciate Stravinsky's genius as an orchestral craftsman, one need only listen to Rimsky's *Golden Cockerel*, Saint-Saëns's *Danse Macabre*, Dukas, Ravel's edition of Mussorgsky's *Pictures at an Exhibition* (a Rimskyan makeover from 1922 also indebted to Stravinsky), and as far back as Schubert, or almost a century to Rossini's overture to *La Cenerentola* (Cinderella), a genial precursor in the orchestral literature of Stravinsky's style of animation. Stravinsky's piano-roll edition of *Firebird* published in 1929 (reissued on Dal Segno, DS PRCD007), like all of his piano rolls, offers a fascinating glimpse of the composer's thematic and rhythmic priorities. Valery Gergiev and the Kirov Orchestra (Philips, 289 446 715-2) showcase the composer's debt to Scriabin while clearly demonstrating the younger composer's superior direction and inventiveness. A vivid 1979 recording of the 1919 suite by the Moscow Philharmonic Orchestra conducted by Dmitrij Kitaenko (Melodiya, 7939-2-RG) nicely highlights the role of exotic percussion sonorities while preserving the original blazing nonstaccato finale. Both Gergiev and Kitaenko versions and a 1966 live Moscow Radio recording by Gennadi Rozhdestvensky of the 1919 suite (Revelation RV 10035) appear to represent uncorrected editions of the score.

* * *

Two Poems of Verlaine (1910) for baritone and piano, orchestrated in 1951 (*Works* 15:4–5).

These two songs are Stravinsky's first settings in the French language, although the melodies appear to have been composed to the accentuation of Russian syllabic translations (Taruskin 654). The second poem, "Un grand sommeil noir . . . ," was set by Ravel in 1895, also by a young Edgar Varèse, at the time a pupil in Paris of Charles Widor, in 1906 (London, 289 460208-2). Partially orchestrated at the time of composition, Stravinsky's settings were reorchestrated in 1951. This is music of an emotional intensity leading one to suspect a time of crisis; in 1951, a corresponding crisis of confidence was about to lead Stravinsky away from neoclassicism toward the countertonality of Schoenberg. What the two Verlaine songs signify for the composer in 1951 is that he had been there before.

In their 1951 versions, these strangely oblique and emotional verses—of which Schoenberg's description of Webern, "a novel in a single sigh," would also be appropriate—carry an intensity of charge, a sense of premonition, out of proportion to their actual duration, a concentration shared with Schoenberg and Webern at this period but more intense, as if Edvard Munch's *The Scream* were expressed with the detailed richness of a canvas by Gustav Klimt. The Verlaine settings also share with Schoenberg and Webern, in dimensions and tone, a sepulchral quality associated with acoustic recordings of the period, the best of which tended to sound like séances. (Just a year later, in 1911 Wassily

Kandinsky and Franz Marc compiled the *Blaue Reiter Almanach*, breaking with the Neue Künstler Vereinigung to form the Blue Rider movement. Following his 1912 meeting with Schoenberg in 1912, Stravinsky is likely to have acquired a copy of the first edition, in which is reproduced Schoenberg's manuscript score of *Herzgewächse*, another specimen of emotionally concentrated writing for voice and chamber ensemble composed to evoke the atmosphere of an acoustic recording [see Kandinsky].)

It would be a mistake to describe these enigmatic works as sketches for a larger work, though they do appear to lead the composer into a Madame Blavatskian region that Debussy and Ravel would consider dangerously close to atonality. (The Rosicrucian Satie, however, would be delighted.) Ravel does not attain a comparable strangeness of idiom until the *Chansons Madécasses* of 1925–1926 (recorded by Boulez on Sony Classical, SMK 64 107); Stravinsky's more radical instrumentation does, however, sound like a serious first attempt at evoking the otherworldly harmonies of *Zvezdoliki* (King of the Stars).

The authorized recording is unfortunately affected by uncertain intonation, also a problem with *Zvezdoliki*, and partly due, I suspect, to a scheme of noting sharps and flats as enharmonic (unequal tempered) intervals deviating from "correct" intonation, at the time a topic of concern to folksong transcribers Bartók and Kodály. The two songs had a muted reception in both St. Petersburg and Paris (Taruskin 655–69), an achievement suggesting that the composer was off on a personal tangent, perhaps in search of that higher plane of existence identified by Debussy with the distant star Aldebaran.

One can see the composition as a warning shot aimed at Debussy; Stravinsky's instrumentation is insolently good, and his prioritizing of Russian accentuation over French could easily be taken as a deliberate snub ("the Russians are taking over"). Why do this? Because Debussy could be suspicious and outspokenly patronizing toward composers of exotic origin. It is a tradition passed down to Boulez, who has been known to express similarly dismissive views of rival Polish and Russian contemporaries. In a 1903 article for the periodical *Gil Blas*, Debussy poked fun at Grieg: "He is a sensitive musician as long as he sticks to the folk music of his own country, although he nowhere near approaches what M. Balakirev and Rimsky-Korsakov do with Russian folk music. Apart from this he's just a clever musician more concerned about effect than genuinely artistic." A young Russian composer reading such a piece would certainly be on his guard.

3

RITUAL FIRE DANCE

With the end of *Firebird* in sight, the meticulous composer—wondering how to handle the climactic "Infernal Dance" in a tactful manner (it was, after all, about eliminating an evil force holding the nation in submission, a subject that could be misinterpreted by the imperial censors, meaning curtains for his career)—did what his father would do. He looked it up and discovered that the name "Firebird" is a literal translation of *flamenco*: in Spanish, a bird with a red breast and talons—and, of course, a style of fierce dance. Overjoyed, he departed from his composing style up to that point, renouncing unnecessary decoration, setting Scriabin and perfumed effects to one side and composed the "Infernal Dance" as a mock flamenco, visualizing the scene in terms of a ceremonial bullfight, taken at authentic speed but with the full weight of the orchestra making it appear all the faster and more terrifying. The style is exact: twelve beats, accented on the offbeat, with a double stamp at the end of the measure. Nobody noticed. At the Paris premiere in 1910, a shell-shocked Debussy introduced Stravinsky to a cosmopolitan circle of friends, including Maurice Ravel, composer in 1908 of *Rapsodie espagnole*, and the Spaniard Manuel de Falla. Among those he befriended from a circle including the child prodigy Arthur Rubinstein, a polyglot Russian pianist well on the way to a glamorous international career, Stravinsky was particularly impressed by Falla, who immediately complimented him on the authentic quality of the "Infernal Dance" and expressed a genuine enthusiasm for the Russian school's respect for antique Spanish music. This was the ancient gipsy tradition that Glinka,

Borodin, and his teacher Rimsky-Korsakov had instinctively recognized as a primeval musical language transcending national identities, a tradition extending across Europe from Iberia to Russia by way of Brahms's parody "Hungarian Dances." "You show respect," Falla said. "I admire you for that. Unlike some people," he added with a shrug. How, he wondered, could composers of such skill and cultivation, geniuses such as Debussy and Ravel, see fit to treat Spanish idioms as pastoral decorations and exotic colors, without attempting to understand their true origins?—and in the case of the composer of *Soirée dans Grenade*, without even visiting the country?[1] In *Firebird*, he said, "I sense an authentic spirit, grounded in your own deep affinity with authentic gipsy musical culture that, as my master Pedrell has demonstrated, unites Old Russia with Andalusia, and Andalusia with ancient Arabic and Moorish traditions of Northern Africa. Listening to *Firebird*, I can hear that what you are doing is more than mere pictorialism—more even than authentic transcription of local color, which is what Bartók is trying to do with his Magyár transcriptions for piano. All they do is capture the outside, but you cannot convey the spirit of a music by reducing it to an outline, if the spirit is not there. What your art is doing, my dear Stravinsky, is what I too am determined to do: our task is to go beyond preserving local color or tradition to reinstate the essence of music as an universal language."

In a chapter on nationalist trends in *Music in our Time*, a survey of postromantic and early modern music, Falla's disciple Adolfo Salazar pinpoints the peculiar cultural politics of the time, particularly as it affected alien composers in Paris:

> Something common to the four artists just mentioned [Schoenberg, Bartók, Stravinsky, and Falla] must be pointed out: it is their quality of being less European; there is in them a certain element which acts as a differential principle or germ of fermentation within their traditionally European cultural organism. This something is a deep root that unites them with the man of the Orient—so different from the classic man, the romantic man, the Central European. Stravinsky carries in his veins the blood of the Slavic peoples; Schönberg is of Israeli descent; Bartók is Hungarian, that is to say, there are within him certain distant Mongolian strains, and of Falla it has been said that he possesses the leaven of the gypsy race. The reader may take this statement with a grain of salt; yet perhaps it will help him to

> understand with what a profound difference the sonorous fact resounds in the consciousness of these musicians as compared with a César Franck or a Debussy in France; a Verdi or a Puccini in Italy; a Strauss, a Sibelius, a Schreker or a Pfitzner, in central or northern Europe. (298)

Stravinsky was intrigued by Falla, this shy, intensely serious friend, small in stature like himself, befriended but also intimidated by Debussy and secretly pained at his culture being used, patronized, by his Parisian colleagues and their superior ways. Stravinsky asked to see some of Falla's music, including piano pieces that had already been introduced to the public by fellow Spaniard, the pianist Ricardo Viñes. They discussed their plans for the future. "I have had it with *Faune et Bergère* stuff," said the Russian. "It is stale, formulaic, Goethe-style classicism, and so too is *L'Après-midi d'un Faune*, for all its brilliance." "Well," said Falla, "as a matter of fact I have in mind, when I have finished orchestrating *El Amor Brujo* (Love the Magician), to compose a modest piece of puppet theater, *El Retablo de Maese Pedro*, based on an episode in *Don Quixote.* Do you have such a character, a Pierrot figure, in Russia?" "Why yes of course," said Stravinsky. "His name is Petrushka."

In 1913 Falla arranged the "Ritual Fire Dance" from *El Amor Brujo* as a concert item for Arthur Rubinstein. Years later Rubinstein would perform the work onstage to great applause in Edgar G. Ulmer's 1947 movie *Carnegie Hall*, one cameo among many. The piece begins with ferocious trills, turning the innocent bumble-bee of Rimsky's 1900 lightweight orchestral study into a buzzing hornet's nest of collective anger, erupting into an angular dance led by an urgent melody in wailing *cante jondo* idiom, a music of great intensity: few moves but every move exact, poised, like a toreador waiting to strike, and ending with an interminable flourish of repeated doublehanded chords, like hammer blows, merciless, defiant, and absolutely final in intention—all faultlessly executed in black and white with a faint smile, effortless calm, and gracefully elevated and arched hand movements, as though the pianist were waving to the crowd.

Stravinsky was transfixed, taken aback, at the ferocity unleashed in the piano music of this mild-mannered individual. "Ritual Fire Dance" had ingredients he was looking for: a sense of control allowing the pianist to take command, like a toreador, stand his ground and face down an entire orchestra by sheer force of personality. Here was an authentic music capable of bending an audience to its will simply by a trill, or a repeated chord—in other words, simply by being there. A trill, a repeated chord—that was all. Music without content. No more scurrying round like a frightened animal. It was manna from heaven. He had already been discussing with Diaghilev a new project to take music all the way back to its primeval roots, a ritual of death and rebirth. The trill and the repeated chord, incessant, punishing, gave him a glimpse of a suitable musical language. The repeated chord was quickly noted for future use. It would become the most memorable and challenging sequence of *The Rite of Spring*.

Diaghilev was surprised, however, when a friendly inquiry about progress on the new work brought a completely unexpected response: sketches for a concerto for piano and orchestra. In *Autobiography* the composer explained,

> I wanted to refresh myself by composing an orchestral piece in which the piano would play the most important part—a sort of *Konzertstück*. In composing the music, I had in mind a distinct picture of a puppet, suddenly endowed with life, exasperating the patience of the orchestra with diabolical cascades of arpeggios. (31)

In fact, Stravinsky had rushed home in a heat of inspiration to compose his own "Ritual Fire Dance" based on the powerful gestural language of Falla, applied to a scenario representing the real, primeval, mortal contest of a bullfight—a dance this time, more than a signature set piece, a genuine fight to the death. (For Stravinsky, "concerto" or "concert piece" invariably meant a contest or fight, as he also intends by the Greek title *Agon*.)

Diaghilev was delighted. "Go ahead," he said, "but dear boy, remember to keep it Russian: we are the Russian Ballet, and Russia is our daily bread. Make sure the melody material you use can all be traced back to authentic Russian sources." So he did. In due course, his "moment of inspiration" would be purchased by Arthur Rubinstein as a companion work to Falla's "Ritual Fire Dance." After a performance of *Petrushka* in London in 1914, Rubinstein plucked up the courage to approach the composer (*Documents* 121–22). In May 1916 Stravinsky joined the Diaghilev Ballet in Madrid for the Spanish premieres of *Firebird* and *Petrushka* (*Documents* 142–43; see also *Expositions* 139). Falla and Rubinstein were there. Rubinstein asked to buy the dedication to the piano score, which was finally published in 1921. For years afterward Stravinsky felt obliged to insist in public that the *Three Movements from Petrushka* had been composed initially for piano solo, as a separate, self-contained composition, and was only later adapted and extended for the stage, not the other way round.[2] It was composed in a virtuoso style suited to Rubinstein, who had studied in Berlin with Karl Heinrich Barth, a pupil of Liszt, who had studied with Carl Czerny, a lineage going back to Beethoven, whence the high-arched hand and vertical drop.

On a return visit to Madrid in 1921, to conduct the first complete performance of *Petrushka*, Stravinsky composed a curious statement for the magazine *Comoedia* that included the following sentences:

> Affinities and resemblances can be remarked between Spanish music, especially that of Andalusia, and the music of Russia, no doubt through their common Oriental origins. Certain Andalusian songs remind me of Russian ones, and I enjoy these atavistic memories. Musically speaking, the Andalusians are not at all Latin, their rhythms being of Oriental inheritance. (*Documents* 143)

In his *Autobiography*, a long-delayed artistic manifesto published in 1935, by which time he had turned into a neoclassicist and Europe was caught up in serious political difficulty, Stravinsky planted a careful tribute to Falla's "remarkable *El Retablo de Maese Pedro*," adding that "he has . . . deliberately emancipated himself from the folklorist influence under which he was in danger of stultifying himself," a comment designed to distance Falla and himself from accusations of a sinister and trivial nationalism.

* * *

Three Movements from Petrushka (1910, arranged in 1921; DG, 447 431-2).

Any doubts as to the Spanish influence on *Petrushka* are dispelled with the first plunge into the "Danse Russe." There is nothing Russian about it except title and composer: clearly a heel-clicking dance in the spirit of

Andalusia, to which a flamboyant use of parallel harmonies adds a Latino, even Mexican taco flavor. In a market governed by labels, the Russian labeling of a manifestly transcultural music drama celebrating a popular idiom of the poor and oppressed across Europe from time immemorial has to be seen, even in 1911, as a marketing ploy concealing a seriously risky political stance. The universal political message of Shrovetide Fair (or *Mardi Gras*) in 1911 is "enjoy life while you may: tomorrow (Lent) you will be fasting for the good of your soul." The choice of a religious festival from which all religious ceremonial is excluded is just as significant. It creates a blank canvas. All nations of Europe celebrate such a day, which is a day for humanity, not for nationalist politics. The choice of such a setting could not be further removed from the costumed elegance of a Tsarist *Firebird.* It is closer to the domestic nursery of *Nutcracker*, as if to describe the gipsy circus entertainers and street musicians of St. Petersburg (or anywhere) equally as society's children. At the same time, the music is also a celebration of the machine, another covertly despised sector of musical culture: the barrel organ, pianola, musical box, and fairground panharmonicon.

Removed from its ballet context, *Three Movements* presses home an original message of mechanical life as real and dynamic. The unanswered challenge of Stravinsky's somewhat puzzling idea of a *Konzertstück* in which the piano is in combat with the orchestra is to imagine the work as a novel concerto for *pianola* and orchestra in which the piano plays itself and the conductor and orchestra are obliged to play by its terms, which makes amusingly provocative sense at a time of increasing public interest in Ampico and Duo-Art *reproducing* piano technology.[3]

Such a mischievous idea also sits well with a composing aesthetic of a classical music having "nothing to declare." Technically, the idiom is consciously diatonic (major scale) and mechanical and surprisingly free of expressive nuance, dynamic shading, as well as timing hesitations. The significant innovation, which Stravinsky owes to Falla and Spanish tradition, is a heightened sense of bravura timing and separation of phrasing, operating within a constant pulse, the beating heart of a machine. That quality of simulation of live action within the constraints of mechanical timing is the stroke of genius that helped to make *Petrushka* an essential reference for Hollywood animation composers in the

1930s. A deliberately mechanical idiom is also a suitable forum for Stravinsky to show off his skill at multiple layering, a distinctively piano-roll skill best appreciated in the pianola edition recorded by Rex Lawson on MusicMasters (01612-67138-2).

* * *

Petrushka: Burlesque in Four Scenes (1910–1911; *Works* 2:1–15).

On the surface, the ballet *Petrushka* is a fairy-tale about a puppet master and a trio of puppets brought to life. Intellectuals would see the puppet master as Diaghilev and Nijinsky as the tragic lead. Under the surface, however, it is about real life—and love—in a Cartesian world where people are regarded as animated machines. The three puppets—Petrushka the clown, the beautiful ballerina, and the fierce blackamoor (the latter do not have names)—reference the wistful Pierrot tradition, the pirouetting mechanical dancer of musical box fiction and (at a considerable distance) an exotic world of "black" music conveniently relocated from Shakespeare's Venice and Mozart's Turkey to the ragtime of contemporary street life in Harlem and St. Louis, an idiom echoed in Debussy's "Golliwog's Cake-Walk" (from the *Children's Corner* suite) and described by him in unflattering terms as *une musique nègre.*

A minor industry has sprung up in the world of scholarship (summarized in EWW 198–200) seeking to pin down the composer's authentic Russian sources of folk melodies. The ploy has clearly worked, and the ballet has ever since been comfortably settled in a niche marked "Russian medley of popular tunes." Those who have devoted time and effort to this enterprise appear to have missed the point that the *national* origin of the materials assembled together in this parlor game of "spot the tune"—actually an exercise in spontaneous random montage closer in spirit to John Cage than Rogers and Hammerstein—is dramatically speaking an issue of no account: the melodies are "found objects" standing for an ubiquitous, amiable, and vital musical presence in civilized life, at a place, on the street, and in the marketplace, where cultures meet and national identity does not matter. The story's real message resides in the *chance of life* extended to the three puppets and how the gift of musical life alters their perception of the world and their possibilities of happiness—or at least one of them: a theme, in other words, that Stravinsky has already spent much of his career thinking about: touching the "life" properly assignable to all music reproduced from notes on paper.

The abundance of music machines active in the score is overwhelming. Of the three puppet characters, only Petrushka truly comes to life to experience love and rejection. One would imagine that audiences could hardly fail to get the message, and yet they still do. The received message of phonograph (machine-reproduced) folk music had been that this material was not only authentic but retained its lifegiving properties and that what were considered crudities and distortions of orthodox tonality were in fact real, subtle, ancient, and significant. Having previously imitated the broken textures of old mechanical instruments and cultivated an improvisatory style in accordance with programming tradition to emulate living gesture in the approximate terms of machine reproduction, Stravinsky faced a new and very different challenge of adapting to the authentic irregularities of real folk traditions. This time round, the mechanical instruments all perform faultlessly.

The underlying philosophical challenge is, "Is the puppet a real person or only a representation of a real person?" It is the same question asked by troubadours from the dawn of time, singing to the tune of a harp: "Are the emotions I am expressing those of a real person or just a representation?" Once such a question is firmly grasped, the rest falls into place, and the music composes itself. *Petrushka* is at the opposite extreme from Alban Berg's opera *Wozzeck*, two works sharing the same agenda and the same basic cast of characters: in the latter case a peasant soldier, his faithless wife, and manipulative science, the difference being that *Petrushka* is Chaplinesque, a silent and poignant comedy of gesture, whereas Berg's opera is heavyweight, verbose, manipulative, expressionist social drama.

This is Stravinsky's second major-length musical project on the subject of a mechanical imitation of nature. In *Nightingale*, set aside to compose *Firebird*, Stravinsky addresses Hans Andersen's romantic fiction of a mechanical bird in a cage, a *serinette,* being preferred in the imperial court over a creature of nature who, when the chips are down, is the one shown to have the gift of life and the power to restore life to the suffering. That the composer may secretly have welcomed the interruption can be judged by his attitude to animation in *Petrushka*, a tale in which the distinctions between life (and connotations of "suffering, freedom and self-determination") and the mechanical simulation of life suddenly no longer appear so clear-cut.

* * *

Two Poems of Balmont (1911, orchestrated in 1954; *Works* 15:6–7).

Petrushka's ultimate triumph over death is a fabulous moment in theater, a transcendent act of liberation that in retrospect makes the life and summary justice inflicted on Richard Strauss's comparable antihero Till Eulenspiegel—indeed, the whole pathetic story—seem morally suspect as well as cynical, manipulative, and socially decadent. *Petrushka*'s fragmented ending, in wisps and shards of sound, leaves the listener in a curious state of elation, and it is precisely that elevated emotion that Stravinsky attempts to recover and develop in settings of two poems by Konstantin Balmont for high female voice and piano, completed in July 1911, along with the inflated but ultimately aphoristic enigma *Zvezdoliki* for male voices and large orchestra, also to words by Balmont.

Scholarly opinion of the *Two Poems* is hard to find. Eric Walter White gives them short shrift: "straightforward lyrics for voice and piano [deserving] no special comment" (White, *A Critical Survey* 37). Richard Taruskin's more recent opinion, based on exhaustive contextual research, is emotionally uninstructive: "[they] conform to the neonationalist pattern established in *Petrushka*: in both songs, chromatically (that is, octatonically) conceived passages contrast and interact with folkishly diatonic ones" (800–801). "Extremely simple, and among the most graceful [songs] Stravinsky ever wrote" is Craft's obliquely laconic view (CD booklet to MusicMasters 01612-67195-2). All very strange because a listener's immediate and overwhelming impression of the two songs is their open and unashamed communication of female ecstasy. These two songs are Stravinsky's entrée to the world of the exquisite miniature, an art of musical calligraphy designed to celebrate the brevity and intimacy of the new medium of recording, the prominence afforded to the singing voice, and corresponding incidental role assigned to a severely reduced accompanying instrumental ensemble. These two songs precede by half a year Schoenberg's equally ecstatic

Herzgewächse for high soprano and chamber ensemble and occupy the same extreme zone of sensual excitement as Berg's *Altenberg Lieder* for soprano and full orchestra, Webern's miniatures for string quartet, and the dazzling erotic canvases of Gustav Klimt. Dedicated, respectively, to his mother and sister-in-law, these gorgeous songs deserve to be appreciated as sophisticated, knowing (and forgiving) responses to his family's preference for the perfumed joss-stick mysticism of Scriabin, saying in effect, "If ecstasy is what you want, my dears, here it is." But there is no hint of irony in the music itself, just the flush of pink-cheeked delight.

Of course, there is more to these enchanting songs than acknowledging the fairer sex. The professional task that Stravinsky addresses is of gaining confidence in control of the voice and interpretation of poetic speech to the level of combined emotional precision and gestural freedom that he had now achieved in *Petrushka*. There was unfinished business in hand with the incomplete opera *The Nightingale*, an opportunity to draw his vocal writing out of reliance on Debussy and—more important—secure control and not be dominated by the demands of a libretto. To capture the essence of a brief, enigmatic, haiku-like verse in real time was all very well, but the problem facing an aspiring composer of music drama, after Wagner and Debussy, was to escape being tied to the literal meaning and relentless sequence of a poetic narrative.

Though unconvinced by the composer's timid recitative style, Stravinsky all the same appreciated Debussy's word setting in *Pelléas et Mélisande* as an attempt at a "natural" speech, very different from the artificial and elocuted cadences of classical opera, designed to allow the composer to remain in control of the action. Debussy's dialogue in *Pelléas* is fragmentary, allusive, and incomplete, as in real life, giving rise to a perception of the drama as residing in what is not said more than what is actually spoken or sung. Such a fragmentation of text is analogous to the deliberate ornamentation and "dithering" applied to plain melody and harmony in mechanically reproduced music: a deliberate incompleteness designed to draw the listener in, to hang on every word, to guess what is really being said, through to the key moment in the play when it dawns on the audience that the characters in the drama are as undecided as themselves, because full disclosure is not an option.

* * *

Zvezdoliki (King of the Stars; 1911–1912; *Works* 20:7).

Such has been its impact on the profession that this long-neglected and enigmatic work—six minutes of solemn choral and orchestral opulence to a text of unfathomable Nietzschean hubris—is more likely to be identified by a casual listener today as title music in the style of Alex North, composed for a Hollywood science fiction fantasy from the 1980s, than authentic Stravinsky from the *Petrushka* era. "Visionary" means very little in musical terms, unless one is talking about Scriabin, of whom the present opalescent musical concoction, it must be said, inclines more toward his fabled "Mysterium" than the orchestral *Poème d'Extase.* Balmont's lyric is set very plainly, in the middle of the frame as it were, as a male-voice choir recitative in natural speech timing, enfolded above and below by a music reaching to the outer limits of aural perception, the very low and the very high, regions of musical space rarely exploited harmonically and particularly susceptible to otherworldly sonorous effects.

Stravinsky's use of the orchestra resembles *The Rite of Spring* in assigning a primary role to wind instruments and a secondary texture and continuity role to the string orchestra, a reversal of classical practice. But in other respects, the two scores are very different: *Zvezdoliki* word bound, solemn, and heavy, the words congested and sluggish, the opposite of *The Rite of Spring*'s translucent textures and dynamic, fleeting gestures. However, the idiom of *Zvezdoliki*, even though a stylistic dead end, is far from being a trivial imitation of Scriabin. Both the work's ritual gravitas and its rich harmonic language are indebted to Russian Orthodox chant, an authentic male-voice choral tradition of genuinely exotic harmony and intense spirituality. Before dismissing *Zvezdoliki* as a category error, a listener is invited to compare the work's style to anonymous medieval motets "Budi imya Gospodnie" and "Sviatui Boshe," as recorded by Peter Phillips and the Tallis Scholars on Gimell (404 902-2) or the anonymous seventeenth-century "May my prayer rise to you" sung in Russian on Saison Russe/CDM (LDC 288 071). Stravinsky is clearly looking beyond fashion toward a genuine Russian choral tradition of great authority and harmonic pungency. That he did not proceed further in this direction is a given. I can think of two reasons: first, the style was inescapably burdened with tradition; second, he had discovered Schoenberg. Varèse had brought Schoenberg's atonal Op. 11 *Three Pieces for Piano* and Op. 16 *Five Pieces for Orchestra* to Debussy's attention in 1912.[4] The future lay elsewhere, with rhythm.

* * *

> *The Rite of Spring* (Le Sacre du Printemps; 1911–1913; *Works* 2:16–29).

Like the strength of a cable, the strength of a myth—even a myth that has been created to order—resides in the number of strands wound to make it. Stravinsky claimed that the idea for *The Rite* came to him in a dream or vision, while he was still working on *The Firebird*. "A dream" is diplomatic jargon that allows the dreamer to take ownership of a topic in general circulation without risking charges of plagiarism or being sued for a share of royalties. What provoked the dream may have been a growing distaste that Stravinsky certainly felt toward the empty symbolism of the *Firebird* myth. The "vision" of a primeval ritual in which a chosen virgin dances herself to terminal exhaustion to ensure the return of Spring is immediately comprehensible as a variant of Christian mythology constructed by an intelligent nonbeliever. In the alternate myth, which claims to antedate Christianity, the sacrificial victim is female, not male; is selected for sacrifice by ritual lottery, not condemned to death for sedition; is a morally neutral member of the community rather than a moral leader and teacher; goes willingly to death instead of being condemned in an act of judicial retribution; does not die passively and in pain but in ecstasy brought on by dance; and in death is venerated by the tribe. The inverse symmetry is exact.

What Stravinsky had to protect was not the theme of pagan Russia, since the only competition in that subject area was Borodin's *Prince Igor* and, in particular, the "Tribal Dance of Men and Boys" from *Polovtsian Dances*. Naturally, he wanted to find out all he could on a theme dear to Russian composers, drawing on a mythical primal existence beyond recorded history, noting what ideas he could extract from published collections of ancient Russian folk music; the way melodies were delivered, repeated, modified, and exchanged between leaders and the tribe; and the nature and pattern of barbarian tribal dance. In all significant musical respects, the involvement of Nicolas Roerich is negligible, leading one to suspect that his role can only have been intended as a distraction or plant to disguise the new work as a distinctively Russian and politically harmless pseudo-prophetic vision. The entire thrust of the finished work, in its musical terms and references, has nothing to do with names and fake identities, like the god Yarilo. Today *The Rite* is accepted at face value as balletic action drama of no names, carrying no traceable cultural or intellectual baggage, as the composer intended. But for present purposes, Roerich was ideal camouflage: a mediocre painter of indeterminate landscapes professing mystical, Madame Blavatskian fantasies about the origins of civilization. Stravinsky knew that he would be safe. Nobody would take Roerich seriously. Between them, the pair concocted a libretto for the new work that Diaghilev could use for promotional purposes, handwritten by Stravinsky, presented as his handiwork, and reproduced in *Documents* (75–76). The florid prose style is unlike anything authentically written by Stravinsky, including his letters to Roerich and Diaghilev at the time. The closest approach to such a style is Balmont's extravagant *Zvezdoliki* text, which Stravinsky would later claim he had only selected for the texture of the words, not for their mysticism. There is a game of charades taking place, or line of dominoes being set up, to ensure that the project goes through, of which national identity propaganda is a part. The real artistic impetus driving *The Rite* would more likely have been Kandinsky, a fellow Russian artist and intellectual of similar age, with musical knowledge and ambitions, who, like Stravinsky, had trained in law before embarking on a career in cutting-edge art aimed at laying bare the ultimate sources of artistic expression in primeval ritual.

Quite apart from its carefully balanced antithetical relationship with Christian mythology, the concept of a balletic ritual on the subject of a young girl dancing herself to death might all too easily have been identified as a countermove to Richard Strauss and Debussy, two of the young composer's more eminent rivals. Such an objective would have to succeed without either composer being embarrassed or feeling threatened. The theme of the *femme fatale*—subject matter ultimately dwelling on the social and personal consequences of following one's natural instincts to charm and seduce—is a romantic cliché of nineteenth-century opera, whether its consequences—in retribution or betrayal—

come in the form of suicide, murder, nature taking its revenge by inflicting fatal disease on the female lead, in abandonment, or in court action. The topic remains a wellspring of the opera industry even today, from Bizet's *Carmen* via Puccini and Berg's *Lulu* even to the late, grotesque, and real-life parody of Mark-Anthony Turnage's *Anna Nicole*. One is driven to wonder whether the conundrum for masculine composers may have been (may even still be) the brutal paradox of why the female of the species was created in the first place, given that men are brutes, childbirth could be a death sentence, and syphilis was a constant risk factor in sexual relations for both sexes. From a contemporary perspective (1910), the idea of a young woman willingly sacrificing herself for the survival of the tribe could be construed as a Havelock Ellis–inspired gesture of female emancipation and acknowledgment of the dignity and natural bravery of women, to be contrasted with a prevailing masculine culture of pointless and destructive tribal warfare.

Stravinsky's search for primal musical ritual led him along two paths: verbal ritual of incomprehensible mysticism supported by a bizarrely rich harmonic language (a direction indicated by Scriabin, Roerich, and Kandinsky), the other a path of primal rhythm and richly intricate and mechanized dance, represented by ragtime, flamenco, and the tarantella. Route 1 led him via the Verlaine poems to *Zvezdoliki*, dedicated to a bemused Debussy and creatively a dead end (a style to be briefly and wordlessly resuscitated after Debussy's death in *Symphonies of Wind Instruments*). Route 2, already indicated by Falla and his enthusiasm for the tradition of Andalusia, would lead Stravinsky by way of *Petrushka* to consummation and success in *The Rite of Spring*.

So why the secrecy? Could it be that Debussy had already composed works bearing the titles *Printemps* and *La Damoiselle élue* and people might accuse Stravinsky of plagiarism? Perhaps because Richard Strauss, another composer whom Stravinsky admired (the admiration was mutual, up to a point), had composed a scandalous opera, so scandalous that performances were banned even in Vienna as well as across the United States, on the subject of a young girl dancing naked and using her wiles to obtain the death and sexual humiliation of a holy man, a self-destructive indiscretion for which she is eventually punished by death, a denouement that even the play's author Oscar Wilde must have realized was a moral cop-out. The antiheroine was *Salome*.

Once again, the antitheses are exact. Strauss's scandalous sensationalism is an expression of a current decadent German cynicism toward cultural history as make-believe, portraying ancestral womankind as knowingly using sexual allure and dance to manipulate justice and public order for whimsical motives of self-gratification: a female version of the delinquent Till Eulenspiegel. (By strange coincidence, Picasso's celebrated 1905 drypoint *Salomé* [from *The Acrobats* series] can be read as the image of a female ingénue auditioning in front of an impassive Diaghilev.) Strauss portrays dance as erotic and manipulative, Stravinsky as elemental and instinctual, with no personal or sensual motive; Strauss's Salome seduces for political and sensual gain, whereas the anonymous Victim of *The Rite* sacrifices herself for the common good; Strauss's myth telling is detached, cynical, and intellectual, whereas the barbarian rite is innocent, formal, and—best of all—*wordless*.

Rimsky-Korsakov disliked *Salome* intensely, analyzed the score, and expressed his moral disgust at the composer's attitude toward women to his pupils (Taruskin 55). So it is a matter of some interest that Stravinsky—who admired Strauss a great deal as a technician and orchestrator—pointedly does not mention the opera among the works of Strauss that he first knew and admired "around 1904 or 1905" (*Expositions* 58), only admitting to have seen the opera for the first time in 1912. He could hardly not have known of the existence of a work condemned in all the newspapers and banned even in decadent Vienna, quite apart from his claim not to know of Rimsky-Korsakov's poor opinion of the composer.[5]

One might equally presume that the composer of *Printemps* and *La Damoiselle élue* might harbor reservations about a rival young composer intending to create a new ballet on the subject of spring eventually to contain dances also titled "Rondes de Printemps" and "Glorification de l'élue." But Debussy's prior interest in such titles and subject matter would turn out to arise from an altogether more tame, pre-Raphaelite vision, inspired by the remote past of Botticelli's *Primavera*, and at a second remove, by Dante Gabriel Rossetti's *Blessed Damozel*, verses of a solitary and unrequited love based on the poet Dante's love for Beatrice and ultimately closer in spirit to Schoenberg's *Pierrot Lunaire*, a reason perhaps why Stravinsky, after seeing a performance of *Pierrot* in Berlin in 1912, came away admiring the composer's ingenuity but unimpressed by the work's dated aesthetics.

Reality is complicated and intriguing. One can imagine Stravinsky going to Diaghilev with his idea for a primeval ritual on the theme of sacrifice. "I have talked to Debussy," he says. (In fact, Debussy has encouraged Stravinsky with a few ideas of his own.) "What do you think?" says Stravinsky, sitting at the piano to play the repeated chord motif inspired by Falla's *Ritual Fire Dance*. Diaghilev is enchanted, also bemused. "But how do I know this music is Russian and not Spanish?" he asks. "It has to be Russian, that is essential." "It's okay," says Stravinsky. "I will get my friend Roerich to help with a scenario." "Just as long as you keep it Russian, or at least Slav," says Diaghilev. "Leave it to me," says the composer.

Strauss's *Salome* is a main topic of conversation and scandal in Parisian musical society. How can any composer trump that scandal? is the question on everybody's lips. Ravel's *Daphnis et Chloé* is a musical inspiration for Kandinsky, who spent time in Paris in 1907–1908 in the hope of arousing the composer's interest in an abstract music and light show called *The Yellow Sound*. What appealed to Kandinsky was Ravel's sophisticated and, for all he knew, synaesthesic handling of orchestral color, along with a use of musical motifs, including a characteristic "galloping rhythm," which Kandinsky identified with the "men on horseback" motif of his own watercolor improvisations. Unsuccessful, Kandinsky would go on to transfer his attention to Scriabin, another synaesthesist, also without success, then to Schoenberg, who, while expressing a profound respect for the idea, also declined to collaborate.

Atonalism is in the air. Debussy recognizes Stravinsky as an exotic, primal force. The Russian composer's idea of a work drawing on antique mystery and ritual from the dawn of civilization was not entirely new. In April 1906, Debussy had been approached by a young poet, Victor Segalen, with a proposal for an opera on the subject of ancient culture, older than *Aïda*, more authentic than Wagner. Segalen had spent two years in French Polynesia studying native culture from a poetic and musical perspective. He had obtained some paintings and possessions of Gauguin after the painter's death, including an inscribed copy of Mallarmé's poem *L'Après-midi d'un Faune*. While in Tahiti, Segalen drafted a novel on the subject of the decline of Maori culture in the face of colonization, to be published in 1907 under the title *Les Immémoriaux* (The Olden Ones; Segalen, *Stèles* 6–7). Debussy briefly entertained the idea of a collaboration but preferred the higher-caste subject of Siddhartha, which carried a certain exotic cachet. Eventually, that project also fell through, partly from the composer's lack of self-conviction (its only vestige the piano piece "Et la lune descend sur le temple qui fut" published in *Images*, book 2, 1907). In late 1908, Segalen volunteered an alternative subject based on a short story, "Voix mortes: Musiques Maori." According to biographer Louis Laloy, Debussy was unable to work up any enthusiasm for this idea either, believing that the subject culture lacked refinement or sufficiently exotic musical possibilities; but he did hold out the option of a Chinese-inspired subject that would allow for a range of special effects and Far Eastern metal percussion (Segalen, *Essay on Exoticism*). Finally, as a last resort, Debussy proposed an opera on the subject of Orpheus, originally suggested to him in 1895 by Paul Valéry as a suitable subject for a "ballet blanc"—however intimating an abstract study from which all reference to color (meaning ethnic origins, primitivism, Andalusian and ragtime idioms) would be carefully excluded (see Orledge). In due course this entire range of exotic subject matter would be greedily taken up by a younger generation of Parisian composers, including Ravel (*Chansons Madécasses*), Charles Koechlin (*Les Bandar-Log*), André Jolivet (*Mana, Danses Rituelles*), Varèse (*Arcana*), and Messiaen (*Turangalîla, Harawi, Iles de Feu I, II*), leaving the topic of a "white" Orpheus to neoclassicist Stravinsky.

Undoubtedly, Debussy was uncomfortable with subject matter of a primitive nature, in part because his interest in the exotic was fundamentally decorative and also, one suspects, out of a certain disdain for "negro music." The question is whether he communicated any of his interest in Segalen to Stravinsky, since he liked Segalen and suspected that such subject matter would be of greater interest to the young Russian. Debussy had nothing to lose by recommending Segalen, had spoken freely with his associates about his admiration for the young poet, and was disposed to help him. Yet, Stravinsky was politically committed to a Russian coauthor, and it would have been counterproductive for him to take on an author whose subject matter would instantly identify him as a French colonial. (In a letter to Stravinsky in 1915, after the scandal of *The Rite of Spring*, Debussy wrote, "Dear Stravinsky, you are a great artist. Be with all your strength a great Russian artist. It is so wonderful to be of one's country, to be attached to one's soil like the humblest of peasants!" [*Conversations* 54]. What the French composer is actually delivering, however, is a none-too-subtle put-down: "My dear, stick with the primitive: it is what you do best.")

Elsewhere in Paris, Matisse was attracting attention with a series of vast canvases of women dancing in a circle in an energetic rite of celebration. Picasso's *Les Demoiselles d'Avignon* of 1907, a talking point in its own way as scandalous as Strauss's *Salome*, depicts a group of women in stylized and inviting attitudes, some of whose faces are transformed into African-inspired masks. The timing was perfect to make a musical statement on female dance as an expression of the life force of the tribe.

Roerich may have had his uses as a researcher, seeking out documentary sources on the subject of primitive song and dance from accounts of explorers such as the German Georg Forster, who had traveled with Captain Cook around the Pacific and witnessed native music and dance ceremonial in Tahiti and elsewhere and had brought the message of primeval culture across Europe to St. Petersburg, to a point where Empress Catherine was about to finance another voyage to the South Pacific, with Forster in charge, had not war intervened. Widely published and hugely popular accounts of travelers, such as La Pérouse (1785), von Langsdorff (1813), Durmont d'Urville, and others, carried firsthand reports, with illustrations and music examples, concerning the *Areoi* of the South Pacific, a priestly cult of music and dance, men and women who performed fertility dances at night, in solemn circles and square formations. Often sexual in nature, these exhibitions were performed with a solemn gravity:

> Their songs were a kind of recitative, harmonious, and generally accompanied by the drum and music. In them they commemorated the creation of the universe, the marvels of nature, great events, and exploits of the inferior gods and heroes. . . . [These included] mythological representations . . . as depicted by living images instead of inanimate figures [of] the two principles of generation in nature . . . a kind of elegy in action, which was not without beauty or inspiration. (Moerenhout 484–503, in Andersen 151–52)

Grigory (the Prussian Georg Heinrich von) Langsdorff, Aulic Counsellor of Russia and a member of the Russian Imperial Academy of Sciences, whose papers were archived in St. Petersburg, left a description of ritual songs of the Marquesas, the islands inhabited by Gauguin, whose music was also studied by Victor Segalen. His account of their ceremonial chants, plaintive wails largely restricted to a four-note scale, with microtonal inflections, in short phrases constantly repeated and varied, are said to have inspired Beethoven's solemn theme of the slow movement to the *Seventh Symphony*. Langsdorff notes that native wailing melody is sung in subtler scale divisions compared to "our Russian sailors, who sing in whole tones," going on to describe the wailing quality and fragmented manner of delivery in terms that also identify the melodies of *The Rite of Spring*, part I:

> It is the peculiar characteristic of the music of Nukuhiva, that it dwells principally upon quarter-tones, not going beyond the minor third from *e* to *g*, except that it sometimes sinks into *d*. . . . It resembles strongly the music of the Romish *Kyrie eleison*, which is still sung in many German churches, in the same manner as the monotonous *oras* of the monks. At every pause in a word or a strophe, . . . the singers are silent for some seconds, then begin again. (von Langsdorff, in Andersen 69–71)

Reports are numerous of fearsome war dances, in boldly stamping rhythms, perfectly synchronized, in crouching postures ending with sudden upward leaps and of bouts of singing and dancing beginning slowly and accelerating with increasing animation to a state of exhaustion.

> The leader of the party stood in the centre, and introduced the recitation with a sort of prologue when, with a number of fantastic movements and attitudes, those that sat around began their song in a low and measured tone and voice; which increased as they proceeded, till it became vociferous and unintelligibly rapid. It was also accompanied by movements of the arms and hands, in exact keeping with the tones of the voice, until they were wrought to the highest pitch of excitement. This they continued until, becoming breathless and exhausted, they were obliged to suspend the performance. (Ellis 317–18, in Andersen 149–50)

The Rite of Spring is composed like the movies, arguably informed by historical scholarship as well as responding to contemporary cultural issues, and represents the highest and most complex exhibition of applied time and motion mechanics ever attempted by any composer (techniques of mechanical music programming designed to simulate the dynamics of human movement). In later life, when Stravinsky declared, "I am the vessel through which the *Sacre* passed," he was finally acknowledging full responsibility for the concept as well as the execution and resulting scandal. *The Rite* is indeed a work of fiction, the vision of the source of all musical being his own achievement, designed as a calculated rebuke to a decadent and cynical central European culture on the cusp of war.

After *Petrushka*, which is vibrant and easy to follow, interpreting *The Rite of Spring* is not altogether easy. There are no familiar characters, no names, no recognizable motivations to the ceremony. If we include smashing the egg of Kashchei, all three great ballets are about death, and in a strange manner all three deaths—of Kashchei, Petrushka, and the Chosen One—are expressions of positive liberation, releasing the clan from the evil monster's clutches in *Firebird*, signaling the triumph of love in *Petrushka*, and celebrating the return of fertility in *The Rite of Spring*.

All the same, there are clues. The ballet is in two parts, day and night. Each half is introduced by a spacious pastoral to set the scene, which then becomes the backdrop for a carefully varied sequence of dances alternating old and young, men and women. Although there are no words, there are melody motifs aplenty that act as a kind of speech: wailing descending chromatic lines in bassoon and clarinet, the same in sunnier diatonic (whole-note) intervals by the flutes; wake-up calls in leaping fourths from the English horn and oboe; then the same more assertively by the trumpet—in other words, an easily intelligible language of call signs passing among the instruments and serving to indicate a variety of moods fluctuating between resignation and high alertness and directed toward a key figure, again announced by the trumpets, in quintuple time (five in the time of four), which becomes a major animating force.[6] In dance terms, the score represents a struggle between duple and triple time. Duple time dominates part I and is about walking, the time of ragtime and the cakewalk, hence about progress and directed motion; triple time dominates part II and is traditionally associated with divinity and circular motion. An army marches straight ahead in duple time, while Vienna waltzes in circles in triple time, everyone rotating around an individual center, in one's own time. Stravinsky dramatizes the struggle and keeps the audience on edge by constantly posing rhythmic riddles in fives. He is not the first Russian composer to do so, but he is the first to push the conflict of duple and triple to the edge of exhaustion.

An obvious opening reference to Debussy's *L'Après-midi* reinvents Debussy's rococo pastoral as a vast and shadowy Poussin landscape populated by tiny figures. Debussy is also the originator of Stravinsky's technique of constant repetition of motifs with constantly altering harmony, enabling the music to be freely developed and recycled without apparently going anywhere. Johann Strauss is another influence, as it were by inversion, in the sense of the endless dance of industrial civilization parodied by Ravel in his out-of-control *La Valse*. Beethoven is another direct influence, particularly in relation to the pounding, primitive, endlessly repeating rhythmic gestures of his "Coriolan" overture and *Fifth Symphony*. Haydn is an influence from whom Stravinsky has learned broken phrasing, how to transform a theme in color and texture in the very act of making it happen, and clever use of repetition and asymmetry. Mozart is the likely source of Stravinsky's functional separation of string orchestra and wind instruments into distinct groups and subgroups: *The Rite of Spring* is ultimately a composition for symphonic wind band with added string orchestra, rather than for conventional symphony orchestra.

The lesson of the movies, the technology that inspired cubist and futurist painting and finds its most compelling musical expression in Stravinsky's ballet orchestrations, is that *perceptual* time and motion and *cognitive* time and motion are two very different things. The movies have shown that in the real world we are exposed to huge densities and complexities of information but are able clearly to apprehend only elements of that complexity for our own purposes and then only retrospectively. At the movies it is impossible to "see" sixteen frames a second as individual still frames; even though the eye registers the frames as separate entities, the brain cannot keep up and hence interprets any consistent pattern of difference between successive frames as movement. In music, Stravinsky knew from his improvisations and studies of ornamentation that by creating uncertainty and adding density in timing and rhythm, after the example of mechanical instruments, it was possible to create an impression of actual rather than reproduced movement. The layered structure of *The Rite* is clearly expressed in recordings of the two-piano reduction (e.g., Naxos, BIS CD-188) and even more explicitly in the drier terms of multichannel piano roll (Pickwick, MCD 25; MusicMasters, 01612-67138-2); but in live or recorded orchestral form, the simple black and white of piano tone gives way to a variety of tonal qualities and spatial cues, adding significant new depth and fuzzy imagery to the listener's task of integration. Multipart music of such density and ambiguity is more than what the listening ear is able to digest, leading the brain to generalize and interpret what is being heard as not only organic movement but accidental, spontaneous actions in real time. With *The Rite of Spring*, Stravinsky has extended the impressionist principle of uncertainty in timing to cover uncertainty in pitch, as with the voices in *Zvezdoliki*, to a point where even solid harmonies become ambiguous and perceptually unstable. The composition of chords is all the same carefully managed to express physical realities—hence, the famous stamping chord of the "Adolescents' Dance" is not only played with a persistent stamping, downbeat action, but literally represents compression in musical terms, an E flat chord above squeezing an E natural chord underneath. Beyond the physical stresses, the music of *The Rite* remains tonally grounded, even static, like the music of Russian Orthodox tradition, with long stretches accumulating and coming gradually into focus over sustained drone harmonies in the bass.

The Rite of Spring is perhaps music's ultimate statement of animation in a movie sense, corresponding to "a perception of movement as the byproduct of structured errors in dense information processes exposed at too rapid a repetition rate for each event change to be clearly apprehended in isolation, the totality for that reason perceived in an approximate manner as coherent and continuous." The composer's achievement deserves to be recognized as a major scientific and intellectual triumph and also (in my view) as an exceptional moral statement for the times in which it was composed. Like an early epic silent movie, the action unfolds in "fixed camera" scenes, each of which is gradually "filled out" by actions of repetition and accumulation, the business of the music to set the scene and then fill out the frame with action, each action building to a climax and separated from the next by a pause for a new title and change of reel, just like a silent movie. In the detail of *The Rite*, Stravinsky plays with melody motifs in analogous fashion, repeating, changing, extending, as if to create uncertainty or suggest coordinated but uncertain direction. In the grand ensembles, however, the reverse is the case: everything is out there, an overwhelming abundance of action and information that no single listener (apart from the conductor, one imagines) could ever fully comprehend.

4

BEYOND TONALITY

Like de Tocqueville in America, Stravinsky found himself an alien observer in an increasingly feverish central Europe. Nineteen twelve was the year that atonality came to public attention. The publication of Schoenberg's Op. 16 *Five Orchestral Pieces*, representations of primal emotions, including a musical version of Munch's *The Scream*, destined to provide templates for future generations of composers of horror and alien invasion movie music; December the same year saw the premiere of *Pierrot Lunaire*, a suite of mock macabre verses for distracted voice and a small group of instruments.[1] Schoenberg came to atonality through meticulous study of the cadences of natural speech. Heightened speech in this case is storytelling speech with enlarged gesture, and Schoenberg's notation of speech in *Pierrot Lunaire* is an exact description of a style of heightened speech already familiar in cameo recordings by famous celebrities from Alfred Lord Tennyson to Florence Nightingale.

Natural speech is atonal for obvious reasons: one, the voice is naturally unstable; two, singing is not natural speech; and, three, the major and minor scales of classical music are inadequate to define the subtleties of normal intonation either in speech or in traditional folksong. (Interestingly, the notation devised by philologist Daniel Jones in 1909 [*The Pronunciation of English*] for transcribing *recorded* speech resembles the earliest plainchant and is deliberately approximate in time and pitch.) New media such as the telephone and the gramophone tend to flatten and compress the natural contours of speech and music to fit very narrow limits of signal variation, introducing listeners to a more laconic style of speaking and a different manner of hearing recorded or transmitted speech.

To scholar composers Bartók and Kodály—gathering folksongs in remote villages with the aid of portable Edison cylinder recorders—technology revealed the inadequacy of classical notation for transcribing ancient speech and song. To Schoenberg and Richard Strauss—representatives of a leading central European culture highly dependent on rhetorical gesture—technology had serious implications for the future of artistic expression; however, for the French pioneers of telephone technology, the relatively uninflected patter demanded by technology came naturally, reflected in the cool *recitativo* style of Debussy's *Pelléas* and laid-back studies of Erik Satie. In a newly technological age, the emotional excesses of nineteenth-century opera were beginning to look and feel overripe and dated. For the core traditions of Vienna and Berlin, rhetoric remained the unassailable key: the face in the mirror—or voice in the loudspeaker—invariably *La Voix de son Maître*: He (or She) Who Must be Obeyed. For French and English audiences, however, the singing voice was invariably Someone Else, the Alien Other, a curiosity to be inspected at a distance. The oppressively overblown subjectivity of German operatic speech both fascinated and repelled the intellectual French, who could be very blasé. It is a matter of some psychological interest that the musical notations of Mahler and Schoenberg's excessively personal speech tend to be overburdened with verbal specifics, as if to say that it is no longer enough for music to describe a sigh; the score has to carry a verbal instruction to "express like a sigh." For a composer to have to resort to such extra baggage signals a growing perception that plain notation is losing its grip or that performers can no longer be trusted to follow instructions: an anxiety vis-à-vis the finished object—"how do I look?"—almost certainly aroused in response to the permanence of sound recording.

Stravinsky was already well acquainted with the art of managed approximation and ornamentation in a rhythmic sense; what he was now seeking to perfect was a vocal writing that captured the emotional contour of a text without unnecessary fuss and within the constraints of classical notation while giving the impression of informality and free association of oral traditions of music making.

"J'aime mieux une boîte à musique qu'un rossignol" (I prefer a musical box to a nightingale; *Retrospectives* 35): puzzling for some but a key observation by the composer of *The Nightingale*, a work of music theater in which a high soprano playing the creature of nature is pitted against an orchestra playing the mechanical imitation, the soprano finally prevailing. What does it mean for a composer to *prefer* a mechanical device to a natural musician? Stravinsky hints at an explanation in *The Poetics of Music*, where he says, "Comparison is not reason" (*Poetics* 23). We gaze admiringly at Monet's water lilies, check the catalogue entry, look again, nod sagely, and exclaim, "Water lilies! How beautiful! How does he do that?" as if that were the point, when in fact the act of recognition of the subject matter as water lilies effectively destroys the viewer's capacity to respond to the painting's real subject matter, which is the mystery of recognition of anything from a first impression of color, light, and qualities of reflection—in other words, the act and moment of seeing, *before* the brain takes over. By implication, learned behavior in the perceptual world amounts to a censorship and reduction of experience to a structure of rules to which the artwork is said to conform or against which is seen to resist. It is hard to imagine Monet—or any of a number of his contemporaries—achieving so masterful a handling of color and light and abstraction of outline and detail, without the assistance of Pathé color photography. At the same time, such a striking sense of instantaneous harmony can only be conveyed by appealing successfully to an ordinary viewer's natural instinct for color relationships, at the moment of apprehension before the brain has had time to digest the relationships as objective features of the real world. For the artist, the target zone of pure awareness lies at the moment before cognition, and it becomes the artist's task to prolong the epiphany and delay the onset of recognition for as long as possible.

The point that Stravinsky is making is that one is more likely to discover how nature is perceived from studying a structure capable of imitating its effect, in this case, a *serinette*, or caged mechanical nightingale, than (say) from emulating Messiaen by making field trips in short trousers with binoculars, rucksack, and cheese sandwich in search of real birdsong to write down in a big round hand in real time in a notebook. The primeval landscape of *The Rite of Spring* is brought to life in a chorus of virtual birdsong based on the orchestral simulation of tiny flute fanfares executed at high speed by programmed miniature pistons created by watchmakers and driven by clockwork. Messiaen's birdsong transcriptions sound nothing like birds; they are rendered simply as interesting figures of musical speech, whereas Stravinsky's flute *fioriture*, though not intended as representations of nature nevertheless fulfill the role of evoking a sense of nature.

Monet's art of dissolving recognizable images into field relationships expressing technically exact color and reflectance ratios, by transferring photographic imagery to tangible pigment on canvas, is a necessary intervention to awaken the same vision in the rest of us. Technology is not enough: we look at the photographic image and see "a color photograph" of this or that, and that is all, nothing more profound. It takes an artist in a nonphotographic medium to demonstrate that technology is able to change how we see and recognize the emotions we feel in association with certain color and shape relations. For Stravinsky, the musical box, barrel organ, and pianola were a means to convey the complicated and primal experience of unfiltered hearing. *Petrushka* contains an abundance of imitation mechanical instruments; indeed, it is as though the composer had been studying the species with Rimsky-Korsakov and the ballet were his graduation exercise. The point of reproducing a musical box is not to imitate a defective technology (as Craft appears to think in *Documents* 165–66) but to bridge the gap between what the technology does and its success in persuading the listener that what is being listened to is music at all. The secret of animation lies precisely in the gap. The eighteenth-century view of people as animated machines assumed that the crystalline tones of a musical box represented the Platonic essence of musical speech, a sophistry leaving the mystery of "animation" out of the equation and out in the cold, unexplored and unexplained. New technologies of image and movement capture were bound to put classical assumptions about nature and how to represent it back under the microscope.

To the managed approximation of melody, rasping textures, and strident tone colors of mechanical instruments, the composer of *The Rite of Spring* brought a new and disruptive narrative style borrowed from the movies, combining saturated action with the violent discontinuities of montage and editing within the movie narrative, and changes of view within the scene. On a more modest scale, Mallarmé had already introduced the idea of interrupted continuity to poetry with his invention of narrative by parenthesis, a technique adopted for music by Boulez in the 1950s. Mallarmé visualized a poetry in which it was no longer necessary to read verses in a fixed order; one could read back and forth at will among adjacent verses without affecting the poetic unity of the whole. That freedom to read stanzas in varied succession had the effect of involving the reader in discovering and following the poet's thought as if it were the reader's own. By the time of *The Rite of Spring*, an art of moviemaking was emerging in which changes of camera viewpoint were becoming an essential part of the drama: not just to follow an increasingly mobile train of events from place to place but as a means of messing with the viewer's head by deliberately interfering with the perception of events, divert attention, or by repetition, close-up, or slow motion to intensify emotional situations. Movies in 1912 were bereft of speech but technically noisy affairs, screened in movie houses to the accompaniment of an ad hoc medley of musical clichés assembled by a band of improvising live musicians in halfhearted attempt to follow the changing moods of successive scenes (a perception within the industry from which the art of music has still not fully recovered). Because music was not intended to intrude on the screen action but to cover the sound of projection and supply an illusion of narrative continuity, the disruptive impact of montage and its often violent dislocations of visual continuity hardly registered on the average viewer. But for a composer the sense of dislocation amounted, in Robert Hughes's phrase, to the cubist experience or shock of the new. Genuine fans of the movie medium, like Debussy, Satie, or Stravinsky, could not avoid noticing the impact of instantaneous changes of scene on the visual integrity of a narrative and accompanying music. These composers embraced the challenge of a musical narrative in ribbons of continuity material devised in such a way that one could edit between them virtually at will to create an effect of suspended time in which multiple characters or viewpoints are experienced sequentially but perceived as coexisting simultaneously. Half a century before Stockhausen and *Momente*, Debussy created *Jeux*, a ballet on the theme of a tennis match, an event that a television viewer today *expects* to experience, cubist fashion, from viewpoints at both ends of the court simultaneously intercut with slow-motion repeats of key moments of play. Stravinsky's *Rite of Spring*, composed at the same time as *Jeux*, employs the same technique of editing between alternate viewpoints but in the context of a music of excessively large numbers, hence with correspondingly greater impact. Stravinsky's musical strategy resembles the visual strategy of D. W. Griffith, the American movie pioneer of the larger view: of scenes of mass crowds, riots, and stampeding cattle. Musically, Stravinsky is transferring an informal technique of musical accompaniment from the silent movie picture house, where it is already familiar, to the world of dance, intending to stir up the conventional unities of time, place, and continuity of traditional ballet. For either a Stravinsky or a Monet, the artistic justification of borrowing and displacing effects from technology is that if the public already recognizes and accepts a mechanically processed image as a representation of nature, that has to mean that the technical process has something to say about how ordinary people actually perceive the world at a subliminal level.

* * *

Three Japanese Lyrics (1912) for soprano and piano/soprano and chamber ensemble (*Works* 15:8–10).

These exquisite miniatures are described in the literature as "moments of relief" for the composer after the hard graft of *The Rite of Spring*. In fact, they form part of an ongoing series of small works for voice and instruments occupying the composer over a decade, to engage with the completely different and equally demanding technical challenge of designing a *nouvelle cuisine* for sound recording while avoiding the elegant *kitsch* of Fritz Kreisler. When Edison developed cylinder foil recording in the late 1870s, the sound quality was terrible, and Edison saw the market for his invention primarily as office dictaphone technology for voice recording and storage. In the 1880s Alexander Graham Bell devised a greatly superior wax recording medium, improving the signal quality to assist the hearing impaired (interestingly Edison, like Beethoven, used a hearing aid, and Bell's wife was deaf). Voice messages are a robust signal, more tolerant of distortion and noise than music; hence, it follows that, reversing the argument, a technology capable of reproducing music to an acceptable standard is bound to be a superior medium for the capture and reproduction of normal speech.

Public interest in recording as a voice medium was promoted by inviting celebrities to record cameo speeches. Through such recordings, the public became aware of the distinctive music of individual speech as an involuntary expression of personality and emotion, a reality very different from the forced and stereotyped emotional world of opera. Among the first to capitalize on public perception of the sound of speech as a gateway to the soul was Sigmund Freud, whose theories of personality and motivation revealed in involuntary speech would eventually be satirized by Bernard Shaw in 1912, the year of *Pierrot Lunaire*, in the play *Pygmalion*, about an ambitious speech expert and his efforts to transform a working-class woman into a lady of high society by altering her tone and manner of voice. For his part, Schoenberg's suite of nocturnal settings of twenty-one expressionist verses for female voice and chamber ensemble are precisely notated to reproduce the histrionic speech of Viennese melodrama (or emulate one of Dr. Freud's patients; Maconie, *Avant Garde* 73–92).

During the early twentieth century, disc recordings of opera celebrities were promoted as a souvenir trade in famous voices, but for young composers, the new technology represented a challenge to develop an original repertoire suited to the modest dimensions of the new medium: an attention span of around three minutes, a lyric art for solo voice or instrument with piano accompaniment, each item complete in itself, and conveying a moment of truth, personality, and emotional location, effectively in a single gesture. Early success was achieved by violinist Fritz Kreisler, whose singing tone and temperament were perfectly adapted to the new medium. Kreisler took advantage of public perception of a recording as a souvenir or relic of the past to drip feed a compliant public with an entire catalogue of lyric pieces in Viennese style, purporting to be arrangements of much older classics but in fact his own inventions: in doing so showing much the same evenhandedness toward historical accuracy as Stravinsky toward the folk music transcriptions that he was accustomed to adapt from scholarly sources.

The *Three Japanese Lyrics* draws together the design limitations of acoustic recording with the emotional concentration of Japanese haiku. These are deliberate exercises in musical calligraphy in which, like a Webern bagatelle, voice and instruments interweave as characters in a single line of poetic inspiration—a graphic metaphor identifying the calligrapher's gesture with the movement of a recording stylus across a wax surface.

Stravinsky composed these beautifully distilled songs in partial knowledge of Schoenberg's *Pierrot Lunaire*, and it is hard to imagine

Schoenberg's ecstatic but rather more detached *Herzgewächse*, composed in December 1912, as uninfluenced by the Stravinsky lyrics. Stravinsky was deeply impressed by Schoenberg's ingenious and multifaceted counterpoint of speech and instruments but did not enjoy the histrionics, not just because the mannerist style was dated but also because he sensed it was inappropriate for a neutral recording medium. Erik Satie caught the measure of the recording medium with a set of brief piano pieces, *Véritables Préludes flasques (pour un chien)*, casual musical snapshots composed without barlines in the manner of strips of film, to be played in a spirit of sublime detachment, their title a kind of crossword puzzle clue to be interpreted as "authentic flabby (or rather, 'flasked' or 'bottled'—that is, 'preserved' or 'canned') preludes for a pet dog"—the mutt in question being Nipper, the His Master's Voice mascot. (Satie's evocation of deflated temporality returns with Salvador Dalí's 1931 painted image of melting watches in *The Persistence of Memory*.) Stravinsky has been accused of unnecessary refinement in deliberately offsetting the *Japanese Lyrics* on the upbeat rather than the downbeat, but for the composer to do so is consistent with a desire to reinforce the impression of an unaccented continuous "ribbon of sound" associated with recording and in keeping with the "single flourish" poetic of Japanese calligraphy.

* * *

> *Three Little Songs* ("Recollections of my Childhood") for voice and piano (1906–1913), instrumented for voice and small orchestra (1929–1930; *Works* 15:11–19).

Too brief to fill just one side of a disc, these invented folksongs, originally composed in 1906, were later revived as presents for his children and private assertions of his Russian identity. Here there is no attempt at elegance or concentration: rather, a machine-like plainness. Each song begins and ends without drama or fuss: the third, a nonsense rhyme, playing with the sounds of speech for purely musical ends, at the opposite extreme of the emotional spectrum from Schoenberg's *Pierrot*, but sensitive in the same way to the role of texture in words and language as elements of a common musical fabric. These "recollections" are an early intimation of his thoughts turning in the direction of *Les*

Noces and search for a modern idiom appropriate for an authentic Russian peasant wedding.

* * *

> *Le Rossignol* (The Nightingale), lyric fairy-tale for singing voices and orchestra (act I, 1908–1909; acts II and III completed 1913–1914, revised 1962; *Works* 14:1–13); *Song of the Nightingale* symphonic poem (1917; *Works* 22:1).

Stravinsky was reluctant to return to the fairy-tale world of *The Nightingale* after the technical advances and upheavals of *Petrushka* and *The Rite of Spring*. One is grateful he did, however, because the simplicity and charm of the Hans Andersen tale and the brilliance of Stravinsky's simulations of mechanical birdlife transcend cuteness. Resuming work on an act I that had previously aimed to bring Debussy's distracted medievalism to heel (*Nuages*, 1899; *Le Martyre de Saint Sébastien*, 1913) allowed Stravinsky the opportunity in acts II and III to revisit the childhood world of Tchaikovsky's *Nutcracker* and Ravel's *L'Heure Espagnole* (Spanish Time; 1911) and *Ma Mère L'Oye* (Mother Goose; also 1911). The libretto, adapted by Stepan Mitusov, is slight to evanescent: in act I, a nightingale is invited into the Imperial Palace to sing for the Emperor of China; in act II, a mechanical nightingale from Japan is presented to the emperor, at which the real nightingale (sung by a high soprano in the orchestra pit) takes offense and leaves; and in act III, the gravely ill emperor is restored to health by the real nightingale's forgiveness and pity. If there is a moral to the story, it would seem to be that the living sounds of authentic nature have a power denied to the clockwork toys of modern technology.

Nevertheless, whatever the story may suggest, in Stravinsky's hands the melodies of nature are nowhere near as fascinating as the delightful challenge of reproducing a mechanical bird, complete with twitching wings, throat clearing, and whirring gears, especially in the context of legendary and bizarre formalities of Chinese court life, in their own way as artificial and stylized as the mechanical bird (they include the character of a Bonze, or Chamberlain, who responds to every question with the same meaningless phrase "Tsing-pé!" in an uncanny premonition of automated telephone help lines today). A storyline revisiting the theme of the illusion of life attributable to a machine compared to a creature of nature, and concluding in favor of nature, would appear to turn the tale of *Petrushka*, a puppet endowed with life, somewhat on its head, though the contest (if that is what it is) has to be adjudged a draw.

* * *

> *Three Pieces for String Quartet* (1914; Adès, 203512); *Pribaoutki* (Peasant Songs; 1914; *Works* 15:14–17); *Three Easy Pieces* for piano duet (1914; Adès, 202922); *Berceuses du Chat* (Cat's Lullabies; 1915–1916; *Works* 15:18–21); *Waltz for Children* for piano (1917; MusicMasters, 01612-67152-2); *Four Russian Peasant Songs* (1914–1917, rev. 1954; *Works* 15:22–25); *Etude for Pianola* (1917; MusicMasters, 01612-67138-2); *Pour Picasso* for clarinet solo (1917; Naxos, 8.557505); *Four Etudes for Orchestra* (instrumented I–III, 1914–1918; IV, 1928; *Works* 11:29–32); *Four Songs* (1918–1919, instrumented 1954; *Works* 15:26–29); *Sektanskaya* (A Russian Spiritual; 1919), for soprano, flute, and cimbalom (from *Four Songs*; MusicMasters, 01612-67195-2); *Tilimbom* (1917, orchestrated 1923, from *Four Songs*; *Works* 15:38); *Piano-Rag Music* (1919; *Works* 13:14); *Three Pieces for Clarinet* (1919; Adès, 203512).

A number of short works and Russian song sets on folk and domestic themes ask to be considered together as a group, as studies in specific techniques looking ahead to the composition of *Les Noces*, a work seeking reconciliation with the composer's Russian homeland, after the Revolution of 1917.

In *Three Pieces for String Quartet*, the composer's attention is focused on the expressive possibilities of bowed strings, a dimension lost to view in the orchestral version (I–III of *Four Etudes for Orchestra*; orchestrated 1914–1918; completed 1928). Terse and poignant, these three tiny but complete works evoke a Marc Chagall pastoral world of rustic hurdy-gurdy and gipsy fiddle. Here for the first time the violin timbre is linked with themes of suffering and redemption, later resumed in works as varied as *The Soldier's Tale*, the *Violin Concerto*, and *Agon*, through to *Requiem Canticles* and the 1968 *Two Sacred Songs*, by Hugo Wolf.

There is more to these primal violin melodies than the pitch collections of textbook theory. Stravinsky appears to be building on Bartók's transcriptions of Hungarian folk melodies by referring his own to the harmonic series embodied in archaic instruments of the pastoral tradition. In I, an ebullient setting of a melody in folk idiom to a viola drone accompaniment and a cello imitating a side drum, the violin four-note melody on G–A–B–C sounds as though it should be in G major, but the accompanying drone on D/C sharp suggests the slightly off-key harmonics 11, 12, 13, and 14 of the D string of a bass viol (or tromba marina). Such a melody is paradoxically harmonious and atonal at the same time. Piece II is a montage of contrasting motifs, like a short movie inspired by the screen actions of Little Tich, a clown with enormously long feet resembling the character of Sideshow Bob in *The Simpsons* (while on the subject, it is worth pointing out that the series' title music, by Danny Elfman, is expertly modeled on Stravinsky of this period and quite possibly on the first of these very pieces). In II, cello harmonics provide a clue that the pitch collection of a longer refrain, in octaves to the tune A–C–E–B–E flat–D flat–B flat, may also correspond to a row of harmonics, in this case 10–12–15–22–14–13–11, of a fundamental F. Treating such tonal/atonal pitch collections as "pastoral oddities" is also a hidden message of the first movement of Beethoven's Pastoral Symphony No. 6, also of the natural horn solo of Leopold Mozart's *Sinfonia Pastorella* (Hungaroton, HCD 12874); and it is certainly possible that Stravinsky referred to Leopold Mozart's *Die Bauernhochzeit* in preparation for his own *Les Noces* (Maconie, *Musicologia* 351–57). III, "Canticle," returns to the liturgical style of *Zvezdoliki*, but the astringent tone of these modestly disciplined string harmonies comes as welcome vinegar after the thick mayonnaise of the earlier composition for male voices.

The *Pribaoutki* are dazzling, ingenious exercises in musical animation for voice and reduced instrumental forces reflecting the austerity of a wartime economy, possibly also composed within the constraints of acoustic recording practice and occupying an aesthetic position midway between Schoenberg's *Pierrot* and Cocteau and Satie's entertainment *Parade*. The instrumentation looks ahead to *The Soldier's Tale* despite an absence of percussion, and it is interesting to speculate whether Stravinsky was seriously attempting to craft an idiom based on imported jazz from the United States. Admired by Webern, *Berceuses du Chat* is of interest technically since the accompanying clarinets can be played without attack, like a harmonium, delivering a smoothness and blend of tone unmatched by most other instruments. To his new arrangement of the *Four Russian Peasant Songs* originally for unaccompanied female chorus, Stravinsky eventually added a quartet of french horns, a different accompanying sonority yet again, in figures suggesting natural horns playing ascending whoops of nontempered pitches. The *Four Songs* (1918–1919) for soprano are a compilation from the earlier sets *Three Tales for Children* and *Four Russian Songs*; in 1954, rescored for voice, flute, harp and guitar: plucked strings, yet another tone color, an interesting choice bringing the work within striking distance of Boulez's *Le marteau sans maître*. A tremulous, weeping melody and steadying drone evoke the stoical gipsy Russia of *Pastorale* in a haunting version of *Sektanskaya* (Russian Spiritual) performed in its original 1919 scoring for soprano, flute, and cimbalom, another hugely poignant premonition of Boulez's exotic sound world (it also prefigures the "Surge, aquilo" of *Canticum Sacrum*). Very different is Stravinsky's jaunty "Manhattan" 1923 orchestration of *Tilimbom*, which might have been inspired by the fire sirens of Edgar Varèse's *Hyperprism* and comes about as close to the style of Gershwin as Stravinsky gets.

The *Three Easy Pieces* for piano duet and another set of *Five Easy Pieces* (1916–1917) contrive to escape into the simplicity of childhood. Both sets reemerge after the war's end as *Suite No. 1* and *Suite No. 2* for small orchestra, transformed into colored musical postcards in the spirit of René Clair. In *Waltz for Children* (reproduced in EWW 248), a piece perhaps not quite as innocent as it appears, the right hand wanders off on its own, after a one-line arabesque by Picasso, a gesture emulated in the brief *Pour Picasso* for clarinet solo, dedicated to the artist and composed literally on the back of an envelope. Heralded by a ferocious bout of musical sneezing, the *Etude for Pianola* draws inspiration from the sights and sounds of Diaghilev Ballet's 1916 visit to Madrid, the irony of Satie, timeless automatism of the mechanical instrument, and wandering fingers of melody in *Waltz for Children* to create a fantasy souvenir of *Petrushka*'s puppet world finally relocated to its Andalusian homeland, a multichannel miniextravaganza to range alongside the *Piano-Rag Music* composed for the two real hands of Arthur Rubinstein. In *Piano-Rag Music* Stravinsky turns the peculiar artistry of piano-roll technology against the conventions of virtuoso pianism, exploiting extreme ornamentation, time voids, and cluster effects with a great deal of humor in a manner startlingly anticipating the piano *Etudes* of Olivier Messiaen of 1949–1950 and even the bravura of Stockhausen's 1961 *Piano Piece X*. Though Stravinsky was doing no more in music than being playful in the spirit of Picasso and synthetic cubism, Rubinstein was unimpressed.

With war had come austerity. The Diaghilev Ballet looked for a new home. Ravel, André Breton, Schoenberg, and pianist Paul Wittgenstein (brother of the philosopher) were among artists who enlisted. There were fewer pianists to play soothingly in hotel lobbies; New Orleans jazz was imported from America; and middle-class homes resounded to the pianola. Along with the distracted twang of the mechanical keyboard, a plaintive air settled on music, from the plagal cadences of Ravel to the pensive melancholy of Satie's *Three Gymnopédies*. For families with loved ones in the trenches, the brittle tone and absent player of a pianola became poignant emblems of mortality and the folly of war. As demand for the player piano spread across Europe, so too did ragtime. Black American jazz evolved in parallel with the record industry and introduced a new style of rhythm-based ensemble music to urban life, performed at uninflected high intensity by groups of solo players chosen for tonal variety in an acoustic recording medium unable to handle the dynamic subtleties of classical music. Among the new sounds popularized by jazz was the tenor banjo, a physical string sound with a distinctive percussive edge. In central Europe the search for an instrument of equivalent penetration led to the revival of the Turkish zither and Hungarian gipsy cimbalom, ancestors of the hammer-action piano of Mozart's time combining the hardness of sticks with the resonance of undamped strings. The clangorous but laconic zither music of Anton Karas's "Harry Lime Theme" captures the bleakness of wartime and is as memorable as the seedy Orson Welles drug smuggler of Carol Reed's 1949 movie *The Third Man*; the music itself, however, is Europeanized ragtime. For an older generation between the wars, the equivalent plucked string sound was the tenor banjo of Vess L. Ossman or Fred van Eps; in Europe, the cimbalom of Joseph Moskowitz.[2] When his new neighbor Ernest Ansermet heard of Stravinsky's interest and took him to a restaurant where the cimbalom was played, the composer was enchanted (EWW 55–56; *Documents* 620). The performer was

Aladàr Ràcz, with whose assistance Stravinsky purchased an instrument for himself.

* * *

Renard the Fox (1915–1916; *Works* 3:5); *Les Noces* (1914–1917; *Works* 3:1–4); *The Soldier's Tale* (1918; Suite: *Works* 3:6–14); *Rag-Time for 11 Instruments* (1918; *Works* 12:6).

With the three stage works, Stravinsky enters the public arena as moralist and librettist as well as composer. His newfound voice and persona, very different from those of Debussy, Strauss, Schoenberg, and Berg, are more aligned to the dry wit of the young Jean Cocteau, Satie, and Marcel Duchamp, though not quite so offhand. All three stage works are on the subject of trust. For the fairy-tale burlesque of *Renard*, the wily fox in priest's clothing represents the seductive danger of fine rhetoric and his intended victim, the cock, naive self-importance. The entire score is composed around the strutting, scuttling tone of the cimbalom, deployed to virtuoso effect. When the episode of seduction, entrapment, and release (by his farmyard buddies) proved too short, Stravinsky repeated the action a second time, a touch of genius. The score desperately needs a decent English translation, and for orchestras without a cimbalom, a keyboard synthesizer with a cimbalom patch should suffice. The writing is sparkling, robust, and unsentimental, with brilliant animations at key moments.

Les Noces began life as a Sacred Wedding, realist counterpart, and emotional corrective to the fanciful anthropology of *The Rite of Spring*. Themes of peasant life and the natural pace of pastoral life have been quietly celebrated in Stravinsky's music for many years; the composer's attachment to realities of suffering depicted in Borodin and Mussorgsky and in literary sources, a kind of protest against the luxurious and exotic image of Russia promoted abroad. An early opulent score for monster orchestra was begun, only to be discarded as impractical and also inappropriate for the earthy subject matter. A second orchestration was started, for smaller ensemble incorporating newly favored timbres of pianola and cimbalom; this too would lapse for practical reasons, including the difficulty of finding players and the virtual impossibility of coordinating a player piano and a live ensemble, including solo singers and chorus. Both incomplete preliminary versions would later be recorded on vinyl by Robert Craft and have since been uploaded to YouTube. Both are delightful in different ways; however, the final orchestration for four pianos and percussion has to be regarded as the best and most appropriate compromise for a conception of ideally mechanical precision for an imaginary Aeolian super-pianola with added bells and whistles, which, however attractive in theory, would never have generated a sufficient volume of sound to fill a concert stage, let alone compete with a substantial body of singers. There is all the same a naively optimistic symmetry to the idea of a timeless peasant wedding in the tradition of Pieter Bruegel the Elder's artwork taking place in post-revolutionary Russia to the accompaniment of the equivalent of a brave musical traction engine.[3]

The music of *Les Noces* is intense and continuous and of unaccustomed loudness virtually throughout. It is a kind of persistence that recurs in the composer's *Cantata* of 1952 and *Abraham and Isaac* in 1963. While such a style is natural for a music designed for outdoors, it speaks of an embedded seriousness and urgency of conviction about ritual in the composer's own mental makeup. The four scenes correspond to ritual actions before and after the ceremony but do not include the wedding ceremony itself. Not very much happens, despite all the activity. Stravinsky is not about complexities of plot development but about concrete situations that are given time and extra definition to fix themselves in the audience's consciousness to a point where actions assume a monumental character and emotions a corresponding gravitas and severity. (Note that Stravinsky's tipsy bass solo in scene 4, "The Wedding Feast" [rehearsal number 127] makes a surprise reappearance as the Dies Irae solo in Benjamin Britten's *War Requiem.*) As in *Renard*, the words of the various characters, including the bride and groom, are assigned to different singers at different times to emphasize the ceremony and its customary exchanges over particular individuals, a very different objective from conventional operatic realism and solo stardom.

In 1994 a newly "authentic Russian" edition of *Les Noces* appeared, devised by Dmitri Pokrovsky (Elektra Nonesuch, 979335-2), along with many of the original village wedding songs from the Ukraine adopted and incorporated by Stravinsky. It offers a fascinating musical insight into traditional song material, as sung by raw peasant voices in native style, a timbre in females closer to the reedy quality of bagpipe music than the rounded tones of the opera house. Because he lacked funding to pay for musicians, Pokrovsky created the piano and percussion accompaniment on an Apple computer, bringing this performance arguably closer to Stravinsky's original conception of a totally automated accompaniment than the default version for live instrumentalists. The resulting impression is of a music of superhuman and instructive precision offset by plaintive voices of wailing intensity and presence.

The Soldier's Tale might have been conceived as a touring entertainment for Lenin's New Russia. Moral ambiguities add deep shadows to Stravinsky's choice of Afanasiev's folk tale of a simple musician lured into permanent exile by the promise of fame and fortune. Where the distinctive emotion of *Renard* is nervousness, expressed by the skittering cimbalom, the emotion of *The Soldier's Tale*, expressed by the solo violin, is an eloquent courage embodied in both the sound and the leadership role of the classical instrument. The simple musician is also a soldier, however, a casualty of war; in a darker sense, we are to understand that he may also be a deserter from the front, not simply a trooper discovered on leave. The moral uncertainty is compounded by temptation in which he gives up his violin—in effect, his soul—in return for security and material success, only to discover that a life without music is also a life without love and thus without meaning.

There is no singing, only dialogue and a voiceover, as though the work were composed for radio (of course, radio did not then exist). Story and music have an emotional range and depth far greater than *Renard*. The violin reigns supreme as the voice of music and of compassion. Though the Devil steals the violin by a trick, he cannot play the instrument, so his action is pointless as well as mischievous. Stravinsky's lively, gutsy music combines the tautness of a Kurt Weill with the layered mechanical rhythms of a Conlon Nancarrow, bringing a terse edge to an idiom previously trialed in the *Pribaoutki* and *Three Pieces for String Quartet*. The septet of players, including a carefully managed part for drums, is jazz-like in makeup and would be an interesting challenge to record by the older acoustic process. Unfortunately, Stravinsky's libretto has not been well served by his Swiss coauthor C. F. Ramuz, who transforms Afanasiev's classic Russian tale into a parody of the Faust legend. The original Faust was a mad scientist who wanted world domination, whereas Stravinsky's Soldier (like Wozzeck in Berg's opera of the same name) is a put-upon rank-and-file loner whose only ambition is to live a peaceful life. More to the point, Faust is corrupted by success, whereas the Soldier, even after he loses his violin, continues to lead a blameless life, corrupting nobody. To save his Princess, he risks everything and confounds the Devil by deliberately losing at poker. These are the redemptive acts of a totally selfless individual. The Devil's revenge, when the Soldier finally crosses the border in a bid to return to his homeland, is an act not of triumph but of moral defeat. This is serious stuff, and alas Ramuz is not up to it, a pity since the music deserves a Brechtian hard-nose realism. Once again the work cries out for a decent libretto, certainly in English and French, less so perhaps in German. It is the reason why the complete CD edition includes the Suite but not the stage version, a sure sign that Stravinsky was not satisfied with the libretto as it stood. Among the many highlights are the Soldier's March, in which every instrument appears to be marching to a different drum, a suite of Three Dances (Tango, Waltz, and Ragtime) by which the slumbering Princess is brought back to life, and the Triumphal March of the Devil for violin and drums, to which the Soldier is led away to his doom as the curtain falls. The jungle drums that finally claim him are also the drums of war and fate.

A brief *Three Pieces for Clarinet*, composed as a thank-you present for Werner Reinhart, a supporter of *The Soldier's Tale*, moves emotionally from the dark low register of pensive lament (a timbre revisited with the *Elegy for J. F. K.* of 1962) to the high-pitched, frantic assertiveness of a solo break in the style of Sidney Bechet. *Rag-Time* sounds like a collection of out-takes from *The Soldier's Tale* but with none of the angst of that work. Instrumentally, it is a delight, a conversational showpiece for the cimbalom in elegant flapper style, with a wonderfully tactile (and tactful) variety of tone qualities. To the good humor and laconic manner of Satie—one thinks immediately of the nonchalant *Parade* (Naxos, 8.554279)—Stravinsky brings a witty athleticism and disarming, twitchy grace.

* * *

Pulcinella ballet with song, after Pergolesi (1919–1920; *Works* 6:1–5); *Pulcinella* (Suite, 1922; *Works* 7:12–22); *Eight Instrumental*

Miniatures for fifteen players (1963; based on *Les Cinq Doigts* [The Five Fingers] for piano, 1921; *Works* 11:21–28).

Following the disruptive impact of hostilities on the Russian Ballet and the company's need to diversify from a hallmark Russian artistic body to represent the best of international modernism, it was Diaghilev's bright idea to lure Stravinsky back into the fold with the chance of working with Picasso on a refreshing Neapolitan song and dance entertainment on traditional characters of *commedia dell' arte* not too far removed from the street players and puppet world of *Petrushka*. The composer's task could not be simpler: to do for ballet using existing music of familiar idiom what Fritz Kreisler had been doing for the classical tradition. His task: arrange and present a selection of songs and short pieces by a little-known master of Italian lyric theater, Giambattista Pergolesi (along, as it transpired, with one or two unnamed composers of the same style and period). The act of restoration would also serve as a restorative for a damaged and divided Europe.

For Stravinsky the opportunity to get to know Picasso led him to appreciate the Catalan artist's genius in reconciling subliminal simplicities of color and pattern with a refined and classical sense of conscious line. Musically, the idiom is light years distant from the layered mechanical primitivism of *The Rite of Spring*, so dear to the Italian futurists of "The Art of Noise"; what gives *Pulcinella* a particularly appealing and poignant charm is a sense of going back to basics and savoring, in real time, the classical idiom of Diaghilev's "found musical objects" from the artist's perspective of simplification to formal and tonal essence. Picasso's flat colors and bold patterns become Stravinsky's instrumental colors and rhythms, and the artist's wonderfully fluid line is matched by the composer's expressively supple treatment of classical melody, an enchanted lyricism new to him and a world away from the nagging insistence of ragtime.

The process of learning a new/old musical language through "reading" the domestic musical recipes of Italian culture appealed to Stravinsky as an exercise in reliving Glinka's encounter with Italian opera in 1830. In his earlier *Easy Pieces* for piano four-hands and again in *Les Cinq Doigts* of 1921 (rearranged in 1963 as the *Eight Instrumental Miniatures*), the composer seems to be striving for a childlike innocence and simplicity of utterance. The readymade idiom of *Pulcinella*, a music by comparison fully formed, is offered to listeners as a guide or treatise in how to listen, while at the same time seeking to pare back the classical idiom in a manner as eloquent as Satie's sublimely understated *Socrate* presents the death of Socrates. By "being still" Stravinsky learned to read the formal tensions and calculated asymmetries of classical Italian lyricism with new clarity and sensitivity, an aesthetic position from which to revisit his own Russian identity and influences with greater awareness. With *Pulcinella* Stravinsky enters the realm of clinical neoclassic revival: the first stirring of a period of revaluation of past tradition to reach its peak with the fatal "*Lux facta est*" (I See the Light) of *Oedipus Rex*.

* * *

> *Concertino for String Quartet* (1920; DG, 477 8730), orchestrated 1952 as *Concertino for 12 Instruments* (*Works* 12:2); *Symphonies of Wind Instruments in Memoriam Claude Debussy* (1920, revised 1947; 1947 version: *Works* 12:15; 1920 version, Naxos, 8.557508).

The *Concertino* is another work deserving to be heard more often in its original version for string quartet. I have a personal interest, having attended a rehearsal by the Parrenin Quartet in which the mechanical Czerny scales of the printed score were played with the sighing, old-style *portamento* of the age of acoustic recording. The effect was to transform a piece of clockwork into a conjuring trick of featherweight gestures and, equally revealingly, to blur the exactly notated dissonances into a much more elusive and convincing atonal language, punctuated in the first movement by violent harmonic sneezes.

In his notes to the Naxos 125th anniversary album, Robert Craft describes the 1947 revised score of *Symphonies of Wind Instruments* (the title means "a sounding together") as "an unfortunate simplification of the original." Since both versions are freely available on disc, the composer's choice remaining with the 1947 version, a decision in favor of either is neither necessary nor required. Debussy died in 1918 after a long struggle with illness, by which time Stravinsky had distanced himself artistically and technically from his elder rival. That the piece was not understood at first hearings may have led the composer to wonder if he had got it right the first time. Its proper location is not the half-empty concert platform of its premiere under Serge Koussevitzky but a galleried cathedral with players positioned high, low, and at all points of the compass as the music itself expresses it. The weight and austerity of Stravinsky's massive harmonies are like those of *Zvezdoliki* but turned to stone: evoking a musical Stonehenge through and across which threadlike woodwind melodies pass like chattering telephone messages, a walled enclosure of columns through which trumpet calls send shafts of brilliance like sunlight through stained glass. Elsewhere the resonant calm is broken by a galloping motif in high-pitched double reeds that might have been inspired by the lively Horsemen of Kandinsky's abstract Apocalypse. But this is not a musical tribute in French style, nor even Russian: rather, the spatial breadth and depth of this somber but deeply grounded idiom take their cue from the distinctively Italian trombones and cornetts of Gabrieli's and Monteverdi's music for the Basilica of St Mark's Venice, a location and setting in 1956 for the equally stentorian trombones of *Canticum Sacrum*.

5

IN SEARCH OF THE LONG LINE

The long line in music is *melos*, melody, the Ariadne's thread that guides the listener out of the scene of battle, back through the labyrinth, to freedom. The scene of battle is human relations (the musical performance) and the labyrinth, the choice of mode and tuning of the harp (the rosette in the center of a lute is carved as a lattice to let music emerge from the interior of the instrument and also to resemble a labyrinth). Stravinsky's encounter with Pergolesi was a touch of genius on the part of Diaghilev, who understood that in the aftermath of war, Stravinsky the musical watchmaker was morally offended and left deeply insecure by the condescending rhetoric of German and Austrian tradition, and this was preventing him from developing confidence in sustaining a flowing line, or sense of leadership, in his own music. Part of Stravinsky's problem was language: European audiences did not understand Russian (they still largely don't) or appreciate that for Stravinsky, as for Janácek, language was personal and a vital sign of musical and national identity. The long line had to do with delivering a message, in words or melody, in terms an audience could understand and at a pace an audience could digest, when previously he had relied on dance actions to provide visible gestures to frame his musical animations. Timing was the problem. Satie understood the importance of timing and not overwhelming the listener with information, but Cocteau and other friends of Stravinsky were excited and seduced by the kaleidoscopic speed, illogical juxtapositions, and authorial indifference of mechanical media, especially the movies. *Pulcinella* was Stravinsky's reintroduction to the remoter past of *Pastorale* and a reminder of the traditional virtues of classical operatic storytelling, recognizing a difference between real-time narrative (in the sense of recitative) and emotional time (in terms of the aria).

After Debussy's death in 1918, Stravinsky sketched a few ideas for the memorial work that became *Symphonies of Wind Instruments*. According to Eric Walter White, he was entering a phase of "feeling particularly hostile to the strings because of their expressive qualities" (*A Critical Survey* 96). The string orchestra is the core of the classical symphony orchestra, providing pliable and controllable ambience and resonance for woodwinds and brass and bulking out the total orchestral sound to fill a concert hall or opera house. For Stravinsky, however, the string orchestra, which he had never been comfortable with, had become a liability. Part of it was custom and practice. The young Swiss German conductor Hermann Scherchen, conductor of the first performance of *Suite No. 1* in 1925, observed,

> German [string] players are subject to a hereditary evil: they do not or cannot sing enough. Often we conductors encounter orchestral playing in which all possible virtues—accuracy, elasticity, evenness, power, &c.—are united, but in which we miss one thing: the soul of music, the song that gives inward life to musical sounds. (29)

String players customarily affected a style of playing using *portamento*, or expressive glide, sliding the finger from note to note like a sticky spider's thread. The technique can be heard in early recordings, for example, Elgar's of the "Pomp and Circumstance" march, recorded acoustically in 1917, a languid style re-created with telling effect in the Smithsonian Chamber Players' performance of Mahler on period instruments (DHM, 054272 77343 2). It allowed a supple and expressive line, the very opposite of piano melody, but in Stravinsky's view, love of the line had become an end in itself, an expression of personal vanity, having nothing to do with what the composer and music might be trying to say.

Yet, he was devoted to mechanical instruments, which had come a long way but were still unable to simulate string tone. So it is of interest to read White describing Stravinsky's original drafts for the *Symphonies*. The *Revue Musicale* asked a number of composers to submit a brief work in Debussy's memory. "For the *Revue Musicale* he wrote a short wordless chorale, which was published in a version arranged for piano" (White, *A Critical Survey* 96). No, it was simply written in short score that readers would naturally assume to be for a piano. Later, White changed his story to read, "He had already (in July 1919) started to draft a work which was originally written for harmonium" (EWW 292). First a piano, now a harmonium. The author continues:

> In writing these Symphonies Stravinsky calculated that he could obtain the dynamic effects he wanted by the juxtaposition of instruments with different timbres playing in their natural *mezzo-forte* throughout and not by directing individual instruments to play more loudly or softly. Secondly, he insisted on metronomic precision and devised a scheme in which the different episodes were carefully geared together on the same principle as in *The Wedding* (Les Noces). (*A Critical Survey* 96–97)

Suddenly it becomes clear. The composer was sketching a work not for piano or harmonium but for an Aeolian *orchestrelle*, a self-playing piano roll–controlled combination pipe organ and harmonium with multiple stops. Such instruments can be seen and heard on YouTube. The composer's original set of conditions: mechanically geared tempi, fixed dynamics, and impersonal manner are all expressive features of the mechanical instrument, so by devising a work omitting the expressive dynamics normally controlled by hand or knee at the keyboard, Stravinsky is signaling that this is a work designed to be reproduced from perforated rolls by luxury instruments in well-to-do houses, however without anyone at the controls, to send a message that "the master of the keyboard is gone": poetic but highly impractical—yet, a musical objective to be borne in mind when the work is performed live in concert, however curious the comparison might appear.

In 1921 the composer and conductor Eugene Goossens was renting mews (garden cottage) accommodation at the rear of a Holland Park property owned, but seldom occupied, by the retired Eastman Kodak mogul George P. Davidson, an arrangement that allowed Goossens free access to G. P.'s music room, which was fitted out with a top-of-the-range model Aeolian orchestrelle.

> One night I invited congenial friends to meet Ravel, who was in London for a short visit. He had hardly been in the room two min-

> utes before he spied the organ console, headed straight for it, and started experimenting with every sonority he could extract from the instrument. Celesta, chimes, harp, and "echo organ" effects were his favourites, and he spent a good half-hour absorbed in what was for him a completely new revelation. . . . "C'est épatant; inouie. Mais, mon cher, vous devez gagner un argent fou pour pouvoir installer une si belle orgue dans une pièce si magnifique." ("Amazing, unimaginable. My dear, you would have to earn a fortune to afford to have such a beautiful instrument installed in so magnificent a room.") (Goossens 156–57)

Among Goossens's other guests on this occasion was the "aescetic timid Spaniard" Manuel de Falla, who "found its mechanics a little awesome and in his meek Castilian French observed that it had "une sonorité très sinistre" ("a decidedly ominous tone quality"). At the time, the premiere of Falla's *El Retablo de Maese Pedro* was still two years away and Ravel's *L'Enfant et les Sortilèges*, some four years distant.

Historians forget the persistent and genuine attachment of leading modern composers, as late as the 1920s, to mechanical instruments or to take account of the influences of such instruments on their handling of musical forces—in Stravinsky's case especially, their contribution to related issues of timing, instrumentation, and musical gesture particularly in the context of music theater and opera.

Stravinsky also faced very different complications arising from his interest in the potential of recording media and concurrent awareness of the inherent obstacles to be overcome for his music to profit successfully from recording. According to Robert Craft, "Stravinsky regarded his recorded performances as supplements to the printed scores. But his overall experience in recording was frustrating. In the early years, from the late 1920s, the recording technology could not reproduce the timbres and volumes of his music, while the divisions into five-minute record sides were painfully disruptive."[1] The frustrations to which Craft refers are unspecified, but violin timbre—indeed, the role of the string ensemble in the modern orchestra, quite apart from the outmoded style and attitudes prevalent among string players—emerges as a major preoccupation for the composer at a time of considerable technological upheaval in sound recording and the movies.

Classical music has always been regarded as the ultimate test of recording standards and remained so after the introduction of microphone and amplifier technology to the recording studio. As the composition of his chamber music clearly indicates, especially the jazz-influenced works, Stravinsky was sensitive to the limitations of acoustic (horn) recording and tried to accommodate to it by composing for small ensembles and imitating idioms, including Dixieland jazz, that he could hear transferred successfully to disc. For larger-scale compositions, the problems of fit were more severe. Stravinsky may have heard via Goossens of a celebrated case from the early twenties in which, determined to make a landmark commercial acoustic recording of Elgar's highly popular and exceedingly grand oratorio *Gerontius*, Joe Batten of Edison Bell set to work to trim the fat from the composer's score:

> Instead of the usual complement of forty to fifty strings, I had to make do with nine. A choir which in public performance consists of anything from sixty to three hundred voices had to be cut to eight; these I selected from picked artistes. Another perplexity was the grand organ, an instrument which never yet had been recorded effectively; fortunately and surprisingly, the bass concertina made a convincing substitute. . . . An orchestra of twenty-four, choir of eight, and three soloists [were positioned] around three small recording horns, greatly cramped for space in a recording studio whose dimensions were thirty feet by eight. (Batten 58–59)[2]

In fact there were a number of conflicting problems facing a composer anxious to work with new media and have his music looked on with favor from a technical perspective as appropriate for distribution in new public and social markets. For a number of years prior to the arrival of public radio, limited concert transmission services had been available via telephone line in major European centers, allowing well-to-do subscribers to listen in to live opera performances by headset from home. With the announcement of plans for public radio in the early 1920s, a potentially lucrative new market was imminently available for music and drama designed for the new medium. For the success of a public and essentially voice-related medium, content would have to be suitable for a mass audience and also of appropriate quality. Public taste was assumed to favor light, melodious music in a conventional tonal idiom, and from a composer's perspective, the change in technical circumstances from relocating the orchestra from a concert hall into a studio environment would have implications for the size and makeup of an orchestra and its relation to the voice. Another issue would be absence of vision: music for radio would have to compensate, he imagined, by enriching the sonic experience—perhaps along the lines of Schoenberg's *Pierrot*. In retrospect we can see that the emergence of neoclassicism in twentieth-century music was dictated less by negative factors, such as capitulation to mass taste or failure of artistic nerve, more by the positive requirements and limitations of audio equipment with which composers were now obliged to deal.

The recording medium is intimate in nature and was destined to stay that way after the arrival of radio, even though radio offered the prospect of an enlarged sound stage and delivery of a more natural concert experience. Unlike a concert hall, where large orchestras were necessary to fill the space, the microphone priorities of a studio recording, with or without a live audience, continued to insist on clarity and separation of voices, leading to reduced player numbers.

Stravinsky had contacts in a position to keep him abreast of technical issues, among them Darius Milhaud in Paris, engaged on projects involving jazz and film, and in London Eugene Goossens, among the first to record electrically for HMV at Hayes in Middlesex. Designed with acoustic recording in mind to maximize volume, the Hayes studio was built like the inside of a violin, though without the curves: it was entirely sheathed in wood paneling, and since polished wood is both highly resonant and sound reflecting, the exceedingly reverberant and "toppy" acoustic was able to improve signal clarity and compensate for the soft and rounded sound of acoustic recording, especially for an accompanying orchestra. Introducing a microphone into such an acoustically "live" environment had the immediate effect of enhancing an already top-heavy, bright sound. As experienced a music lover as Compton Mackenzie, founder of *The Gramophone* magazine, was, he reacted with horror and distaste to the harshness and brightness of the changeover from acoustic to electrical recording.

Particular criticism was directed at the string orchestra, about to resume normal working conditions after more than a decade of having to record acoustically in small numbers using Stroh instruments, which are little more than fingerboards with trumpets attached at the bridge to direct sound at the recording horn. The unexplained noisiness of the string orchestra was only one aspect of a greater problem for composers and producers having to reacquaint themselves with the acoustical role of the strings in a traditional symphony orchestra, an orchestration issue that Stravinsky had hitherto done his best to avoid, even in his best-known ballet scores. From the baroque era of Vivaldi and Bach—whose concerto works deserve to be studied from the perspective of practical research into balance and separation issues respecting the composition of a baroque orchestra and its relation to a unifying acoustic—the role of the string orchestra can be construed, in effect, as providing a *programmable acoustic* for a lyric music of constantly varying tonality. String instruments en masse amounted in modern terms to a tunable reverberation chamber, providing a diffuse enveloping ambience instantly adaptable to the modulations of a solo voice or instrument and by which soloist and accompaniment would be able to remain in tune.

Schoenberg's path to atonality was certainly guided by acoustic recording, since the older technology was practically anechoic, there being no room response, therefore nothing to assist the soloist to stay in tune other than an innate sense of pitch. In the absence of natural room response, a listener's focus of attention passed from blended harmony to multiplicity of parts and lines and the use of timbre contrasts among woodwind, brass, and horns as major elements for projecting musical form. Such priorities were reflected in mechanical organs such as the orchestrelle, designed to be heard up close in acoustically damped domestic or upper-class music rooms. With the arrival of electrical recording, listener attention was suddenly refocused on the role of ambience or room reverberation and the string orchestra as an ambient "spatial" component of the listening experience.

Since there was no established science of acoustics to which they could refer, in the early days BBC engineers grappled intuitively with the problem of a boxy studio sound by reverting to the conventions of acoustic recording and lining the broadcast studio walls with sound-absorbent materials and drapes. That was resisted: musicians were uncomfortable with having to perform in an acoustically dead environment in which they were unable to hear themselves play. To get the best out of early carbon microphones, the "meat safe" models of which were intimidatingly large, studio engineers demanded smaller orchestras, in particular fewer string players, to achieve a clean, uncluttered sound. Instead of creating a pleasant airy ambience, large numbers of string instruments created unpleasant noise and interference. However, reducing the string orchestra to a group of soloists altered the chemistry of the orchestra, creating serious balance issues for the composer, as well as the conductor of traditional repertoire.

* * *

Mavra (1921–1922; *Works* 14:14).

Stravinsky staked a great deal on the success of this one-act comic opera and was deeply depressed at its lack of popular success. On the plus side, the music reveals a new generosity and beauty of melodic line, a direct legacy of his experience of setting Pergolesi's Italianate melodies. In principle, *Mavra* should have succeeded as an early example of a new postwar genre of domestic one-act comic operas, treating jazz and movie themes, borrowing freely from popular song, and catering to flapper-era audiences with a taste for the surreal and bizarre.[3] A surge of activity in domestic opera composition coincided with the arrival of domestic radio as a live entertainment medium in 1922–1924; a development followed in rapid succession by electrical recording in 1926. Both media were destined to transform the industry from the realm of dreams and fantasy of acoustic recording and silent movies to a hard-edged information medium for the newsreel age. The change in public taste arising from the arrival of electrical recording is an effective subplot of the Gene Kelly–Stanley Donen movie musical *Singin' in the Rain* (1952): its subject matter, the launch of Al Jolson's *The Singing Fool*, a "Vitaphone" movie with synchronized disc-recorded sound. Followed by Walt Disney's animated cartoon *Steamboat Willie*, 1928 marked the end of the silent movie era and the beginning of a dramatically new streetwise medium of talking pictures with synchronized sound and music.

In 1922, the year of *Mavra*, none of these technological innovations had yet taken place. The media as we understand them now (radio, newsreels, electrical disc recording) did not exist. Lightweight, frivolous, and surreal musical entertainments were composed simply to fill an entertainment void created by the war and cater to an appetite for ironic and diverting entertainment among an emotionally damaged and exhausted civilian population. All the same, the rapidfire action and vertically complex instrumentation of *Mavra*, including greatly reduced string orchestra split into treble and bass groups playing purely accent roles, already show clear signs of microphone-influenced planning.

Considered on its own terms, which are personal and technical, *Mavra* is a delightful and accomplished musical achievement. The storyline is an attempt at Russianized Feydeau farce, based on Pushkin. But it is Feydeau transported to a Russian nineteenth-century upper-middle-class domestic setting, viewed from the perspective of a nervous exiled composer still being henpecked by his elderly mother, a joke so flat it might have passed muster as a silent one-reel piece of Buster Keaton slapstick. The beautifully composed lyrics are in Russian, a language incomprehensible to a majority of listeners, words that furthermore clog up any action (an adequate English translation remains sorely needed). With the exception of heroine Parasha's opening song (published alone as "The Russian Maiden's Song"), which rises above its rhythmic complexity, the majority of arias and ensembles, while beautifully executed, are impossibly densely written, even for chamber opera. For a story unfolding in real time at the speed of a silent movie but with added sound, there are simply too many factors in play and changes of instruments competing for attention and distracting from the voices, and neither the action nor the individual exchanges of dialogue allow the audience any time to draw breath and reflect on what is being said and what it might imply—adding more to the impression that the composer has conceived the opera for radio or cable telephone transmission, rather than for live performance, on the assumption that in the absence of a visual dimension, the narrative must necessarily proceed at a faster than normal pace. (Perhaps an answer might be to stage the opera with an orchestrelle performing on set as virtual *deus ex machina*, directing the action as a substitute for the orchestra or at least replacing the woodwinds and brass. The roll running out would then provide a suitably comic rationale for the current damp squib ending.)

What Stravinsky appears not to have learned from Pergolesi is that, apart from the cognitive requirements of the audience, in opera the singing voice and associated text have an auditorium to fill and an audience to impress. They need space and time to make their point. Judging by its complexity, Stravinsky may have ventured a little too far for comfort into the contrapuntal idiom of Bach or Schoenberg. In addition to the kaleidoscopic speed of the earlier *Pribaoutki*, a listener now has to deal with multiple threads of song instead of just one voice. Stravinsky may also have misjudged the speed of his action by comparison with the pace of silent movies, which create comedy through accelerated motion.

One has the impression that these problems of delivery and timing in real space either have not been worked through or the composer has taken the example of Schoenberg and others at face value as assurance that so compressed a style of writing is musically viable as well as dramatically (or at least, comedically) effective.[4] That the comedy itself strikes a listener today as pointless and unworthy of the composer's gifts may be another indication of misplaced priorities, given that characters and subject matter appear intended to allude to familiar stereotypes in Russian literature (including the pivotal sexual ambiguity of a bearded lady destined to reappear years later as Baba the Turk in *The Rake's Progress*).

Density of part writing and concentration of idiom are temptations associated with mechanical instruments. When the sounds you have in mind can be played back immediately and automatically from a paper roll on an instrument only a few inches away, it is all too tempting to expect that same density of rapid transitions and combinations of line and harmony, easily executed at the keyboard, to translate just as easily to live performers on the opera stage, a much more spacious environment demanding considerably greater simplicity of outline and more generous timing. It is not enough that the effects required are playable, if they happen too fast for the listener to keep up. When excessive speed is applied to human emotions, where timing is the essence, the loss of connection can be ruinous. Were the accompanying music to be performed by a machine onstage or heard from offstage, its effect might be less overwhelming.

A music composed for synchronization with a movie production would have to adhere to precise clock times to fit—either live or on disc—with the action on the movie screen. It is possible that *Mavra* may have been conceived as a silent movie comedy with parallel music track, given that in both *The Nightingale* and *Renard*, the solo voices are located in the orchestra pit, their roles mimed onstage. Rex Lawson is not convinced that the tempi of Stravinsky's piano rolls can be entirely trusted, implying that playing speeds could be slower than those indicated. Yet, Benjamin Zander's adoption of "authentic" piano-roll tempi for the Boston Philharmonic's *Rite of Spring* (Pickwick, MCD

25) has shown that even a 20 percent higher speed for the Danse Sacrale is practically achievable by live performers. In considering the implications of Stravinsky's mechanically geared tempi, it may be helpful to distinguish changes in ratio of tempi from the running speed of a performance as a whole. The speed at which a roll is actually played depends on the person operating the mechanical instrument, who in 1922 may be working the pedal-action bellows with foot power as well as controlling dynamic shutters and swells with knee and hand controls. When the role of the operator as "timekeeper" is considered alongside the singing tradition of Pergolesi—or indeed, of folk tradition, given that the "Russian Maiden's Song" can be interpreted as pure and unashamed *klezmer*—it is possible to interpret Stravinsky's attitude to timing as *organic* and *driven* by an executant (the solo voice, the keyboard operator) rather than by a machine. Such a perception of timing is analogous to record playing, where the operator has the option to set the turntable speed but on the understood terms that the speed selected should be right for the music, not distort it. Tempi slower than Stravinsky's marked metronomic indications might then be viable, if the result is heard to be emotionally and dramatically effective. The same question has arisen elsewhere, over Beethoven's and Bartók's metronomic indications, alleging that their metronomes are at fault. When a composer stipulates excessively fast tempi, however, it can also be a normal consequence of living too close to the metronome and forgetting to allow for audience reaction and reverberation time in a concert acoustic. As long as the inner proportions are maintained, the choice of a slower pulse may be acceptable, even desirable. I have the distinct impression of greater emotional control in Marie Mrázová's voice-led performance of *Pribaoutki*, a shade slower than normal, on CDM (PR 250 057).

* * *

Octet for wind instruments (1922–1923; *Works* 12:3–5); *Concerto* for piano and wind orchestra (1923–1924; *Works* 10:1–3); *Sonata* for piano (1924; *Works* 13:18–20); *Serenade in A* for piano (1925; *Works* 13:6–9); *Suite No. 1* for orchestra (1925: from *Five Easy Pieces* for piano duet; *Works* 11:2–5).

The *Octet* is a happy piece; like *Mavra* it ends abruptly, with a polite cough. Stravinsky says the idea and choice of instruments came to him in a dream, but the high spirits also coincide with his meeting and falling in love with Vera Sudeikina, an encounter engineered by the wily Diaghilev. Though composed for wind instruments (and therefore still overshadowed by the mechanical organ), the idiom is a refreshing change from the jousting, cubist block harmonies of earlier works, including *Mavra*. The principal reason for the change of mood is easy to hear: a freedom of line extended to every instrument and a relaxed, unforced sense of timing. Counterpoint and invention are abundant but all done with an admirable lightness of touch. Shortly after completing the work, Stravinsky purchased a Renault car for the couple to travel by road across Europe, and even though it antedates the children's book by several years, I hear the *Octet* all the same as a musical jaunt through the country in the spirit of Babar the Elephant, a promenade on wheels with stops along the way to enjoy the view. The theme and variations constituting the bulk of the journey are introduced by a characteristic ascending scalewise ritornello that evokes the swing action and sound of cranking an automobile, the engine ticking over, then misfiring and gliding to a stop (a gesture recalled in the interludes of *Agon*). Others may hear a warning allusion to the *Dies Irae* concealed, Dalí fashion, in the trombone part of the same interlude. This time Stravinsky seems to have got it right in terms of pace and length in relation to musical ideas. The music is more open, at times closer to Dixieland in spirit than to the slightly manic mechanical quality of (say) the *Etude for Pianola*.

Circumstances, including the need to seek alternative income at a time of financial stress, led Stravinsky to compose a piano concerto with a view to performing it himself. After the *Piano-Rag Music*, which had quite possibly alienated rather than pleased its dedicatee Arthur Rubinstein, Stravinsky needed a pianist he could rely on, and he was not quite ready to give that responsibility to younger son Soulima, who was being groomed for the role. The style is ebullient and interesting and shows not only the composer in charge but also some influence of Busoni's equally sparkling Bach-influenced set pieces (e.g., "Chorale Prelude on 'Nun freut euch, lieben Christen g'mein,'" Hyperion, CDA66566). For Stravinsky, contrapuntal fluency, another aspect of "the long line," is matched by a new vigor acquired from renewed piano practice and finger-strengthening exercises in the tradition of Carl Czerny, a step up in weight from the Clementi tradition of his early piano studies. The music alternates lightfingered baroque and strutting jazz. A solemn introduction in A minor in mock-heroic French overture style could be interpreted as a comment on the outcome of the recent war, just as the sinister marchlike rhythm of the third movement, dissolving into Milhaud and Poulenc-style French dance rhythms, also appears to comment on recent events and outcomes. In between, an uncharacteristically rich, slow movement alternates solemn and unusually heavyweight chordal harmonies with plangent oboe and English horn melodies: very definitely, "wail and hug" music of a soulful character to become a hallmark of Stravinsky's slow movements.

Schoenberg was deeply unimpressed at Stravinsky's reversion to "imitation Bach," and it is worth noting that despite being in control, Stravinsky remains mistrustful of the string orchestra, omitting all but bass viols from the accompanying ensemble, making the concerto (his first, after *Petrushka*) effectively a duel between keyboards: solo piano and wind orchestra represented by the *orchestrelle*—a kind of memento of *Petrushka* in its earlier conception of a *Konzertstück*. At times the relationship of piano solo and orchestra appears to foreshadow *Movements* for piano and orchestra. The piano-roll edition combining solo and orchestra is issued on Dal Segno (SPRCD 007).

Included on the Dal Segno CD, the *Sonata* of 1924 is a particular favorite of mine: white music, reduced in speed, totally poised, and in control—the message "no need to fight." The slow movement is a particular joy, with meticulously written-out melody arabesques in the right hand against a laconic, steady left hand, a cross between Chopin and a Beethoven slow movement. Here the melody line is at its most unhurried, expansive, and luxuriant. This is the sense of executant-directed timing that a listener perhaps ought to feel with the vocal line of "Russian Maiden's Song," here translated into the keyboard domain. There is also a glance back at the shimmering gracenote figurations of the earlier *Pastorale* and associated tranquility of mood.

Serenade in A is an odd creation in four short movements, like a sundae of four scoops, each timed to fit nicely on one side of a ten-inch gramophone record. It is the first overt intimation in Stravinsky of deliberate interest in the gramophone medium, no doubt because the year of publication was also the year that electrical recording was launched in the United States. To demonstrate the dramatic improvement in audio range and definition afforded by the change, the EMI Centenary Edition Sampler (EMI, 7087 6 11859 2 8) has thoughtfully provided comparison recordings of the same music (an excerpt from the Rossini/ Respighi *La Boutique Fantasque*) recorded acoustically in 1921 under Adrian Boult and electrically in the same studio in Hayes in 1925 by Eugene Goossens (tracks 10 and 11). The quality of these early recordings is still a long way from perfect, but the new electrically assisted sound opens out and incorporates a new breadth, inner balance, and consistency of room ambience, which amount to a revelation, at the same time acknowledging a benchmark for radio transmissions of music that the competing record industry will henceforth be obliged to match. At a stroke, electrical recording signaled the obsolescence and imminent decline of the orchestrelle and reproducing piano. The electric medium of radio would assist in restoring Stravinsky's faith in the string orchestra.

Serenade in A for piano solo has a deliberately spacious and dignified quality that—in the first movement, "Hymne," especially—may remind listeners of Aaron Copland or Virgil Thomson. Perhaps because Stravinsky recorded the work personally for Columbia, the idiom has embedded itself in American musical consciousness. Its austere plain style, evoking Shaker tradition, returns in Copland's *Fanfare for the Common Man* and continues to resonate in movie contexts emblematic of the pioneer American spirit, an example Dennis McCarthy's title music to the television series *Star Trek: Deep Space Nine.*

* * *

Pater Noster for choir (1926; *Works* 20:10); *Oedipus Rex* (1926–1927; *Works* 18:1–2).

For a nonpracticing believer of the Russian Orthodox faith, Stravinsky's setting of the *Pater Noster* in Slavonic is a tiny but significant petition in advance of *Oedipus Rex*. A Latin version of the prayer setting was made in 1949.

The 1914–1918 war had forced Stravinsky to leave his friends in Paris and seek a place of safety in Switzerland. The war's end saw punitive economic sanctions imposed on Austria and Germany, pressures leading to a reawakening of social and political prejudices against gypsies and minorities. In a gesture of reconciliation with their Austrian colleagues, composers Darius Milhaud and Francis Poulenc and soprano Marya Freund traveled from Paris to Vienna, where Alma Mahler, the composer's widow, arranged meetings with librettist Hugo von Hofmannsthal and Schoenberg, Berg, Webern, and associates, out of which came the idea of a double performance of *Pierrot Lunaire*: a French interpretation with Marya Freund, conducted by Milhaud, and a Viennese version conducted by Schoenberg, with Erika Wagner as solo voice.[5] Schoenberg was touched at this expression of solidarity from a French composer of outwardly very different aesthetic loyalties. What they did have in common was a Jewish heritage, and this act of friendship may have contributed to Schoenberg's decision a year later in 1923, in defiance of a rising current of anti-Jewish feeling in public life, to identify himself publicly as Jewish and an outsider and soon after to refuse the offer of a teaching post at the Bauhaus because of rumors of antisemitism within the organization (Schoenberg 88–93).

Such acts of cultural diplomacy form part of an important but neglected background to a composer's musical development and aesthetic choices, a reason why Stravinsky's comment on the publication of Schoenberg's letters, even as late as 1964, in a review for the London *Observer*—a review dwelling more on moral and economic issues than on aesthetics—may provide a clue to the Russian composer's own family recollections of adjusting to the loss of his personal possessions and identity after the Revolution of 1917, while bearing in mind his history of attachment to the musical traditions of disenfranchised minorities. When Stravinsky says,

> The lenses of Schoenberg's conscience were the most powerful of the musicians of the era, and not only in music. Indeed, . . . one rubs one's eyes at, for example, the dates of the letters to Kandinsky, with their references to Hitler—that they were written in 1923, not 1933, (*Themes* 133–34; *Conclusions* 249)

the composer seems also to be speaking of his own experience of political and ethnic rejection.[6] Stravinsky's sense of isolation during the 1920s was especially acute since, in addition to being vulnerable to criticism as a modernist, he was a political exile and potentially stateless.

Darius Milhaud was connected to Stravinsky through Jean Cocteau, their joint attraction to jazz and mutual respect for Satie. In 1926 Hermann Scherchen asked Milhaud to reduce the score of his one-act opera *Le Pauvre Matelot* to thirteen instrumentalists as a companion piece for Stravinsky's *The Soldier's Tale*. Based on an actual news item, *Pauvre Matelot* (Poor Sailor) is a tragic farce about a serviceman detained abroad who at the end of hostilities becomes successful in business, returns anonymously to his village an ostentatiously wealthy man, and is offered a place to stay by his faithful wife, who, not recognizing him, murders the stranger overnight for his wealth to secure her husband's release (Milhaud 169–72).

As Paris intellectuals, Cocteau and Milhaud may have been content to interpret the original news episode (which involved a Rumanian student returning to his village after gaining an education abroad) as a trivial but brutally amusing example of life imitating Greek tragedy. For Stravinsky, already in consultation with Cocteau on the libretto of *Oedipus Rex*, the drama of the exiled hero, reinstated in society but unrecognized for who he really is and fatally betrayed by the vanity of his own success, was no frivolity but a moral fable of unsettling personal relevance. The Oedipus of Stravinsky's music drama is the plaything of the gods, and the gods in this case are implicitly cast as smart set intellectuals of postwar Europe who do not realize that the world has changed: that the balance of power—especially people power—is changing, and the change is radio. The political message underpinning *Oedipus Rex* is that actions have consequences and that leaders are answerable *to the people*. It is a richly sensitive political message to deliver at a fragile moment in European history, and Stravinsky accomplishes his chosen task in two ways, first by setting the text in Latin and thereby universalizing the message, second by expressing the drama in the static terms of the new medium of radio.

Diaghilev was frankly nonplussed at having a work dedicated to him that contained neither dance nor choreographed action of any kind. The collected edition recording (*Works* 18:1–2) even sounds like a period BBC radio broadcast (I confess a special weakness for an earlier Philips vinyl recording in mono with Cocteau as reciter in the original French). The drama is consciously faithful to the classic French tradition of unities of time, place, revelation, and denouement. The chorus is both Greek chorus and a representation of the public voice and the public's right to know in the new era of mass communication. For Stravinsky to have achieved so compelling a mastery of the new medium so early in the history of radio is a mark of his vision. Much of the drama turns on whether various leaders, messengers, and commentators can be trusted to tell the truth. Equally interesting, the story endorses "the people" represented by the chorus as the ultimate foundation of a democracy, enjoying the right to decide whether the leader remains or is removed from power. At a time when most of his contemporaries, even Schoenberg, are continuing to dabble in situation comedy, *Oedipus Rex* is an astonishingly brave and risky political statement for an exiled composer to make.

Stravinsky would later describe the work as a *Merzbild* after Kurt Schwitters, in other words as an assemblage of stylistic bits and pieces from a range of sources, among them references to Mozart, Beethoven, and Verdi. The association of Oedipal hubris with a lyric tenor voice, rather than a Wagnerian *Heldentenor*, is a thread that persists through *The Rake's Progress* and *Cantata* to the character and demeanor of Lucifer in *The Flood.* The stage setting suggests a cross between Verdi's *Aïda* and a movie set by Fritz Lang. In paring all stage action from the core drama, Stravinsky is denying himself the dramatic possibilities of a secondary role to compare with Falstaff in *Henry V* or the night watchman in *Macbeth*, in the interest of direct reportage and attendant sense of audience participation in actions unfolding in real time and designed for radio. Unlike the *St. Matthew Passion*, the chorus remains rather one-dimensional, as though Stravinsky were deliberately emulating the sublime modesty of Satie's *Socrate* but on a larger scale; however, the chorus's final farewell to the blinded and disgraced king ("Gently, gently, his people drive him away. Farewell, farewell Oedipus, we loved you") is among the most moving in all opera. With *Oedipus Rex*, the dragging upbeat octave sweep, a flourish straight out of the piano practice exercise books of Czerny and Clementi and previously encountered in *Concertino* and *Octet*, assumes a note of apocalyptic menace to be recalled, at the defeat of Nazism, in the opening thunderbolts of the *Symphony in Three Movements.*

* * *

Apollo (Apollon Musagète), ballet for string orchestra (*Works* 4:1–10).

Stravinsky's conversion to the string orchestra is so sudden and so total that commentators have struggled to explain *Apollo* ever since as a consistent, inevitable, and deliberate choice by the composer of *The Rite of Spring* and *Symphonies of Wind Instruments*. The work was commissioned by the Elizabeth Sprague Coolidge Foundation in the United States, whose only conditions were that the ballet require no more than six dancers and last not more than half an hour. Stravinsky himself chose to base the ballet on the legend of Apollo and the Muses, the latter reduced to three in number. Just as the classical story of *Oedipus Rex* could be seen to be chosen for its contemporary relevance (as a meditation on the downfall of those who believe in a divine right to power), so too the choice of Apollo is informed by the composer's awareness that the master of the lyre was also master of the bow and arrow, a god of war and bringer of harmony. The strings are Apollo's instrument and companion of his eloquence; even so, a reader may struggle to accept the composer's fulsome words of praise for the string orchestra and the tonal language—no doubt also intended to ingratiate him with American listeners—so soon after his repudiation of the string orchestra as a sonority in *Mavra* and the *Piano Concerto*. Once again the answer may in part be technical. Along with photographs of featured composers Schoenberg and Bartók, in its *Handbook 1929* covering events of the previous year, the newly restructured BBC offers useful hints and tips to musicians with ambitions to work in radio. A note to pianists warns,

> The piano never sustains tone at level intensity. Immediately after a note has been struck, the tone drops to about half-strength, and gradually tails off to nothing. This is not very noticeable in a concert hall, but the microphone, never being deceived, transmits exactly what it gets from the piano. . . . The ideal attributes of a broadcasting pianist are these: a clear, bright tone, a clean technique, and a first-class sense of shape and rhythm. Rigid economy in the use of the pedal is essential.[7]

All of which makes very good sense in relation to the piano style of *Concerto* and the *Capriccio*. On the subject of string sound, however, a note to composers has this to say:

> The transmission of music is now so faithful that all music broadcasts more or less satisfactorily; but there are some combinations of instruments, and some types of music, that seem to be more naturally adapted to broadcasting than others.
>
> A string quartet, or a string orchestra, being composed of instruments which all have the same tone-quality, always transmits well; so does a brass band, for the same reason, and an unaccompanied chorus. Orchestras and—in a less degree—military bands, being composed of groups of instruments of different qualities, are not quite so foolproof to broadcast; they can, and usually do, reproduce faultlessly, but they require constant care in balancing the strength of the various instruments. The same is true of most chamber-music combinations.
>
> As to the type of music that is easiest to broadcast, classical music is more generally satisfactory than modern. This is chiefly due to the simple fact that only the best and purest classical music has survived, whereas modern music has not yet stood the test of time. But there can be no doubt that the more elementary harmonic system of the former is an advantage, as the microphone's natural reverberation, while enriching simple texture, tends to render the complex confused.
>
> An essential in good broadcast music is a strong vein of melody. Melody—which really represents personality in music—is even more necessary in the studio than in the concert hall. The necessity is so far-reaching that contrapuntal music, the texture of which is a combination of melodies, is nearly always more satisfactory in transmission than large masses of harmony.
>
> As broadcasting goes on, the technique of special composition for wireless will be explored more fully; but however thoroughly this art—in some aspects an entirely new one—is developed, the same root principles will always lie at the bottom of the best broadcast music: strong melody and simple texture.[8]

Stravinsky might have composed *Apollo* to these exact specifications. Choreography of the Paris production (for Diaghilev) was by the young Russian émigré George Balanchine. Melody is supreme; textures are generally spare and include an unprecedented cadenza for solo violin ("The Birth of Apollo") as eloquent as the same in *Agon*, to be choreographed by the same Balanchine nearly thirty years later.

Stravinsky has enlarged the string orchestra from quintet to sextet, adding a second cello voice; this both enriches and creates a warm string texture without cluttering the high register with excess resonance. It also reinforces the bass, as he has previously done in the *Piano Concerto* and *Mavra*, and will carry on doing in *Capriccio* and the *Symphony of Psalms* on the clear technical understanding that bass frequencies are good karma in the studio. Of the change in preferred sonority from piano and winds—typically marcato, "digital," and mechanical—to legato strings, as an act of reconciliation, not only does it compel a beautiful line from performers, being idiomatically written for the instruments, but the very texture of the string orchestra also seems to have the effect of putting the brakes on the composer's previously febrile invention by acknowledging the fact that string tone takes longer to speak. The tradeoff is a bloom of harmonic resonance more pungent and sustained than is possible with winds or piano. That the more relaxed pace works for dancers and in the theater as successfully as in the recording studio is an added bonus.

6

THE ART OF NONEXPRESSION

From line comes form. The role of line (melody) is to maintain focus and a steady hand, to complete an action in a controlled manner without losing the thread. The art of rhetoric compels the attention of others by tone of voice and the power of gesture, but these are mere appearances and have little to do with musical content, only with the impression of authority. A surgeon in the operating theater may be a great actor and a powerful presence, but to perform well requires one to follow procedure and demonstrate a steady hand and brain, along with an intimate knowledge of human physiology. An operation is teamwork. It is not enough to execute moves with grace and finesse: they have to be prepared and implemented in an order that makes sense, smoothly, without undue assertion or haste, and equally without unnecessary delay.

By taking on the role of concert pianist, then as a conductor of his own music, Stravinsky inserted himself into the world of performance as an active participant. The unfortunate *Mavra* experience had shown once again the importance of pacing musical and dramatic action to take account of natural delays in performer, orchestra, environment, and audience reaction time and the amount of information—density of part writing—an audience (or, indeed, a microphone) is capable of handling. Radio spoke to the world but did so invisibly and from a fixed and limited perspective. Channeling information by radio required a simplified and coherent signal, with emphasis on consistency of tone and continuity of speech. A benign impersonality is appropriate if the delivery of information is regarded as paramount; however, as a medium for dictatorships, the reverse may be the case and rhetoric, more important. Stravinsky's success with *Apollo*, at a time of adjustment to a powerful new medium, can be attributed in part to the music's coherence of speech and formality of gesture, the composer's courtesy in identifying the medium of radio as the voice of musical enlightenment and to his treating the radio public as a discriminating audience. The radio industry was not prejudiced against modern music, certainly not in Britain and central Europe. This was a time when technical expertise in microphones and balance engineering was coming to terms with the limitations of equipment and signal distribution in an early stage of experimentation, at the same time developing a new science of studio acoustics, while seeking out and testing new microphones and ensemble arrangements for improved balance. In the early days of radio, composers of modern music, including such pioneers of percussion as Edgar Varèse, were welcome guests of the BBC on account of the specific challenges their music posed to technical staff. For their part, technical staff appreciated the challenge of new music that was intelligently designed and clearly focused in its technical and acoustic requirements.

Stravinsky's uniquely meticulous interest in the timing and mechanical ratios of tempi in his compositions endeared him to manufacturers of piano rolls and concert planners and gave him a potential advantage in negotiating with the record industry, radio, and the movies, for all of whom accurate timing was always a priority. Attention to chronometric timing in relation to expressive timing, though not a concern for a majority of art composers (except perhaps Bartók, who was interested in time as an architectural dimension), is a skill of particular relevance to the movie industry, especially movies of the disc-synchronized Vitaphone variety but in due course also for movies with optical sound. A radio producer may only be interested in how long a piece may run, but a movie composer is rather more concerned with coordinating and pacing music relative to the intervening action. So when Stravinsky recalls Nijinsky at rehearsals of *The Rite of Spring*,

> "I will count to forty while you play," Nijinsky would say to me, "and we will see where we come out." He could not understand that though we might at some point come out together, this did not necessarily mean we had been together on the way,

one recognizes it as the recollection of a movie-aware composer who understands that the important issues are not beginnings and endings but the alignment of music and dance in between (*Expositions* 143). Even as outwardly minor a composition as the *Serenade in A* is, a reminder that the task of composing four different styles of music to the same timespan amounts to a study in the relationship of "performance time"—and associated audience perception of a specific emotion—in relation to an impersonal measure of "clock time."

* * *

> *The Fairy's Kiss*, ballet (1928; *Works* 5:14–22); *Divertimento*, symphonic suite (1934; EMI, 7243 5 69675 2 6).

Pulcinella had been a series of set piece orchestrations of Pergolesi and others, held together by an agreeable if flimsy plot. The music is delicate and humorous, and the characters are stereotypes of the kind encountered in *Petrushka*. After the success of *Apollo*, Stravinsky was eager to apply his melodic and lyric skills to a Russian story line with genuine emotional resonance and in the service of Tchaikovsky's music, a composer whose fortunes had suffered from criticism of decadent (or at least, uninspiring) formalism. Ravel had revisited the fairy-tale world of *Nutcracker* with his childhood opera *L'Enfant et les Sortilèges*, to a libretto by Colette. Stravinsky was more interested in revealing the inner adult in the character and emotional complexity of Tchaikovsky's familiar music, and *The Fairy's Kiss* is in part his portrait of the composer, through music experienced as it were in close-up, as in a movie, rather than experienced at a distance, as in the concert hall.

For the back story, he returned to Hans Andersen, reawakening memories of Debussy's contemptuous dismissal of Grieg, and implied disdain toward Rimsky-Korsakov and all Russian music from "north of the border." The story of a young man doomed in infancy and spirited away by the Ice Maiden in the prime of life has elements of Oedipal tragedy, while musically speaking, it evokes scenes of domestic tranquility overshadowed by an unknown threat, not too far removed from the endgame of *The Soldier's Tale*. Apart from the wider relevance of such a story to the composer's life in politically uncertain times, the tale of a doomed child may indicate some emotional connection to Stravinsky's sense of himself, his wife and family living under the shadow of tuberculosis, which had become a matter of concern in 1925, at the time of *Oedipus Rex* (*Documents* 260–61).

The symbolism of ice, however, is also the symbolism of life permanently locked in recording media, whether photograph, piano roll, or film. It is as though the composer were determined to reanimate himself, as well as the music of Tchaikovsky, in a music in which the customary formalities are dispensed with in favor of a stream-of-consciousness narrative flow, each melody merging into the next, as if in a dream—at one juncture a frozen solo cello harmonic transformed magically and seamlessly into the mobile sound of a clarinet. The music moves and unfolds as a movie camera moves and enlarges the scene in view: not as a background or stage set but as an experience of life in transition. In a further concession to radio (and possibly with the movies in mind), the composer avoids full orchestra set pieces in favor of structurally articulate smaller ensembles geared to particular episodes; in this fashion, the instrumentation takes on a concertante function of defining the narrative itself, a technique to return with advantage in his later serial music. From a practical perspective, the use of smaller ensembles is appropriate for radio's modest sound window and helpful in a production sense for keeping track of a recording process executed in segments of five minutes at a time, in addition to ensuring clarity and transparency in the recorded sound.

For a composer working with "preloved" thematic material, the task of revisiting an earlier tradition is more than a matter of simple orchestration: rather, more an obligation, paraphrasing structuralist theory, to recover a sense of "how the music thinks itself"—an aspect of which, for radio listeners, is an audible continuity of flow perceived to be emotionally as well as thematically coherent. Diaghilev took offense at Stravinsky's acceptance of yet another commission from Ida Rubenstein for a rival ballet company, deploring the work, with a few reservations, for its drab story and chocolate-box scenery (cited in EWW 347–54). His description of the work as "stillborn" and reported objections (EWW 353) that the sets were altogether "Swiss" and that Stravinsky's arrangements "lacked vitality" can be read as the disappointment of a connoisseur at being left behind by an emerging art deco aesthetic in an electrified world embracing radio and the movies as distribution media.[1] The world was moving on, and these simplifications were necessary to appeal to a wider audience and focus more on music's role in character development than traditional set-piece actions. (Stravinsky's deft handling of timbre as a tactile projection of form is truly Webernian at times and returns in more energetic guise in the later serial works. One can even imagine *The Fairy's Kiss* being composed with Walt Disney in mind, since the US moviemaker's *Silly Symphonies*, despite the title, were attracting admiration among movie intellectuals Sergei Eisenstein, Rudolph Arnheim, and Kurt London for their skillful integration of image and music.) While modesty of conception is the ballet's most notable asset, Stravinsky's personal self-effacement behind the mask of Tchaikovsky is no doubt intended, after *Oedipus Rex* and in times of Hitler's rise to power, as a gesture of reverse hubris and the antithesis of a personality cult.

* * *

> *Capriccio* for piano and orchestra (1928–1929; *Works* 10:9–11); *Symphony of Psalms* for chorus and orchestra without violins or violas (1930; *Works* 9:8–10); *Concerto in D* for violin and orchestra (1931; *Works* 10:12–15); *Duo Concertant* for violin and piano (1931–1932; *Works* 13:1–5).

"In the domain of music the importance and influence of its dissemination by mechanical means, such as the record and the radio—those redoubtable triumphs of modern science that will probably undergo further development—make them worthy of the closest investigation" (*Autobiography* 152). Stravinsky made a number of interesting changes to the balance and registration of the orchestra of *Capriccio* from the bottom-heavy wind band (plus bass viols) of the earlier *Concerto*, even going so far as to forbid the two works being scheduled in the same concert, at least with himself as soloist, declaring the technical differences between them to be too demanding. The full string orchestra is reinstated in the *Capriccio* but divided in two groups, a concertino quartet of solo players: violin, viola, cello, and bass, and a support ripieno group, again with a single division rather than the customary first and second violins. The alteration of string balance—along with other details, such as a frequent doubling of parts for simultaneously plucked and bowed strings—puts one in mind of Schoenberg's venture into neoclassical territory, the *Concerto for String Quartet and Orchestra* after Handel's *Concerto Grosso* Op. 6, No. 7 (Naxos, 8.557520), except that Schoenberg's corresponding essay into neoclassicism was completed five years after Stravinsky, in 1933. What is not disputed is that both composers were disposed to modify the conventional layout and balance of the string orchestra at a time when microphone technology and balance engineering standards were rapidly evolving. In both cases the altered distribution of forces can be read as measured responses to changing conditions of radio broadcasting, in which the number of microphones was severely limited compared to present practice. For Stravinsky, the solo string quartet provides a clear and resonant foil for the percussive piano; in a broader sense, the larger string presence and timpani together acknowledge a more lively working acoustic than the relatively anechoic studio environment of former times.

The first movement of this good-humored work opens with a variant on the composer's now signature upward surge, a double fit of pianistic sneezes to which the solo strings offer an emollient response. The mood is upbeat, and in contrast to the somewhat clotted bass register of the *Concerto*, here the low-register theme is articulate and fast, with a nice presence, a quality of sound indicating a significant and welcome enlargement of the frequency window. The same airiness in the bass register gives rise at the end of the first movement to a nicely understated (and technically instructive) sequence of exchanges among piano, timpani, and plucked cellos and basses.

The slow movement is characterized by decoratively assertive postures drawing on earlier cimbalom style, harking back to the ornamental figurations of *Pastorale* but delivered with greater urgency and weight and offset by melodious woodwinds of a melancholy sweetness. In the third movement, further echoes of the cimbalom—or, indeed, the balalaika—are heard in passages of sustained repetition of the same note, a strumming effect substituting for natural resonance that once again speaks to the relationship of changes in piano technique to changes in studio recording conditions and microphone sensitivity. Stravinsky's interest in the repeated note sound for the piano—as if to reinvent the instrument as a cimbalom—is pursued further in the *Duo Concertant* and *Concerto for Two Solo Pianos*; years later the tremolo makes a discreet reappearance in *Movements*.

After *Apollo* and the *Serenade in A*, signature works conceived in an imaginary American pastoral style already being actively promoted by Nadia Boulanger among US pupils, including Aaron Copland and Elliott Carter, the commission of a symphony by Serge Koussevitzky to mark the fiftieth anniversary of the Boston Symphony Orchestra might have been expected to inspire, perhaps on a larger scale, another composition in pre-Copland, Boulanger-influenced tonal idiom. But rather than repeat himself, Stravinsky seized the opportunity to transform and deepen a message of celebration of a landmark achievement in American musical life, into a plea for sanity (or singing telegram) from a Europe descending yet again into chaos and war, addressed to a United States fast becoming a refuge for persecuted minorities, if not for civilization itself. In eliminating violins and violas and substituting voices, ideally to include clear and pure children's voices, enhanced by additional woodwinds, the composer has created a new species of ensemble, without soloists, of a grandeur and resonance to fill a large auditorium but at the same time acoustically managed to sound effectively in broadcast media. The employment of a sung text, in Latin, selected from the Vulgate, by implication turns a work of absolute music into a propaganda statement perceived to have meaning for contemporary audiences, even though a majority may not be expected to understand the words. However, the attention of an American listening public was always more likely to focus on a music including voices than a music without words. Stravinsky's substitution of voices for violins can also be understood as a smart move to ensure a suitably "plain style." Other innovations include the additional anchors of timpani, bass drum, harp, and two pianos, an exceptionally resonant combined bass register suggestive of transparency and spaciousness, over which voices and higher wind instruments may be heard to float suspended and, at times, to soar.

The entire work has a spacious and numinous formality and unexpected emotional intensity after the busy scampering of *Apollo*, as if to say, we live in serious times. It is a work without leaders. Employing voices instead of upper strings was a touch of genius, since a choir is a considerable presence, while at the same time words are not always easy to make out and demand special attention from an audience. In providing a human focus for what is ostensibly an abstract three-movement form, Stravinsky shrewdly humanizes the listening experience for

American listeners while at the same time ensuring that the solemnity of his message—a plea for sanity and restoration of peace in world affairs—is not lost on audiences of any political or religious persuasion. The two-note rocking melody of the first movement "Exaudi orationem meam" is more primeval and minimalist than any Russian folk melody of *The Rite of Spring* or *Les Noces*. The slow and deliberate pace of events is offset in apotheosis by woodwind and brass harmonies of unparalleled radiance and complexity, almost in defiance of recording technology of the day, making the *Symphony of Psalms* perhaps the first example of what the French call "spectral composition" in modern times (an acoustic spirituality compellingly acknowledged by unbeliever Boulez in 1999 with the Berlin Philharmonic on DG, 2989 457 616-2).

For one so fluent in writing for the solo violin, it is surprising to read of Stravinsky's eager, even anxious cooperation with the young Samuel Dushkin in further developing a technique already demonstrated in the starring instrumental role of *The Soldier's Tale*. Although the composer's "off again, on again" approach to the string orchestra over a decade can partly be explained as a consequence of technical acoustic problems related to recording and radio, the gipsy fiddle music of the older work is expertly composed and fully justifies its symbolism as the voice of the soul. No doubt Stravinsky's interest in consulting Dushkin had to do with matters relating to the characteristics of a more sophisticated string technique in a conventional orchestra context, since he was going through a patch of feeling uncomfortable with the role of the string orchestra and saw a need to come to terms with string sonority in general. Another reason may have been an awakening interest, through Nadia Boulanger in Paris and Swiss conductor Ernest Ansermet, in music of the Italian baroque, and emerging new talents Hermann Scherchen and Paul Sacher, the latter a specialist in the musical arts of Vivaldi, Corelli, and others of the Pergolesi era. Other correspondents in the United States, in particular Leopold Stokowski, were aware or involved in researches in new microphone techniques aimed at eliminating existing problems with multiple string sonorities.

The collaboration with Dushkin was suggested by Willy Strecker, a director of the music publisher Schotts Söhne, based in Mainz, a firm that had recently acquired rights to publish a small number of Stravinsky's early compositions. Dushkin was Jewish, so for Strecker and Stravinsky publicly to endorse the partnership in dangerous times amounted to a gesture of political and humanitarian solidarity as well as a purely musical commitment. In four movements, the concerto is a restless and relentless tour de force: strangely passionate, sardonic, at times deeply melancholy, and at other times seeming possessed, evoking the Tartini of "Devil's Trill" fame or the legendary Paganini. For Stravinsky, the emotional index is huge, almost unprecedented: a far cry from the austere reserve of *Oedipus Rex* or even *Apollo*. Far from eliminating the gipsy ingredient of violin style in *The Soldier's Tale*, it is as though he has enlarged and extended the range and power of the traditional idiom as a tactic of deliberate confrontation. As an exercise in abrasive violinistic resistance and demonstration of moral leadership, the concerto deserves to rank in concentrated impact alongside the later and better-known violin concertos of Alban Berg (1935), Schoenberg (1936), and Bartók (1937). The first performance, in Berlin on 23 October 1931, was indifferently executed by the Berlin Radio Orchestra in what may have been an attempt to discredit both soloist and composer, an act of bad manners rebuked in the media by none other than Paul Hindemith. Fifteen months were to elapse before the Nazis seized power; even so, for Dushkin and Stravinsky to premiere a violin concerto of such eloquent ethnic character in Berlin at such a moment in history seems in retrospect to have been a gesture of extraordinary courage. In his autobiography, published in 1935, the composer goes out of his way to acknowledge Dushkin's Jewish musical heritage and encourage Jewish musicians to be proud and not call themselves by Russian diminutives, such as Sasha, Yasha, or Misha (*Autobiography* 166).

Following the *Violin Concerto*, Stravinsky pursued investigations into the relationship of violin (bowed) and piano (struck) strings in the *Duo Concertant*, a collection of five movements to be regarded as studies in sonority relationships rather than as a suite or sonata in the conventional sense. He needed concert items for a projected tour with Dushkin, but these otherwise slight pieces have a deeper interest, suggested by the choice of title that in Stravinsky's terms implies a contest of equals. The collection can be regarded as test pieces in the acoustical balance of violin and piano in relation to a microphone.[2] A note on the piano fades immediately, leading to a situation where the pianist is forced to keep playing notes to retain the attention of a listener; the violin, however, has the advantage of being able to sustain a note at its initial intensity more or less indefinitely and furthermore can modulate the tone continuously in intensity and pitch and so requires fewer actions to retain the attention of an audience. (A similar relationship of difference had already been explored, to comic effect, in the trombone-bass viol duo of *Pulcinella*.) At a further remove, the pieces resemble excerpts of an ongoing Socratic dialogue, conducted by the composer with himself, on the subject of leadership in a musical (baroque) sense, as shared between the composer-conductor at the keyboard and the concertmaster or lead violinist. Traditionally, the keyboardist is the designer who has planned the entire musical strategy and is therefore the higher authority; however, in practice, the concertmaster is the executant leader in the field of battle whose responsibility is to make the action flow smoothly and coherently. Stravinsky describes the relationship in exact and classical terms evoking the singing voice of Orpheus and his lyre:

> The spirit and form of my *Duo Concertant* were determined by my love of the pastoral poets of antiquity and their scholarly art and technique. The theme that I had chosen developed through all the five movements of the piece which forms an integral whole, and, as it were, offers a musical parallel to the old pastoral poetry. (*Autobiography*: 171)

* * *

> *Credo* for unaccompanied voices SATB (1932; *Works* 20:9); *Persephone*, melodrama in three scenes for tenor, narrator, mixed chorus SATB, children's choir, and orchestra (1933–1934; *Works* 19:1–3); *Ave Maria* for unaccompanied voices SATB (1934; *Works* 20:8); *Concerto for Two Solo Pianos* (I, 1931; II–IV, 1934–1935; *Works* 13:10–13).

As with the *Pater Noster*, composed at the time of embarking on *Oedipus Rex*, the composition of *Credo* and the *Ave Maria* comes across in context as small petitions for divine blessing on larger works of potential significance for the composer's immediate future. The drama *Persephone*, a second Ida Rubenstein commission (after *The Fairy's Kiss*), brought the composer into collaboration (and conflict) with the writer

André Gide. Gide's verse play belongs to the same prewar French literary culture as d'Annunzio's *Le Martyre de Saint Sébastien*, set to music by Debussy, and while Gide may have anticipated a similar musical treatment of an antique myth of comparable doctrinaire formality, for Stravinsky the musical challenge of a young woman abducted from the world of the living, eventually to return voluntarily, as it were on annual loan, to restore the cycle of the seasons to a world in desolation, ran the risk of implying a return to the pagan subject matter of *The Rite of Spring* and, in some senses, a self-criticism or repudiation of the earlier work.

Persephone would be his way of making yet another political statement, continuing the message of *Oedipus Rex* and *Apollo*, a show of defiance toward the Nazi propaganda message of the 1933 "Victory" Nuremberg Rally filmed by Leni Riefenstahl and distributed under the title *Der Sieg des Glaubens* ("Victory of Faith"), while maintaining a position of political neutrality or separation of art and life (or church and state). He was certainly determined to avoid composing in mock Debussyan style, or pursuing the art deco aesthetic of *Oedipus* and *The Fairy's Kiss*, another tale of abduction by the gods, though of a young man. The new orchestration is larger than life, ranging in style from expressionist abstraction to resplendently colorful. Despite serious aesthetic reservations, he was effectively insulated from press criticism—given the political risk of promoting a message of healing and reconciliation at a time of financial devastation and rising militant socialism—by Gide's prestige in the world of literature; he also saw attractive expressive opportunities in Gide's austerely melodious verses and subject matter that he was determined to treat with the luminous clarity and sublime indifference of Erik Satie's *Socrate*.

The poet for his part was somewhat taken aback at the composer's plans for an extreme formality and absence of action and apparent treatment of the lyrics as a kind of news *reportage* held together by the device of a narrative voiceover. It was all the same a strategy building on the success of *Oedipus Rex* and allowing the production to succeed in the terms and confinements of a movie production or radio broadcast as effectively as for an audience in the concert hall. Like *Momente*, Stockhausen's 1964 choric testament to love, *Persephone* is a drama that takes place not in real time but in flashback, in the memory of the composer and listener. For that reason (which has partly to do with the way we experience radio and the movies as well) *Persephone* may appear to lack motivation or dramatic urgency in the conventional sense. *Oedipus Rex* is at least a drama of revelation; *Persephone*, however, resembles a sublime dream of which everything is already known, and there are therefore no surprises, only a succession of intensities of feeling. It is a narrative whose constituent elements erupt from a single point of consciousness, rather than follow one another in conventional narrative terms: resembling a movie in disguise, comparable in effect to Cocteau's *Orphée* or Renais's *L'Année Dernière à Marienbad.*[3] Stravinsky would later express regret (*Dialogues* 36–37) at some of his choices, at the old perfume of Gide's lyrics, and at the idea of a narrator: these, however, remain relatively minor challenges to overcome in relation to some of the most sublime and mysterious music of his entire career, a thread stylistically connecting the celestial harmonies of *Symphony of Psalms* with the coded messages still to emerge in the *Symphony in C*, the forgiving flutes of *Ode*, the harp of *Orpheus,* and children's voices of the *Mass.* And in despite of his own reservations, the role of narrator duly returns in the *Sermon, Narrative, and Prayer* and again in *The Flood*, a melodrama conceived for television. Roman Vlad has said "in *Persephone* some of the most deeply hidden spiritual premises of Stravinsky's art have at last found full expression" (Vlad 114). I am inclined to agree. This is a work whose considerable—indeed, extravagant—riches remain incompletely realized and insufficiently acknowledged.

Stravinsky did not take kindly to Diaghilev's claims of Markevitch's genius, not because the young Ukrainian-born composer was lacking in talent, but because Diaghilev, Cocteau, Milhaud, and others were behaving pettily in a way calculated to create a reputation for the "second Igor" (Markevitch) at the expense of "first Igor" (Stravinsky himself). More to the point, Diaghilev clearly had a hand in advising Markevitch on an unwise choice of subject so obviously political in implication that any association with it ran the risk of undermining the altogether subtler and more delicately nuanced messages of *Oedipus*, *Apollo*, and the composer's collaboration with Dushkin and implicit support of Jewish culture.

Stravinsky was nevertheless curious to evaluate a student of Nadia Boulanger and Scherchen, whose ballet score *L'Envol d'Icare* (1932) had attracted the "second Igor" epithet and whose planned cantata *Paradis Perdu* (1935) might conceivably distract critical attention from the philosophical message of *Persephone*. There were other issues. As a pupil of Scherchen, in 1933 Markevitch had recomposed *L'Envol d'Icare* for two pianos and percussion, a radically symmetrical arrangement (Largo, 5127) attracting the instant approval of Bartók, whose *Sonata for Two Pianos and Percussion* (1937) not only acknowledges the influence of Markevitch's work but adopts many of the same figures of musical speech (CBS, MK 42625).[4] Another person of related interest is Sacher, who commissioned the *Music for Strings, Percussion, and Celesta* in 1936 from Bartók and in 1938, the *Concerto for Double String Orchestra, Piano, and Timpani* for a virtually identical formation from Bohuslav Martinu (Chandos, CHAN 8950).[5]

Scherchen was a scholar and conductor with a natural interest in recording technology (he would go on to found Ars Viva Verlag after the 1939–1945 war, publish new music scores, and launch the periodical *Gravesano Review*, dedicated to new music and technology research). Nadia Boulanger in Paris and Paul Sacher in Basel combined interest in contemporary music with devotion to reviving neglected music of the Italian baroque, which has a technically challenging spatial dimension, expressed relatively starkly in the polychoral works of Gabrieli and with particular richness in Monteverdi, whose *Vespers* of 1610 strikingly prefigures *Persephone* in subtlety and complexity, as well as symbolic distribution of forces to left and right, front and back of the performing space (Telarc, 2CD-80453; Maconie, *The Second Sense* 101–17).[6] That Stravinsky was acquainted with Markevitch's two-piano reduction of *Icare* may be conjectured from the fact that work on his *Concerto for Two Solo Pianos*, interrupted in 1931 ostensibly because the composer "could not *hear* the second piano" (EWW 389), was resumed with enthusiasm in 1935 in the months before the December premiere of *Paradis Perdu* (Naxos, 8.370773). Since his pianist son Soulima was also a student of Nadia Boulanger, Stravinsky had reason to be kept informed about the younger composer with whom he was being compared, as well as occasion to check out a two-piano score attracting effusive praise from Bartók.

Elsewhere on the technical side, Stravinsky could hardly fail to be aware of US research ongoing from 1930 involving Leopold Stokowski and the Philadelphia Orchestra with RCA and Bell Labs, activities intended to develop high-fidelity optical sound recording for the movies, a market of important potential for classical music. Compared to disc recording, live radio in the 1930s offered marginally superior sound quality and no time barriers, but both media remained invincibly mono. Stereo and full frequency transmission researches in the United States from 1930, taken up in Britain from 1933 by Alan Blumlein for HMV, using a completely different approach, were focused on developing panoramic sound system technologies capable of delivering a stereophonic signal of unprecedented frequency range and quality. That Paul Sacher, an enthusiast for Italian baroque and polychoral music, was interested in the possibilities of stereo can be inferred from his commissions in consecutive years of three substantial concert works, by Bartók and Martinu, in movie stereophonic (triple-channel symmetrical) formation.

The *Concerto for Two Pianos* is musically dense and coruscating, not distant and relatively undifferentiated like the pianos of *Les Noces*, but engaging, intricate, and close up, as if the two pianists were arm (or, at least, finger) wrestling. The musical idiom is nothing like Markevitch or Bartók but all the same subtly stereophonically conceived in the way that motifs are shared and integrated. Color, texture, and imagery are resolutely black and white, diatonic, and uniformly high resolution, closer in spirit to Stockhausen's *Mantra* (1970), though without the electronics, than Boulez's *Structures* (1952) and a world away from Debussy's *En Blanc et Noir* (1916). It is as though the new assertiveness of the *Violin Concerto* were transferred to the two keyboards, though for all that the new work shares with Debussy the introspective character of a private music oblivious of an audience and unconcerned to make grand rhetorical statements. Stylistically, the score is dotted with classical and formal sophistications, including a fugue and inversion more elaborate and complete than the double fugue of the *Symphony of Psalms*. Other enrichments are near-cluster parallel chords for melodies, a chromatic blurring of lines of force, and reinventing the piano as a super-cimbalom with vastly extended treble and bass registers.

* * *

A Card Game, ballet "in three deals" for orchestra (1936; *Works* 4:27–29); *Preludium* for jazz ensemble (1936–1937; *Works* 12:1); *Concerto in E flat*, "Dumbarton Oaks," for chamber orchestra

(1937–1938; *Works* 11:10–12); *Symphony in C* (1939–1940; *Works* 9:4–7).

A game of poker is the suitably Western (cowboy style) US subject of Stravinsky's next ballet, commissioned for Balanchine while the composer was visiting the United States in the year of publication of his autobiography. A game of cards is a game of chance and an uncomplicated metaphor for a Europe whose future is at risk of being gambled away. Perhaps there is no better way of introducing American audiences to a form of abstract play based on the idea of the bet as a last resort for negotiating with the future and implicitly on submission to the fall of the cards as an alternative to reason. Long before the Batman franchise, the figure of the Joker as Ringmaster is a benign presence in Chaplin's *The Circus* (1928), turned sinister in Alban Berg's opera *Lulu* (1928–1935); here he returns, not as the Devil of *The Soldier's Tale*, but as the Joker in the Pack, hence no longer a superior and malign force, just another card in the game of destiny. That Stravinsky's most celebrated observation, in *Autobiography*,

> For I consider that music is, by its very nature, essentially powerless to *express* anything at all, whether a feeling, an attitude of mind, a psychological mood, a phenomenon of nature

has been endlessly discussed but remains resolutely misunderstood in the field of music criticism to the present day, including the writings of high academia and the philosophy of Theodor Adorno, has something to say about the remoteness of musical knowledge in the West from a basic grounding in communication studies or philosophy. It is an important statement for the composer to affirm at a time when national broadcasting authorities across Europe and around the world were negotiating with one another on the practical necessities of sharing information and the importance of agreeing protocols of impartiality and truth in the information to be shared.[7] For Stravinsky to say that "music"—not just his music but *any* music—is powerless to express anything, is a way of saying that, like the news, its role is to deliver information impartially and without bias: not that music has no meaning or does not convey a world view but that *expression* has nothing to do with attributing meaning to what music represents, which is order and pattern, along with a certain kind of energy. On the one hand, it is a statement that requires audiences to listen rather than watch (a rejection of the airs and graces affected by conductors that Stravinsky continued to maintain in public through to the era of Herbert von Karajan and Leonard Bernstein); on the other hand, he is offering a *moral* caution against professional interpreters in general and not only of the news. Fortunately the abstract idioms of Stravinsky and Schoenberg protected both composers against accusations of misleading public taste, as well as helping to defend them from the frivolous attentions of members of the press.

A Card Game sparkles with the composer's delight at resuming a working relationship with Balanchine and the ballet: a willfully entertaining work, his choice of subject a distant riposte perhaps to the labored puzzle of Markevitch's *Rebus*, an unrealized Massine collaboration from 1931. The work sounds more than ever like a Schwitters *Merzbild* or scrapbook compilation, in comparison to *Oedipus Rex*, to which Stravinsky applied the description. The mood is *Octet* all over again but with larger forces and choreographic extensions of range. Significantly, the work begins and ends in major keys, ducking and diving, often at frantic pace, through a dazzling succession of tonalities and fashion designs, most of them in a major key, interspersed with flash cards of quotations and other allusions to the classics. In both title and wayward informality conception and execution suggest a carefree, improvisatory approach to form of a distinctly American (if not quite John Cage) character. Above the bustle of activity the composer has placed a warning quotation from La Fontaine, roughly translated as

They sue for peace who still desire our doom:
Be vigilant for war, or die at home. (reproduced in Craft, *A Stravinsky Scrapbook* 8)

A Walt Disney caricature survives from the composer's visit to the Walt Disney Studios in 1939, an unflattering image conveying the composer's squat posture, bug eyes, and prehensile lips. What the great movie animator sensed in the composer of *The Firebird* and *Petrushka* looks like a canny premonition of Jiminy Cricket, the diminutive, opinionated, and chirpy conscience of Pinocchio, the animated puppet.[8] The analogy works on a number of levels. Stravinsky's idiom, especially *Petrushka*, was already a favorite with Hollywood animation composers for its supple dynamism and ease of coordination to cartoon action.

Masterminded by Leopold Stokowski, whose involvement with RCA and Bell Labs in the development of a high-definition movie sound system had already led to a guest appearance by the conductor playing himself alongside Deanna Durbin in the Universal movie musical *A Hundred Men and a Girl* (1937), the meeting was a staged formality to agree Disney's terms for use of *The Rite of Spring* as musical accompaniment in one of a concert sequence of classics to be interpreted in a new movie, *Fantasia*, in precisely synchronized and choreographed animation and recorded in a novel approximation of surround sound.

Disney was keen to exploit the commercial possibilities of quality music in animation and had previously funded a pilot nine-minute short, starring Mickey Mouse as the Sorcerer's Apprentice, to the energetic and illustrative orchestral work of the same name by Paul Dukas. The commercial cachet of music, classical music in particular, was not only that it provided a demonstrable index of technical and artistic quality but that as an international language, the market for such movies was relatively unaffected by the language barrier that had arisen in 1931 with the first dialogue movies in synchronized sound. In an effort to minimize the disadvantages of American speech for foreign audiences, Disney had already moved to reduce the role of dialogue to a dadaist poetic of more or less abstract sound characters: Donald Duck as an angry kazoo, Mickey Mouse a diffident squeak, Goofy a muted klaxon, and Pluto to the sound of excited panting—a tactic also deployed to comic effect by Harpo Marx of the Marx Brothers.

For the *Fantasia* project financially to break even, a full-length feature was the only option. Having recently recorded *The Rite of Spring* in 1933, Stokowski was eager to demonstrate what technology could bring to the interpretation of so radical a score. Stravinsky was curious to know more and perhaps become involved in an industry whose arts of montage and sound balance had long influenced his approach to form and style. Though publicly disapproving major aspects of Disney's treatment of *The Rite*, which involved cutting and reshuffling the sequence of dances and altering the scenario from primitive rite to a cosmic chronicle of Darwinian evolution, it is fair to say that Stravinsky had only himself to blame, having previously seen fit to do the same by creating orchestral suites of *The Firebird* and other works, including *Petrushka* and *The Fairy's Kiss*, to suit alternative markets. He had even defended the practice in an interview with French composer Georges

Auric: "My later scores are conceived and constructed as separate musical entities, independent of their scenic purpose" (EWW 398–99).[9]

Almost certainly influenced by Hollywood and sounding today like an outtake from Disney's *Melody Time* (1948), the charmingly aphoristic *Preludium* for jazz band, rearranged in 1953 for a quartet of saxophones, sextet of strings, guitar, and percussion, including glockenspiel, was composed as low-resolution title music for a jazz series, but its French-accented idiom seems closer to Marcel Mule or Boulez than Paul Whiteman. However, the clarity and disposition of unfamiliar timbres are a significant indication of a new impressionist aesthetic of instruments treated as instant colored noises (bright, high, fuzzy, etc.) rather than as time-dependent melody elements.

As a work in progress, Stravinsky described the "Dumbarton Oaks" *Concerto in E flat*, as "a little concerto in the style of the [Bach] Brandenburg Concertos" no doubt aware that his French interviewer André Schaeffner would understand such a description to imply a minor work in pastiche neoclassical idiom. The allusion to Bach is not trivial but technical, at least for those who recognize the Brandenburg Concertos as scholarly exercises in dynamic counterpoint designed to weave a maximum density of information, differentiated by tone color, into a strictly mechanical time frame (Maconie, *The Second Sense* 163–65). However, this work is a commission for American clients at a time when the composer is continuing to develop a technique of instrumentation geared to the possibilities of studio recording and very much with the spatial balance of multiple forces in mind, in particular strings in relation to woodwinds, a major issue. The distinctly new properties of the *Concerto in E flat* are immediately evident when considered in the context of recommendations to composers of movie music by Leonid Sabaneev (1881–1968): Stravinsky's contemporary, a former pupil of Rimsky-Korsakov and Taneyev, and disciple of Scriabin. Sabaneev's *Music for the Films*, published in English in 1935, is rife with cautionary hints such as the following:

> As a rule the number of performers should be limited to twenty-five. . . . Subtle differences in the timbres of the various instruments disappear or are greatly diminished when recorded on the film. The characteristics of a group of instruments (the strings, for example) are levelled down, and the contrast between the different categories is lessened. . . . Harmonies, if at all complex, begin to sound unpleas-

> antly harsh and discordant, and, owing to the mixing of the harmonics in the middle register, produce an impression of cacophony. . . . The principal melody and its counterpoint represent the utmost polyphonic luxury permissible without risk of obtaining an undifferentiated chaos of sounds. (Sabaneev 69–70)

The existence of a substantial literature on the philosophy and aesthetics of sound film provides a technical framework against which the distinctive innovations of a "minor" score like "Dumbarton Oaks" are better appreciated. With this work more than ever before, a listener is made aware of Stravinsky's mental agility and skill, acknowledging Bach, in utilizing counterpoint, imitation and instrumental color contrasts to pack a maximum of information into a small and perfectly formed acoustic package. The ghost of the piano is all but vanished, creating a cloud of dispersed sonorities whose actions resemble a corps de ballet and maintain perfect balance between strings and winds, front and back of stage, in a lively eighteenth-century acoustic designed to convey a distinct impression, even in mono, of breadth and depth. This is music from a period in Stravinsky's career that Boulez has had reservations about, ironically since he is one of the few composers of his generation capable of appreciating the maze of relationships—at times approaching Webern on speed—and the more so because Boulez's own early forays into orchestral composition are predicated on very similar principles of fragmentation and continuous variation. A 1982 recording by Boulez and the Ensemble Intercontemporain, reissued as a foil to the Berg *Chamber Concerto* begins dispassionately, but by the third movement the ice has broken and conductor and ensemble are clearly enjoying themselves (DG, 447 405-2).

Composition of the *Symphony in C* began in 1938, in Paris, was resumed in mid-1939, and was completed in Hollywood in 1940. Beethoven is often mentioned as an influence, but to me the tone is not as close to the heavyweight German tradition as much as a return to the lighter Viennese tradition of Mozart and Haydn: Mozart in the expert integration of string orchestra and winds, which attains a new level of sophisticated accommodation, and Haydn for his sense of nervous energy and occasionally wayward fantasy, features of the London symphonies, along with such theatrical tricks as the introductory crescendo, almost a crib of the signature timpani interruption of the "Surprise" symphony. Mozart and Haydn were also composing at deeply uncertain times.

More than ever Stravinsky appears to seek dramatic continuity throughout an entire movement, along with motivic integrity and economy, and equal rights between strings and winds. An introductory motif of a thudding crescendo terminating in an inconclusive falling fourth evokes the approach of a diving warplane center screen and Doppler effect as it passes low overhead, followed by ascending scales suggesting a scramble of troops out of the trenches. From the outset it is plain that the composer is still nervous around the string orchestra, quick to substitute steadier woodwinds and subordinate the strings to a lyrical oboe line that seems to be instructing the first violins in how to sing. It is a *moto perpetuo* that is more about marking time than preparing for action. At the end of the first movement, the sturdy woodwinds are again on hand to shepherd the violins toward a safe and precise conclusion. The gigantic sneezing fit that acts as an unexpected coda breaks a potentially fatal trance, seizing the day with the first of several outbursts of "harmonic noise" that, while tonally intelligible in a strictly neoclassical sense, are of interest chiefly as concrete effects of an explosive and tangible physicality.

The slow movement that follows, an extended lullaby of pervasive melancholy, is sublimely moving and ample evidence of the composer's continuing grief and loss at the deaths in 1938 of his daughter Ludmila and the following year of his wife, Catherine, and his mother, from tuberculosis. The most interesting new ingredient of the composer's language to come to attention is the momentary pause or arrest in midgesture: in ballet terms, the equivalent of suddenly freezing, holding a pose as if in a photograph, which in real life is very hard to do and extremely intense, since absence of movement in ballet is in many respects harder to achieve than executing movement. What it signifies in the composer's vocabulary is renewed confidence in the long line, because only after mastering the long line (or extended melody) does the insertion of breaks make sense and acquire meaning and dramatic purpose. The somewhat Zen-like conception of meaningful absence of movement is likely to have come to Stravinsky from Balanchine, but it also signals a new relationship with the string orchestra. The somewhat stagey formulae in the first movement are set aside to mourn, and once again, the violins are taught a lesson in tact by the flute and oboe. There are echoes of slow, graceful dance, and sounds and reminiscences of the Russia of *Pastorale*, as if composed for a movie by Ingmar Bergman.

In the third and fourth movements actions are preceded by pauses, not just edited together, a touch of military precision that for the same reason allows each new action to be perceived as considered and therefore intentional and goal directed, rather than impulsive or passive responses to external forces. The third movement awakens with a jolt and describes a growing pattern of complexity and coherence of activity, encouraged by winds, that reaches a peak of optimism and organization with the arrival of distinctively American-sounding and cheerful brass, including tuba, at which everyone seems to perk up. To this point, Stravinsky's orchestration—certainly on record, less evident perhaps in live performance—has followed his traditional practice of focusing musical activity in the midrange, musically speaking the middle distance, with relatively little action at ground level in the bass. While this arrangement creates buoyancy and allows the composer freedom of maneuver and change, it conspires against an audience's sense of tonal position and security. Hence the welcome arrival in the fourth movement of a powerful and resolute motif in the cellos and bass viols, following the tense prison escape of a shadowy two-voice counterpoint of bassoons crawling under the wire and eluding a baleful searchlight beam of horns and trombone. Success leads to a brief but jubilant resume of cheering chords, treated as white-note noises, the symphony ending in watchful suspense, echoing the *Symphonies of Wind Instruments* with a slow reprise of austere, spacious, and chill woodwind harmonies, pent-up emotion broken at the last moment by a sigh of relief from the full string orchestra, filling the air and gradually fading to silence.

7

TESTAMENT OF ORPHEUS

For Stravinsky as for Schoenberg, Hollywood promised life and liberty but only limited prospects for the pursuit of happiness. When optical sound for the movies arrived in 1929, Schoenberg composed his Op. 34 *Accompaniment to a Cinematographic Scene* (Sony, SMK 48 462) to show the industry how it should be done, not realizing that his concept of music for the silent movie was now out of date or indeed that he had already achieved his goal in 1909, by composing the Op. 16 *Five Orchestral Pieces*. On its compositional merits, Stravinsky admired and studied the Schoenberg *Accompaniment* score, slyly describing it as "by far the best piece of real film music ever written, an ironic triumph if there ever were one, for the film itself was imaginary" (*Memories* 108 [UK], 102 [US]).

In general, European composers regarded a movie as a production to be negotiated around the wishes of their music, like an opera or ballet, and were ill-prepared and reluctant to cut and paste an "already perfect" score (Schoenberg's phrase) to suit the whim of a fellow exile who happened to be sitting behind a megaphone. In the glory days of the silent movie, composer and conductor led a symphony orchestra in sympathetic, if no more than approximately synchronized, accompaniment to the action on screen, molding the music to fit in real time. When the opportunity arose for Richard Strauss to conduct his music for the German film version of the opera *Der Rosenkavalier*, he was distracted and upset at being expected to beat time in accordance with cue marks and timing indications scratched on the movie image. As late as 1941 Schoenberg's pupil Hanns Eisler, also an exile in Hollywood, composed *Fourteen Ways of Describing Rain* as a birthday tribute to his former teacher, a loyal gesture doomed to fall a little flat given that the instrumentation, based on *Pierrot Lunaire*, dated back to the era of acoustic recording, and the rationale of the entire work was essentially bespoke for the age of the silent movie (Ars Vivenda, 2100236).

If any major composer in 1940s Hollywood was close to understanding the movie medium and principles of montage and exact timing, that composer was Stravinsky, but even Stravinsky found it difficult to deal with the politics of an industry determined to impose its way of working on musicians whom it regarded as little more than sound effects technicians. Disney stood out as the exception who understood that a musical composition was an organic whole and that it was necessary for a successful animation to be choreographed to fit the music, not the other way round. For *Fantasia* the choreography was planned and filmed in black and white to existing Stokowski recordings, and the movements of dancers used as templates for color animations (the Rotoscope method). But even Stokowski was frustrated at having to rerecord his own interpretations in "Fantasound" surround sound to a click track played back to him on headphones.

> Each section of the orchestra, divided into seven choirs, was enclosed in a three-sided partition. . . . The unvarying rigidity of the click-track upset Stokowski frightfully, since his own conducting marked a flexible rhythm, which naturally conflicted with the mechanical beat. The partitions, which did not enable the musicians to hear each other, diminished their impeccable standards. (Chasins 172)

Because he knew the score, Stokowski wanted to be allowed the freedom to fit music with which he was familiar to the animation, which is what a conductor is trained to do. The production team however, obsessed with the need for exact synchronicity, expected him to be able to conduct to the tick of a clock, not understanding that a click track, even though based on Stokowski's own recording, was a click track all the same.

* * *

> *Tango* (1940, instrumented in 1953 for jazz ensemble and string sextet; *Works* 12:7); *Danses Concertantes* (1941–1942) for chamber orchestra (*Works* 22:2); *Circus Polka* for orchestra (1942; *Works* 11:17); *Four Norwegian Moods for Orchestra* (1942; *Works* 11:13–16).

Tango is another inscrutable gem of abstracted jazz, perhaps equivalent in musical terms to Salvador Dalí's portrait of Mae West with invitingly upholstered lips.[1] Composed in 1940 for wordless voice and piano, the piece was orchestrated for Robert Craft in 1953 as a companion piece for *Ebony Concerto*. This tango is only partly an exercise in American jazz. Over thick chords in the bass, the dance moves with solemn deliberation, a remote, haughty rite of foreplay putting the listener just a little in mind of the Tango in *The Soldier's Tale*, a work of magic designed to reawaken the Muse. There is all the same a sly wit in an instrumentation that exploits poise and phrasing to pass the musical lead back and forth among contrasting groups of instruments: left and right, forward and back, in imitation of the rocking motion of the dance itself. What is recognizably "American style" about the work, like the *Preludium*, is Stravinsky's treatment of groups of instruments as background splashes of color, here overprinted by a thin melodic line on guitar. The instrumentation is highly interesting in its balance of lean guitar, lyrical strings, and podgy brass. Craft's recording is spacious and slightly more upbeat (MusicMasters, 01612-67195-2), but Stravinsky's laidback version retains an air of melancholy, like the empty stage of a De Chirico painting.

Texture is key to the *Danses Concertantes* (a title in essence identical to *Agon*), commissioned for the concert hall but conceived and executed as a suite of dances. The collected edition recording is conducted by Robert Craft. A remastered 1954 Swiss Italian live radio concert program conducted by Stravinsky, including *Danses Concertantes*, was issued in 1995 (Ermitage, ERM 156), the interest of which is that the recording is a nicely balanced mono, compared to the Sony version, which, while in stereo, is strangely less coherent spatially. In mono all groups of instruments are centered, meaning that the various layers of music and structural distinctions are aligned to a common axis from violins and cellos at stage front by degrees to the brass and timpani at the rear (on this occasion including the attractively pinched sound of muted horns). With such an arrangement, the composer has to ensure a clear separation of cues and musical actions by a combination of color, texture, register, natural amplitude, and distance from the microphone. Many listeners might assume that the balance of an orchestra is the job of a sound engineer at a studio mixing desk, but since the baroque era, the role of assigning weights and numbers of instruments had been the responsibility of the composer and conductor (in modern times, only occasionally the same person, a Richard Strauss, Stravinsky, or a Mahler).

For a live radio broadcast, where microphones are at a minimum and the layout of players on the platform conforms to standard concert practice, the achievement of satisfactory clarity is largely down to the composer's orchestration. It is tempting to regard Stravinsky's decision on this occasion to compose for the orchestra as though it were a corps de ballet—in other words, treating solo instruments and sections as virtual dancers—as an idea triggered by Disney's *Fantasia*, not only from Stokowski's division of the orchestra into widely separated groups in recording the movie soundtrack, but because in the movie it is actually the sounds of the orchestra that are heard to dance around the auditorium, above and behind the heads of the audience, leaving the animations on screen confined to the picture plane. It is possible that Stravinsky may have created *Danses Concertantes* with spatialized sound projection in mind, because the composition of the work is so effectively spatial (and certainly implies a specifically tailored approach to recording in stereo). So when the composer discusses stereo in the following terms (in *Conversations*),

> Stereophony has already influenced composed music, too. At one level this amounts to the exploitation of the stereo effect (the stereo fault, rather) by "building" it "in," i.e., creating distance and separation by reseating the orchestra, etc. (When I listen to this sort of music, I find myself *looking* in the direction of the sound, as I do in Cinerama; "direction" therefore seems to me as good a word as "distance" to describe the stereo effect.) (*Memories* 124 [UK], 120 [US])

one cannot help but imagine he is speaking from personal experience of conducting and monitoring at a studio mixing desk as well as listening at home.

Reduction to mono does not eliminate a listener's awareness of depth, tending instead to reduce acoustic space in depth to the screen's vertical plane surface. As with the ballet stage, so too the picture plane of an animated movie corresponds to a field of action in which things are expected to be happening in the background as well as in the center and side to side in the foreground. The art of total animation, after the model of an animated Bruegel painting, had taken just such a turn in 1920s Hollywood, reinventing the screen as a canvas to be filled front to back with incident and, to save time, often recycling the same background incident (say, of children playing) from one movie to the next. Such a piecemeal approach to filling the animated canvas became a trademark of Max Fleischer and compares with Stravinsky's habit of recycling musical gestures—or indeed, with ballet practice in general, to be sure. Of the many genres of Hollywood moviemaking, animation attracted Stravinsky's particular attention in relation to his musical art, so much so that when Robert Craft alludes in a book review to

> the sense of frustration that some people have felt in Disney's full-length animated movies (though another factor is an inadequate spatial depth, something that even the use of the multiplane camera did not entirely dispel). . . . What if Max Fleischer, rather than Disney, had dominated the animation field? . . . Disney seems to have borrowed back Fleischer's idea of combining live-action films with animation and his rotoscope method of filming actors to guide the animators.[2]

it is reasonable to assume that the "some people" to whom Craft refers included the composer.

Circus Polka is a jolly if rowdy item in the style of a Sousa march with a side order of Schubert's *Marche Militaire.* It was composed for a *Khorovod* (Russian dancing circle) of elephants, creatures of excellent hearing who it transpired may have preferred to work to a music more gentle and melodious. Misunderstandings arose with *Four Norwegian Moods*, composed at the request of a producer, only to be rejected because the movie had not then been made.

> Igor Stravinsky showed some interest in writing film music but no interest or understanding in how the process of scoring was resolved. Columbia hired him to score *Commandos Strike at Dawn* (1942). At the initial discussion of the film, the plot was outlined to Stravinsky—Norway during the war, the underground resistance of the Norwegian patriots, the raids of British commandos, etc. Stravinsky said he

> found all this fascinating. Some weeks later he called the producer and said the score was ready, which surprised the producer because the film wasn't. (Thomas 42)

Perhaps it was the studio's misunderstanding of a goodwill gesture on the composer's part to show that he was ready and able to compose to order at short notice. At least the music has not been lost. One can imagine the conversation,

> *This music is very nice, but it is not what we want.*
> So tell me, what do you want?
> *I can't say, because we haven't yet made the movie.*
> But we had a meeting. You asked for mood music on Norwegian themes, and I have composed mood music on Norwegian themes. Four Norwegian moods, in fact.
> *The meeting was just to give you our ideas. We cannot know exactly what music we require until the movie is in the can.*
> But if you have not made the movie, how do you know the music I have composed is not what you want? Mr Walt Disney did not complain that I composed *Le Sacre* before he made his movie.
> *That was a musical. We work differently. We are paying you to compose music so we can decide if it is what we want after the movie is made, not before.*

One can also be kind and interpret the speed of the composer's unilateral action as a spontaneous expression of solidarity with the people of Norway and homeland of Grieg. The four short movements adapt themes from Norwegian folk music, and it is understandable if, having been suitably inspired, Stravinsky was reluctant to have his score interfered with and withdrew from the project.

Ernest Ansermet, who took it upon himself to take care of Stravinsky's interests in Europe in the composer's absence, complained that the *Symphony in C* was only pretending to imitate classical symphonic form, which is supposed to resemble a formal debate in which contrasting themes or points of view are stated at the outset, discussed in the middle, and reconciled at the end. A mathematician by training, Ansermet had a logical mind, and to a logician, inconsequence sounds like helplessness. The thematic processes in *Symphony in C* did not add up.

> When he turns to the *Symphony in C*, he finds that its form is static and its motives fail to grow in meaning. "On their reappearance," he says, "the fundamental motives are no more significant than they were on their first appearance." (EWW 409)

Ansermet has known Stravinsky since *The Soldier's Tale*, but like many of his generation, he fails to see that the composer has *never* composed along classical sonata-form dialectical lines: not just because he doesn't approve of German style musical argument but because he has never believed in the practice, which is old-style Glazunov-era academicism. The traditional notion of dialectic is one in which ideas are exchanged and there is a winner. But the world of ballet does not argue; rather, it presents male and female contrasting characters and invites them to dance together, and at the end they remain contrasting characters, but the point has been made that they can all the same dance together in harmony; it is not necessary for one to be declared the winner and the other to be defeated. In reverting to a version of tonality, first in *Pulcinella*, subsequently in *The Fairy's Kiss*, Stravinsky was responding to the radio medium. Apart from preferring tonality because it is easier for a radio listener to monitor, the composer's treatment of tonal material indicates an awareness of listening to radio as a species of channel hopping between coexistent realities, each of which follows a different logic. The medley of Tchaikovsky melodies in *The Fairy's Kiss* does not amount to a logical process: it is simply one way of experiencing multiple realities, and the defining issue is not the content of experience (or transformation of themes) but the quality and execution of the sequential process, presented as a fantasia or stream of consciousness. In imagining *The Fairy's Kiss* as a virtual radio experience of tuning between channels, it is possible to grasp John Cage's rationale of a music of twelve radios (*Imaginary Landscape No. 4*, 1951) and Stockhausen's of a music for rearrangeable segments (*Momente*, 1964), the two reconciled in Stockhausen's *Hymnen* (1966–1967) and *Opus 1970*, a version of *Kurzwellen* in which a quartet of players manufactures connections between virtual radio channels engineered to be playing Beethoven related material.

At this time, much the same dilemma—whether successive thoughts "add up" to a logical train of thought or only amount to an accidental conjunction of coexistent thoughts—was provoking Wittgenstein in philosophy and filmmaker Sergei Eisenstein's probing inquiries (in *The*

Film Sense) into the psychology and aesthetics of montage. Stravinsky is not alone in seeking to redefine or replace classical narrative logic in response to modern perceptions of the world as a multilayered simultaneity. The message that Ansermet fails to register in *Symphony in C*, as of *The Fairy's Kiss*, is that "at the end, nothing has changed"—apart from the listener's perception of the world in general, having probed a currently stratified reality by radio, as it were, or visual reality through the camera lens. For a majority of Stravinsky's intellectual contemporaries, however, the propaganda experience of radio or the movies had to be logical or be rejected as an aberration. Exceptions are typically poets: an Ezra Pound, for example, or a William Carlos Williams (who served in the military during the war). T. S. Eliot, whose *Four Quartets* (1935–1942) examines the idea of history as simultaneity, sums up the prevailing culture of inconsequence in *The Waste Land* (1922) in the riveting image of a young woman who, after casual sex, "Smooths her hair with automatic hand / And puts a record on the gramophone."[3]

* * *

> *Elegy* for unaccompanied viola or violin (1944; DG 477 8730); *Ode*, elegaical chant for orchestra (1943; *Works* 19:4–6); *Babel* cantata for male chorus, narrator, and orchestra (1944; *Works* 20:23); *Scherzo à la Russe* for jazz band (1944; MusicMasters, 01612-67113-2), for orchestra (1943–1944; *Works* 1:23); *Scènes de ballet* for orchestra (1944; *Works* 5:1–9); *Sonata for Two Pianos* (1943–1944; *Works* 13:15–17).

Purged of all rhetoric, the glowing timbre and reserved melancholy of *Elegy* for muted solo viola acknowledge Hindemith and Bartók and would inspire Balanchine to a choreography of statuesque restraint anticipating Merce Cunningham. With more light and shade, the *Ode* contains some of the most serenely moving and lyrical music in all of Stravinsky. Commissioned by Serge Koussevitzky in memory of his wife Natalie, the work is notable for a slow and continuous build of emotion in the first movement and equally gradual dissolution of tension in the last movement, of a darkness suggesting a personal sorrow, as though the composer were still grieving for his own family.[4] The complete works version and Michael Tilson Thomas's even quicker version (Red

Seal, 09026-68865-2) seem a shade brusque compared with the composer's 1945 recording (on Columbia Graphophone, 33CX 1100, a personal favorite). For some reason *Ode* is routinely disparaged in the literature as a makeweight, a discarded hornpipe forming the incongruous middle of a sourdough sandwich, put together for a client Stravinsky did not particularly like. I don't agree. The two outer movements are perfectly matched: the first for string orchestra, a lamentation, gaze downcast; the final movement a nocturne for flutes, somber, spacious, and celestial, gazing upward; between them the call of hunting horns, evoking the autumn chase at midday, which has its own classic symbolism. To me the emotion is intense, heart wrenching, genuine tears: an elegy less for the dead than for the living, whose journey is bound to continue.[5]

Babel was Stravinsky's interesting choice of text to participate in Nathaniel Shilkret's *Genesis Suite* project, a cycle of minicantatas based on key passages from the Book of Moses (*Genesis* in the Old Testament). Shilkret is an interesting and underrated talent, a Hollywood arranger with experience as a bandleader and producer for Victor Records in the acoustic era.[6] It was his idea to assemble an international group of composers to create a musical joint manifesto for peace and compassion at a time of war. Schoenberg, Alexandre Tansman, Milhaud, Mario Castelnuovo-Tedesco, Ernst Toch, and Stravinsky accepted; additional invitations were sent to Bartók, Hindemith, and Prokofiev, but they declined.

Such ventures are rare but not unknown: the 1921 ballet *Les Mariés de la Tour Eiffel*, devised by Jean Cocteau, incorporated music by *Les Six* members Auric, Honegger, Milhaud, Poulenc, and Tailleferre. The unusual interest of *Genesis Suite* was Shilkret's generous determination, as an American-born movie composer and publisher, to unite high-ranking composers and musicians from the Los Angeles community of European exiles—a group of diverse and routinely conflicting aesthetic persuasions—in a declaration of mutual opposition to state persecution of minorities, particularly the Jewish people. Shilkret's *Genesis Suite* brought Schoenberg and Stravinsky into the same room, if not to adjacent chairs, for the first time in many years.

In 2003 the complete suite was reassembled and recorded by the Berlin Radio Symphony Orchestra under Gerard Schwarz (Naxos, 8.559442) in a commission for the Milken Archive of American Jewish

Music, making it possible to compare all seven contributions under the same conditions, including sensitivity to Jewish musical protocols. In such distinguished company Shilkret's contribution, "The Creation," holds up remarkably well—at the very least enabling a listener to grasp significant differences in tone and musical symbolism that distinguish European composers of different nationalities and aesthetic persuasions from one another and from conventional Hollywood practice. Perhaps against his better judgment, Stravinsky agreed to use a narrator but drew the line against any representation of the voice of God, whose words are delegated to a male voice choir. The choice of *Babel* as subject matter might be construed in the circumstances as a reflection on the conflicted state of modern music;[7] however, Stravinsky has chosen to clothe his contribution in a music of dignified formality, with mysterious hints of *Ode* and even distant memories of *Zvezdoliki*. While avoiding a temptation to depict a confusion of dialects in musical terms (one to which a Darius Milhaud might well have succumbed), the scattering of tribes is illustrated ballet fashion in scampering and scurrying episodes after the style of *Danses Concertantes*. Memories of this engagement with religious subject matter and recollections of Schoenberg's contribution return to haunt the advanced serial language and symbolism of later biblical settings: *A Sermon, Narrative, and Prayer* (1961), *The Flood* (1962), and notably *Abraham and Isaac* (1963–1964).

The four-minute *Scherzo à la Russe* was commissioned by Paul Whiteman for his band, to be used in a movie set in wartime Russia. Evoking a tickertape parade with set piece interruptions, the work is a fascinating portrait of American big band jazz experienced through Russian ears, orchestrally speaking an essay in variable density sound track creation. Its characters, too good to ignore, are destined to be assimilated, developed, and expanded in the *Symphony in Three Movements*. Stravinsky commented, "I wrote it originally to exact specifications of [the Paul Whiteman] ensemble, then rewrote it for standard orchestra—which gave me some trouble, as the volume of mandolin and guitar in the Trio canon was so much lighter than that of harp and piano" (*Dialogues* 53). The work is a likeable comedy of weights, thin and thick sounds, a headache for a balance engineer since the opening refrain, full band, and Trio are seriously different ensembles in density, texture, and transparency, in effect corresponding to the too-hot, too-cool, and just-right bowls of porridge in the fairy-tale of *Goldilocks and the Three Bears*. Whiteman, who (according to the composer) took the premiere at too fast a pace, claimed to hear hints of *Petrushka* in the piece—no doubt in error for the "Village Fête" sequence, scene 2 of *The Fairy's Kiss*, which is based on the "Humoresque" Op. 10, No. 2, by Tchaikovsky. *Scherzo* is hardly jazz in the regular sense, rather an interesting and laconic use of the big band medium as a source of jovial differentiated noise effects in the spirit of *musique concrète*. The initial jazz version, with a quartet of saxophones, is recorded by Robert Craft on MusicMasters (01612-67113-2). By comparison the complete edition symphonic version, dating from the same year, is brazenly noisier and acoustically intoxicating, an exuberant chaos conveying a feeling of being swept away in the crowd. If any work of Stravinsky after Stokowski's *The Rite of Spring* for Disney's *Fantasia* merited recording in surround sound, this would be it. The character of this musical carnival is all the same more American than Russian, and the most revealing comparison might be a polychoral symphonic happening by Charles Ives or a Stockhausen battle scene.

To come to terms with *Scènes de Ballet*, a neglected masterpiece, it is essential to listen—preferably at length—to Aaron Copland, ideally *A Lincoln Portrait* (1942), and the *Symphony No. 3* (1944–1946). For many listeners this period of Copland represents the apex achievement of a recognizably American national style: noble, plain, assertive, at times also long-winded, even filibustering. These same virtues were instilled in the American composer by Nadia Boulanger, the great teacher and defender of neoclassicism, so the idiom is one for which Stravinsky himself must bear some responsibility. Of Boulanger's teaching, Copland recalled, "At the period when I was her pupil she had but one all-embracing principle, namely, the desirability of aiming first and foremost at the creation of what she called '*la grande ligne*'—the long line in music" (Copland 89–90).

At the time Copland was maturing as a composer and writer, Stravinsky's influence on American music was as much political as musical:

> It is these plain tunes [from Russian folk song, in *The Rite of Spring*] that make Stravinsky's music sound so very Russian. They are also responsible for the accusation, heard repeatedly, that Stravinsky seriously lacked any real melodic invention. . . . What was less obvious at the time was the historic role Stravinsky's ballets were to play in the

> reorientation of music away from the German tradition. (Copland 61–62)[8]

Copland would appear to be expressing a wider consensus in concluding,

> It is the rightness of his "wrong" solutions that fascinates one. Marcel Proust must have had something of the same notion in mind when, in considering Flaubert's prose style, he talked about "great writers who do not know how to write." One might say Stravinsky doesn't know how to compose in the sense of Hindemith or Milhaud. (*Copland on Music* 93–94)[9]

Marcel who? It is as a response to such disingenuous criticism—of which Stravinsky was no doubt fully informed—that the merits of *Scènes de Ballet*, a Billy Rose commission, deserve to be appreciated. In this, yet another programmed sequence of abstract ballet movements, Stravinsky emerges in total mastery of the string orchestra as an expressive resource and connective tissue. The neoclassic rhetoric routinely despised by Boulez and other Europeans is Stravinsky's acknowledgment of the plain style, one in which harmonic complexity and the blending of instruments reaches new heights of refinement while at the same time continuing to develop, long before his encounters with the Darmstadt school, a Schoenbergian "through the microphone" perception of dynamic composition as an exact chemistry of noises and "tone qualities." The mood is upbeat, and emphasis is on corporate discipline; brass are cool and strings feminine and voluptuous (including a sneak peek at a gorgeous opening quartet of violas, echoed later by woodwinds, that might have been inspired by the Andrews Sisters). Lawrence Morton, champion of modernism, friend of Stravinsky, and founder of the Los Angeles Monday Evening Concerts, expressed dismay at an exposed trumpet theme (imitating a cornet) that he considered "vulgar" (EWW 345), not appearing to recognize a carefully placed allusion to Copland's semiofficial rhetoric and to the US anthem "The Star-Spangled Banner." Yes, to a connoisseur the tune may appear vulgar, but it is also honest in a wistful kind of way, an echo of Satie's use of music hall tunes. Stravinsky is paying his respects to a people's idiom and "plain style" endorsed by American composers Ives, Copland, and Virgil Thomson and treats its naivety with tact and dignity.

By contrast, the reserved and fastidious tone of *Sonata for Two Pianos* puts a listener in mind of France, especially Francis Poulenc. While the plaintive opening three-note motif recalls the oboe folk melody of Bartók's *Concerto for Orchestra*, fourth movement (Decca, 421 443-2), composed the same year, its serene continuation and diatonic mode are more characteristic of the cool simplicity inspired by Erik Satie (and in fashion by Coco Chanel), styled by Stravinsky in the mid-1920s with the *Sonata* of 1924, and pursued as it were under license by Poulenc with understated charm. Unlike the percussive insistence of the *Concerto for Two Solo Pianos*, the new *Sonata* has an air of otherworldliness, as if it were music transmitted from another planet, also a quality of Poulenc's imitation gamelan music in the 1932 *Concerto for Two Pianos and Orchestra* (EMI, 7243 5 62647 2 4), not to mention the *Balinese Ceremonial Music* (1940), transcribed for two pianos by Canadian composer Colin McPhee, a former pupil of Varèse (Chandos, CHAN10111).

* * *

> *Symphony in Three Movements* (1942–1945; *Works* 9:1–3); *Ebony Concerto* for clarinet solo and big band (1945; *Works* 12:12–14); *Concerto in D* for string orchestra (1946; *Works* 11:18–20); *Orpheus* ballet in three scenes (1948; *Works* 6:6–16).

A symphony is defined by its opening gesture. In *Symphony in C* the opening gesture is a stuttering crescendo; it rattles like the strafing gunfire of an approaching fighter at troops on the ground—an image re-created by Alfred Hitchcock in the Cary Grant chase sequence in *North by Northwest*. The prevailing emotion therefore is *fear* and motivation to "do something, fast, but not to panic." At the end, the music says, "The storm is still to come, but at least we are secure for now." In the *Symphony in Three Movements* the opening gesture says "My God! My God! We've won!" the piano solo responding "Yes! Yes! Wow!" Now the emotion is *elation*, whereas the prevailing sensation of *Symphony in C* is containment, of holding one's breath; in *Symphony in Three Movements* it is a sensation of letting go, of breathing out, of pent-up tension giving way to enthusiasm.

"Dionysiac or Apollonian?—Symphony or Concerto?" asks Eric Walter White of the *Symphony in Three Movements*. Of a major work marking the end of hostilities, asking such a question is the equivalent of a cub reporter asking a victim and witness of disaster what it feels like. The Dionysian strain supposes a music of action without thought, and the Apollonian, of thought without action. Such simplicities were addressed long ago in the ballet *Apollo*, the subject of which is the Greek god of music and archery (in other words, of war). In *Apollo* the composer summons the power of music to reason and persuade, but in the history of art, the same Apollo, his violin representing music as an art of *negotiated* relations, is challenged by piper Marsyas, whose panpipes represent the world of numbers or *exact* quantities. In the legendary contest of art and science, King Midas decides in favor of Marsyas, at which Apollo enacts a terrible revenge, flaying the imposter alive (fair recompense for having a thick skin; Maconie, *The Second Sense* 129–30). Stravinsky has already given an answer, in *Scènes de Ballet* and verbally in *The Poetics of Music*, to the effect that music does not inspire by appealing to conviction but in consequence of good design. A music that provokes listeners to jubilation is not bound to do so, or be said to do so, because the composer says so, but because it succeeds in igniting a response in the listener. The emotions created are the listener's own, the music only a trigger. A composer does not hold a copyright on emotion; otherwise, Stravinsky might have claimed a royalty from Olivier Messiaen for the appropriation of opening motifs and instrumentation, including solo piano, in *Turangalîla Symphony*, another Koussevitzky commission.

The *Symphony in Three Movements* is a robust statement of exceptional drive, initially reduced complexity, and arguably greater urgency compared to *Scènes de Ballet*. The character set, including piano and harp in dialogue relationship, draws on the *Scherzo à la Russe* and extends and deepens the pivotal role of these two Apollonian instruments (arguably corresponding to reciprocal temperaments: plucked strings the passive, hammered strings the active), respectively, Muse and Leader of the community of players. The upward sweeping gesture is a familiar device from the *Concertino for String Quartet*, employed in unhurried stepwise fashion in the *Symphony in C* and serving in a similar way to *Octet* as an ignition device—though on a monumental scale in the *Symphony in Three Movements*, say the equivalent of turning the keys of a four-engined B-29 bomber, rather than the modest Renault tourer of *Octet*. The hammer blows that follow, however, are of Schoenbergian force, recalling the Op. 42 *Piano Concerto*, a work Stravinsky admired (Philips, 289 468 0332). The emergence of the piano as a motivating force, overseeing busy strings, is a particular delight given the composer's history of nervousness at the combination of struck and bowed string sonorities: a sign perhaps that Apollo is finally in tune with himself. The graceful slow movement is poignantly feminine, the exuberant final movement a cheer in C major that could be interpreted as the long-awaited answer to the questioning E minor–C major uncertainty of the ending of the prewar *Symphony in C*. Its ultimate climax, building up *Rite of Spring* fashion over an oscillating ground to the rhythm "Hip! Hip! Hooray!" appears designed to bring an audience to its feet in jubilation and contains some of the most complex and densely written orchestral textures ever composed. Among a wealth of available interpretations, a 1962 Otto Klemperer recording with the Philharmonia Orchestra combines courage and determination with matter-of-fact precision (EMI, 7243 5 67337 2 5): a buoyant 2007 recording by Simon Rattle and the Berlin Philharmonic (EMI, 50999 2 07630 0 8) also worth considering, the orchestra arrangement, with bass viols in the center, adding a mellow timbre of attractive coherence and gravitas.

Ebony Concerto is "an artist's impression" of jazz, the most extreme of Stravinsky's jazz-inspired compositions, and in many ways the most self-revealing. The composer has said that the ebony in the title is a reference to the role of the solo clarinet, which is made of that wood. What he really means is that this is "black music," in Debussy's sense of *la musique nègre*, as opposed to the "white music" of his French neoclassical style. Not a case of Dionysiac versus Apollonian, then, but music of feeling (touch) and approximation as opposed to music of reason, of pattern and balanced design: and not only "black music" but a *concerto*—that is, a contest of jazz styles in which a dignified slow movement in traditional blues idiom shows respect, in the midst of big band choric effects mainly for excitement. The work was commissioned for Woody Herman's band, at a time when Herman was a fellow recording artist for Columbia. For whatever reason, shortly after recording *Ebony Concerto* in 1945, the orchestra disbanded, an event that jazz historians consider as marking the end of the swing era. Woody Herman and fellow clarinetist Benny Goodman (soloist on the 1965 collected edition recording) were among a group of jazz crossover artists who took classical music seriously and commissioned uncompromising new works from leading composers—among them a 1955 *Prelude, Fugue, and Riffs* composed for Herman and new lineup by Leonard Bernstein.

Like the classic "artist's impression" of a wanted criminal, Stravinsky's portrait of jazz is designed to sound nothing like the real thing—to convey, in fact, a sense of shock of the new, in Robert Hughes's phrase. It is a strangely smeared and blurred suggestion of energetic and purposeful collective noisemaking. At the same time, the idiom connects profoundly with the composer's roots in the rustic pastoral tradition of decorative out of tuning and reedy, resonant, and textured sounds. *Ebony Concerto*, *Scherzo à la Russe*, *Tango*, *Preludium*, and *Piano Rag-Music* belong to the same group of works as *Pastorale*, *Petrushka*, *The Nightingale*, *Concertino*, and *Symphony in C*, in all of which the sounds of mechanical instruments are deliberately imitated and blurred for dramatic effect, including false intonations and incidental noises.

The title also hints at "the dark side": the *Enfer* into which Orpheus descends. Woody Herman perceptively described *Ebony Concerto* as "a very delicate and a very sad piece." To others *Ebony Concerto* may evoke a monster computer, a Colossus of exotic design, winking lights and enormous power, delivering a ticker tape of chattering distortion from a speaker system in overdrive. Like the barrel organs in *Petrushka* and the mechanical songbird in *The Nightingale*, the machine simulation is meticulously observed and exactly composed of familiar, if unorthodox, orchestral combinations, in this case extending into the upper audio spectrum with honking saxophones in staccato, needle-sharp trumpets with Harmon mutes and snare and suspended cymbal highlights glinting around the edges, as if the ensemble were a Fritz Lang monster consuming its worker slaves, chewing them up and spitting out the bones. It is surely no coincidence that by the end of the piece the solo clarinet, Herman or Goodman, has been totally absorbed and digested by this ravenous Beast of Broadcasting in a cloud of smoke.[10]

There is a significant unstated tactical connection between Stravinsky's imitation of mechanical distortion for comedic effect and Schoenberg's harmonic tensions and notated speech for emotional effect, in *Pierrot Lunaire*, *A Survivor from Warsaw* (1946), and the opera *Moses und Aron*. Both Schoenberg and Stravinsky are exploiting a perception of relative musicality in noise and speech as effects of audio recording and transmission systems with distinctive resonances (the ringing Westrex outside broadcast microphone comes to mind). For Stravinsky the aim seems to be the effect of a radio "not quite tuned" to the transmission frequency, producing sideband distortion. To appreciate the *aesthetics* of distortion, it is necessary to listen in a more detached fashion to the range of sound and contrasts of a work as a whole. For example, when saxophones are driven hard, their tone and pitch become attractively distorted and approximate, and when muted trumpets and saxophones alternate chords at speed (a brilliant effect like masticating mechanical teeth), the tonal function of the chords quickly vanishes, leaving a stroboscopic impression of flickering brightness and texture. This could be called Stravinsky's contribution to a trend in jungle music impressionism pursued in the fifties and sixties by exponents of musical exotica Les Baxter,[11] Shelly Manne, Martin Denny, and others and in avant-garde music by Stockhausen and Ligeti.

Compared to the Woody Herman recording (reissued on Everest, EVC 9049), the complete edition recording conducted by the composer with Benny Goodman as soloist is strangely unbridled, one in which the gracious soloist appears gradually to fade from the spotlight (this may be a remix issue, since another version of the same recording [Columbia MK 42227—a compilation incidentally including the Bernstein *Prelude, Fugue, and Riffs*] is noticeably clearer, if still oddly balanced). From comparing the layout and mix of a token half-dozen versions, including Boulez (DG, 447 405-2), Edo de Waart (Philips, 442 583-2), and Craft (MusicMasters, 01612-67195-2), clearly this is a work exploiting extreme contrasts of color, texture, and depth that represent an enormous challenge to balance engineer and producer alike. Added reverberation is another issue for a music conceived anechoically for execution in a studio environment. As a concert experience, it teeters on the chaotic and may be difficult or impossible to present without the aid of spot microphones. It is most likely to succeed in recorded form either as an example of extreme monophony or as music in the round for headphone listening from a vantage point in the middle of the mêlée. After it, Stravinsky no longer had any excuse to ignore Varèse, the master of noise.

The *Concerto in D* for strings is part of the cluster of works that lead in the direction of *The Rake's Progress*. They deserve to be considered as a group for the very good reason that, along with *Ebony Concerto*, all partake in the Orpheus legend of the musician descending into the Underworld to plead for the return of his lost muse. The plot is outlined in *Ebony Concerto*, a musical action where the clarinetist is swallowed up by the band, and the band behaves at times like accusing counsel, at other times like Furies, and the ritual centerpiece is a funeral march. Commissioned by Paul Sacher, the "Basle" *Concerto in D* is an unexpectedly ferocious, savagely ironic work, most unlike the Swiss temperament. In retrospect and in conjunction with the *Ebony Concerto*, it is as though the composer has transferred his attention from an ensemble of mainly winds, to string orchestra, with the deliberate intention of rehearsing in advance the destruction of Orpheus by avenging Furies, either to prove it is possible for a string orchestra to behave in ferocious mode or to get it out of his system. Choreographer Jerome Robbins found the music "terribly driven" and choreographed a ballet around praying mantis–like insects, the females of which decapitate and eat their male partners at the peak of the sex act.

For Stravinsky, this is massed string music of extraordinary savagery and weight. Like the winds of *Ebony Concerto*, the strings are forced to play out of their comfort zone so that their tonal quality becomes abrasive, blurred, and distorted, in this case by the scrape of bow on string (a texture relieved at key points by piercing chords in harmonics of searing pain).

In the middle movement, at a quieter pace, described no doubt ironically by Craft in a liner note as "a long-line melody, one of the most lighthearted Stravinsky ever wrote," the composer enters the narrative in person by demonstrating the art of composing a melody in unedited real time as a sequence of failed initiatives and dead ends, false starts, and abrupt stops, clearly expressing the frustration of a composer whose muse has left him. The final Rondo for incessantly buzzing strings is a terrifying evocation of paranoia or intoxication.

Orpheus is based around the idea of a "song without words" or music drama in which voices are present but unable to speak, a powerful image derived from John Dowland's *Lachrymae* (1604), songs for an absent voice (hence the tears of the title). Not being able to speak, the Furies cannot reason with or warn the blindfolded Orpheus on his ascent from Hades with Eurydice, so when he mistakenly removes the blindfold too early, believing himself back on Earth, the revelation of failure through acting too soon and Eurydice's disappearance provoke the Furies to inarticulate frenzy. Stravinsky's return to Greek mythology, to meditate yet again on an universal drama of music, love, hubris (in this case, Orpheus's misjudgment of the gods' compassion as weakness), and loss of vision, like the blindness of Oedipus, deserves respect as a sober reflection, almost Japanese *gagaku* in its formality, on life after death, in other terms on the complicity of music in war and the composer as a lost soul seeking redemption. Stravinsky reverts to the static presentation of *Oedipus* and *Persephone*, but as dumb show, a silent movie of formal dances in black and white against a plain music for strings and just the occasional wind instrument standing in the role of narrator but speaking a foreign language. The music is unusually literal for Stravinsky, from the measured descending staircase of the opening measures, pointed by harp—a descent repeated at the conclusion, after Orpheus's violent dismemberment, in a bleak and devastating acknowledgment of failure—to the "Lux facta est" critical moment, the same as Oedipus, expressed in music of terrifying clarity, the fading of Eurydice from sight, expressed as a sudden void in the flow of music and the furious rage of retribution that follows. The musical action seems to be defining Orpheus's fate as a sin of pride: that he should have realized that in persuading the gods to release Eurydice, he was actually demonstrating that the muse was still capable of inspiring him, revealing his motive in seeking her return to the world of the living as a selfish desire to challenge fate and unbalance the universal order, rather than accept grief and turn it to music to serve humanity.

> We [the New York City Ballet] commissioned *Orpheus* from Stravinsky in the fall of 1946. This collaboration between him and Balanchine was one of the closest since Petipa dictated to Tchaikovsky the precise duration of each section of *The Sleeping Beauty*. . . . The action in *Orpheus* and its musical springboard are exceptionally concentrated if deceptively bland. . . . Balanchine conceived *Orpheus* as a ritual ceremonial, in its plangency and pathos. It is rare in the theater for artists of like intensity and talent to work together in harmonious tension. (Kirstein 99–100)

In *Orpheus* as in *Persephone* there is no drama, or rather it is drama observed from a great height. In Jean Cocteau's attractive but distinctly mannerist 1950 movie *Orphée* the poet and his muse descend to Hades by Rolls Royce, and the Furies are reinvented as coeds on motorbikes; but the movie still turns on the poet's crisis of lost inspiration and a futile (though in this case, not doomed) effort to retrieve his muse from limbo. All the same, Cocteau's perception of Orpheus's (and Stravinsky's) dilemma remains acute:

> The entire mystery of free will resides in this, that it seems that the thing that is *need not be*, as is illustrated by the amazing words of Christ: "Abba, Father, all things are possible unto Thee, take away this cup from me." . . . The princess dares to substitute herself for destiny, to decide that a thing *may be*, instead of being, and plays the part of a spy in love with the man she was appointed to watch and whom she saves by losing herself.[12]

8

THE RAKE'S PROGRESS

Over dinner at Chaplin's, Stravinsky proposes that they make a movie together. War has not been declared. They have been sharing experiences as cultural exiles in Hollywood, of life in America, and (for the actor-director) the challenge of adjusting from silent to dialogue movies. Stravinsky expresses pleasure at the scene in *Modern Times* where Charlie, as a restaurant waiter called upon to stand in for a missing vocalist and entertain diners, invents an intensely funny *pribaoutka*, or patter song, in Franco-Italian nonsense syllables to the music of a Brazilian rumba.

What the composer has in mind is a drama in which the hero is totally unlikeable but redeemed at the end by love. Horror and fascination go together in Mozart's *Don Giovanni*, about the legendary Don Juan whose charm and other personal accoutrements make him irresistible to women, ultimately damned through blindly pursuing his natural appetites for pleasure to the exclusion of all other moral considerations. Someone like Douglas Fairbanks (senior), perhaps. Chaplin (who has enjoyed his share of affairs and regards Fairbanks as a mentor and friend) considers how to respond. "Why not Hitler?" he asks. "Hitler has no redeeming features," says the composer. "His only virtue is rallying German public opinion to a political cause based on revenge and a perversion of social justice." Chaplin makes a mental note to start work right away on a comedy about Hitler. "What I am really looking for," says Stravinsky, "is someone like the tramp: a person entirely virtuous, whose actions for good are doomed to be perceived as undermining society, as in *Modern Times* when Charlie picks up a discarded flag in the street and finds himself unexpectedly leading a parade of striking workers."

Chaplin improvises a scenario set in a nightclub around the figure of speech known to music hall and stand-up comedy artists as "dying on the night" or "being crucified."

> It should be surrealistic, I said—a decadent night-club with tables around the dance floor, at each table groups and couples representing the mundane world—at one table greed, at another hypocrisy, at another ruthlessness. The floor show is the passion play, and while the crucifixion of the Saviour is going on, groups at each table watch it indifferently, some ordering meals, others talking business, others showing little interest. . . . As the show progresses, a drunk, being under the influence of alcohol, is on a different plane; he is seated alone and begins to weep and shout loudly: "Look, they're crucifying Him! And nobody cares!" He staggers to his feet and stretches his arms appealingly towards the Cross. The wife of a minister sitting nearby complains to the head waiter, and the drunk is escorted out of the place still weeping and remonstrating. The maestro's face became very grave. "But that's sacrilegious!" he said. And so the subject was dropped. (Chaplin 429–30)[1]

Weeks later, having reflected on their conversation, Stravinsky writes to Chaplin to ask if he is still interested in the proposal. But Chaplin is already way ahead of him, immersed in writing *The Great Dictator*, in the political currency of the day a seemingly impossible comedy subject, akin to blasphemy.

In making the change from silent movies to dialogue movies, Chaplin has acquired the gift of speech, and in acquiring speech, his public persona has consciously altered from comedian to political activist. He makes fun of Hitler the demagogue by turning his speeches into nonsense; then in 1947, his image changes irrevocably from mute and innocent tramp into a modern-day Don Juan: *Monsieur Verdoux*, banker, seducer, and serial murderer of rich women. In finding a voice, Chaplin's public image is unsettled, then compromised, his private life becoming increasingly the focus of unwelcome intelligence to a point where he is forced into permanent exile.

Monsieur Verdoux is a shade of Don Giovanni, whose character of unrepentant evil is destined to become a shadowy inspiration for *The Rake's Progress*, Stravinsky's greatest and most absorbing music drama. For Stravinsky, the political challenge of opera is the same as the dialogue movie for Chaplin: in possessing the gift of speech and being identified ideologically with a libretto, explicit words in a character's mouth that convey sentiments open to attack and misrepresentation by people to suit their own political agendas. The same issue is raised in Schoenberg's opera *Moses und Aron* (1932), in which the words and intentions of the prophet Moses are undone by the publicist and demagogue Aron, to a point where Schoenberg as author has found himself unable to continue beyond the prophet's bitter rebuke ending act II: "Oh Word! Oh Word! That I lack!"[2]

The ending of hostilities brings shocking revelations and intense recriminations. In 1946 Schoenberg composes *A Survivor from Warsaw*, a brief cantata in terse, newsreel style, in which the composer, speaking in the first person, breaks silence over the fate of Polish concentration camp victims. Spoken narrative—along with the commands and counting voices of prison guards—the dreaded "*Abzählen!*"—is offset by the sublime music of faith with which, in the final measures, the prisoners confront imminent death. Both spoken (factual) and sung (spiritual) messages are overlaid on a music of extreme emotional tension composed in the composer's abstract—and according to some critics, inhuman—twelve-tone musical language (Koch, 3-7263-2). The moral message, of redemption through music of lost souls imprisoned in a concentration camp counting house, is not lost on Stravinsky and added reason for his taking an interest in the young Robert Craft, a newcomer to the Stravinsky circle who has already made friendly contact with Schoenberg and is in a position to assist communication and future understanding between the two composers.

In the same year, 1946, exiled author Hermann Hesse is awarded the Nobel Prize for Literature for his wartime novel *Magister Ludi* (also known as *The Glass Bead Game*), a philosophical fiction about a future world in which images of musical abstraction and the abacus (the glass beads of the title) come together in a new vision of civilization devoted to numerical play—a startling prediction of today's information society inspired in part by the abstract music of Schoenberg and Webern. Among others, Hesse's novel references the exiled author Thomas

Mann, whose novel *Doktor Faustus*, published the following year, in less forgiving mode characterizes Schoenberg's twelve-tone method of composition as a pact with the devil: a moral fable in which the gifted but unpleasant composer Adrian Leverkühn pays the price for fame and fortune by going mad and dying of syphilis contracted from his liaison with an infected muse. Stravinsky is one of a number of experts consulted by Mann, the composer's neighbor in Beverly Hills, for his views on the twelve-tone system; however, the definitive characterization of the fictional demented composer is heavily influenced by Theodor Adorno, an ambitious former student of Alban Berg whose conversion to a revisionist aesthetic parlayed in elusively Freudian rhetoric has been the younger man's passport to intellectual respect as an expert on musical modernism, a theoretical construction in which Stravinsky and Schoenberg are represented as opposite poles, and Stravinsky casually diagnosed as a closet sadomasochist.

Stravinsky is dismayed at Mann's attribution of moral and mental disorder to a composer who has suffered so miserably for so many years and just as repelled by Adorno's insolent characterization of modern music as a cultural battleground fought over by equally disreputable antagonists.

In 1947 Hitler is over, and Richard Strauss a disgraced shadow of his former self. What is one to think of the values of the idolized composer of *Till Eulenspiegel* and *A Hero's Life*, golden boy of the cynical, decadent early twentieth century, who hitched his wagon to Nazism and was destroyed intellectually and morally? How respond to the views of a Thomas Mann, whose latest novel attempts to blame the decline of society on Arnold Schoenberg, of all people, for the sin of having discovered a musical language answerable to no political power but only to humanity?—the same Thomas Mann, incidentally, whose *Death in Venice*, picturing an aged aesthete whose last hours are spent vainly stalking a young Adonis in a plague-infected city, is destined to become the subject of Britten's last and arguably greatest opera. Along with the newly fashionable pessimism of Sartre ("Hell is other people"), intellectual conversation turns to the philosophical amorality of the Marquis de Sade, the perils of existentialism, and bleak reflections on the meaninglessness of life in general.

* * *

The Rake's Progress, opera in three acts (1948–1951), libretto by W. H. Auden and Chester Kallman (*Works* 16, 17).

Nineteen forty-seven is also the year Stravinsky signed with the British music publisher Boosey and Hawkes, a move guaranteeing security for the composer after many years of financial uncertainty. He wished to make a gesture in gratitude by composing a major work in English. Ralph Hawkes agreed to commission the libretto. A neoclassical opera in English would be Stravinsky's tribute to the integrity of a culture and language that had prevailed against the deadly Wagner-inspired rhetoric of Nazi propaganda. In that sense, *The Rake's Progress* can be seen as a parable of twentieth-century values that have been tested in the war and led to the disgrace of a number of leading cultural figures, along with the forced exile of many others. (One realizes with a shock how precisely the same emotional landscape of *The Rake's Progress* is addressed, albeit from a different perspective and at considerably greater length, by Stockhausen in the opera cycle *LICHT*, even to Stockhausen's co-option of the Orpheus myth in the character of Michael and his descent to Earth, and parody of Duke Ellington and his band in *Luzifers Tanz*, a reworking of Stravinsky's *Ebony Concerto*.)

A Rake's Progress is the name of a set of paintings, published in engraved form as a moral fable, by the eighteenth-century artist William Hogarth. Their nominal subject is a young man who on the promise of an inheritance leaves an idyllic and uneventful pastoral existence for the City of London, is led into a life of debauchery, gambles away a fortune not once but twice, enters into a disastrous marriage of convenience, is sent to a debtor's prison, and finally goes mad. The morality is one aspect; its peculiarly English subject matter and moral intention, a second. To a reader raised on La Fontaine's edition of Aesop's fables, the fate of a country squire depraved and corrupted by city life has elements in common with the folktale of the country mouse and the city mouse, along with allusions to Stravinsky's former life and times as an ambitious young newlywed persuaded by Diaghilev to exchange the idyllic world of his Ustilug country estate for the fast life in Paris.[3] The English connection is significant linguistically and culturally because the moral component of Stravinsky's earlier fables *The Soldier's Tale*, *Les Noces*, *Renard*, and the *Symphony of Psalms* is all too easily overlooked, and the stage dramas *Oedipus Rex* and *Persephone* are delivered in the style of formal ritual, with a minimum of stage action. In principle, an *opera buffa* in homage to Mozart and delivered in English would ensure there could be no question about the composer's message. The language of the BBC and the British temperament represented cultural and human values corresponding to his own musical values of precision and impartiality.

I am not sure that many around the composer, even Craft, certainly Auden, were fully in tune with the composer's firm moral intentions. Any idea that *The Rake's Progress* has nothing to do with his private life is clearly bizarre. Hogarth's comic parody of London as a world trade and finance metropolis and pinnacle of high society is Stravinsky's Paris and also his Hollywood, not to mention the Berlin of Christopher Isherwood. Hogarth's caricature figures and Stravinsky's have identifiable analogues in the composer's own lifetime: for Hogarth, Handel, for Stravinsky Cocteau, Nijinsky, the garrulous but charitable Gertrude Stein, the formidably unpretty but dignified and secretly passionate Edith Sitwell (what wonderful surnames these poets have!), along with a plethora of Ugly Duchess *grandes dames* of modern music: the Ida Rubensteins, Princesses de Polignac, and Peggy Guggenheims, not forgetting the Machiavellian presence of Diaghilev himself.

Would Stravinsky recognize Hogarth's depiction of gambling and whoring as a prim rural Puritan caricature of the life of London merchant bankers? Or the Rake's descent into madness as a literal or metaphorical syphilis? Does it matter? It does not matter. In the engraving "False Perspective" Hogarth cautions the viewer "do not believe everything you see"; in other words, "a picture can deceive." By the same token, different interpretations of a deliberately ambiguous moral message may be equally valid: the choice you make is the meaning that makes sense for the individual viewer. From the way the opera evolves, it becomes clear that Auden had a very different view of the leading character, seeing the poet's role, through the hero, to bring order and definition to a world of chaos and conflicting interests. The preoccupied Auden does not take Stravinsky's earlier fables into account or discards their messages. His childhood induction to Stravinsky is the *Three Easy Pieces* for piano. Had he studied *The Soldier's Tale* more closely, for instance, Auden might better have understood the dramatic potential of a different, more sympathetic hero, redeemed by the love of a woman, whose tale of failure and descent into madness we may finally see, in an inversion of the *Oedipus* myth, as in some sense sympathetic and honorable, like the abdication of Edward VIII for love, or even Thomas Mann's wretched aesthete Aschenbach, pomaded and rouged, gasping for breath in vain and unrequited pursuit of an unattainable and indifferent Adonis.

Stravinsky has long wanted to make a statement to match or update, in the public mind, the impact of *The Rite of Spring* and secure him a place in the world of opera. For so important a mission divine blessing is obligatory. He has already composed *Ebony Concerto*, the "Basle" *Concerto* for strings, and *Orpheus*, all instrumental studies in extreme emotion, all potentially available to serve as orchestral and ballet interludes for a neoclassical opera: the dissolute *Concerto* for strings as a prelude to act I, scene 2 (the brothel scene), *Ebony Concerto* a comic orchestral pantomime of the Infernal Machine as intermission between acts I and II and *Orpheus* as a sobering ballet intermission between acts II and III. Now he composes the *Mass*, a petition for blessing of considerably greater substance than the *Ave Maria* and *Pater Noster*, and inspired, so he says, by "some Masses of Mozart that I found in a second-hand music store in Los Angeles in 1942 or 1943," works of faith knowingly described as "sweets of sin" (*Expositions* 77).

Years before, commenting on *Oedipus Rex*, a teenaged Britten observed that the tenor role should best be taken by a lyric tenor able to manage the high notes with ease, not a heroic tenor for whom the high notes are an effort.[4] As a Boosey and Hawkes composer, Britten's settings of English poets, along with the works of John Dowland, Henry Purcell, Handel, and the Arthur Sullivan of *Iolanthe* and *The Gondoliers*, are ready to assist Stravinsky in his musical scansion of the English language. Peter Pears's tenor in Britten's *Serenade for Tenor, Horn, and Strings* (1942) is clearly modeled on Eumolpus in *Persephone*. To Stravinsky the admirable features of English speech and temperament are clarity, precision, and BBC objectivity—hence, the collected edition performance of *Oedipus Rex* in which a British-speaking voice evoking wartime BBC announcer Alvar Liddell, substituting for author Jean Cocteau, announces "The King . . . is dead."

Auden is recommended to Stravinsky, we learn, by Aldous Huxley, a close friend and neighbor in Beverly Hills. The reality is a little more contrived. Auden recommends himself by association with Britten, a now established and highly regarded opera composer, but is also known to Balanchine through fellow Russian composer Nicolas Nabokov, a cousin of the novelist Vladimir Nabokov, the future author of *Lolita*, a study of literary decadence in parody inversion of Mann's *Death in Venice*. Balanchine and Nicolas Nabokov are close colleagues of Lincoln Kirstein at the New York City Ballet. All three are on intimate terms with Stravinsky, and by coincidence all have previously known and worked with Diaghilev. Since the war's end Kirstein and Nabokov have seen active service with American occupation forces in Europe, assigned to tasks of cultural rehabilitation in which Auden also plays a brief, memorable, and conspicuously eccentric role. Another mutual friend from the poet's Oxford circle is exiled Russian philosopher and Turgenev scholar Isaiah Berlin, whose linguistic expertise Stravinsky would eventually consult in setting the Hebrew text of *Abraham and Isaac*.

Kirstein was a considerable poet on his own account. By the time *Orpheus* was commissioned for the New York City Ballet, Nabokov had risen to a position of formidable influence in US-sponsored cultural affairs of greater occupied Europe. Auden's name is much more likely to have surfaced as favored librettist in conversation over flagons of Gallo burgundy in New York than in table talk over bean sprouts with Aldous Huxley in Los Angeles, though Huxley's endorsement would carry authority.[5] A grandson of the great Thomas Huxley, Darwin's defender against Bishop Wilberforce, Aldous is tragically going blind, but like the seer Tiresias, his mind is absolutely clear. Auden, by contrast, is an intellect so dazzling it leaves nothing in the field of vision but floating purple and green afterimages.

Auden is chaperone at Robert Craft's first meeting with the composer and his wife, at a Washington hotel in 1948. Craft tells a charming story against himself, the point of which appears to be that Vera's beauty left him lost for words.

> "Tell me please," she says, "what means 'doctrine'?" and the word comes out so French-sounding—"doctreene"—that I answer "a female doctor." (*Chronicle* 5)

An intriguing conversational gambit: "doctrine" suggests "doctrinaire" with the meaning of "maintaining a position by appealing to form rather than reason." The description could apply to Auden or Stravinsky, though if applied to Stravinsky he would already have looked it up for himself. So *doctrine* has to refer to somebody else. Imagine the repartee as it might have been, in table talk over dinner:

> Vera: Now, Mr. Craft—Robert—Bob. Perhaps you can help. We were asking the other day Mr Huxley what is the difference between *dogma* and *doctrine.* Aldous says that a *dogma* is a pet that you keep for love and protection, who ends by eating all of your food, taking your bed, and ruling your life. So now, what do you think, is *doctrine*?
>
> Craft [*in his best Dr. Johnson manner*]: Why Madam, a *doctrine* is a fruit, like a peach, sweet to taste, but unlovely to be seen in the eating of it. [*Cries of "Bravo!"*]

Stravinsky has a very clear idea of the opera he wishes to write. Auden, however, is out of his comfort zone. The outline libretto (*Memories* 154–76 [UK], 156–67 [US]) reveals as much, as do subsequent changes, not all of which are improvements. The composer has a personal motive, if not a duty (okay, you win: *he had a score to settle*), to ensure the opera may conform to a truthful expression of his own life and times and defend his personal reputation against widely circulating impressions of him, authored by Copland and others, as a musical pretender—a Russian primitive lured into sophistication in the court of Diaghilev, who converted to neoclassicism, the aesthetic of dictatorships—and to defend Mozart's reputation, whose *Don Giovanni* was perceived not only as falsely glamorizing the worst in human nature but also as the composer's revenge on a Viennese high society that treated him as a lowly servant. (Stravinsky's Mozart allusions in *The Rake's Progress* are frequent, obvious, deliberate, and knowing. They are part of the composer's moral message, and Auden for one does not get it.) It is in Stravinsky's interest that his hero be seen as a tragic innocent, in Aesop terms a country mouse who falls prey to the machinations of city life or as a mute victim in the tradition of Chaplin and Keaton.

Hogarth's engravings form a tableau or series of panels, a presentation appealing to the composer because it reduces the course (or *Progress*) of an adult life to a sequence of contrived snapshots, frozen in time, for which the viewer has to imagine the connections. The Rake can be seen in one sense as an antihero and the opposite of Apollo and Oedipus: the opposite of Apollo, because his actions appear to betray no sense of altruism or commitment to harmony, and the opposite of Oedipus, because he demonstrates neither aptitude nor inclination to a life of service. He is that strange combination, a creature of instinct and natural goodness, part Voltairean optimist (a character type revisited by Leonard Bernstein in the musical *Candide*) but at the same time religiously anti-Faust and anti-Fantômas, the antithesis of a power-hungry demagogue. His weakness is to be cooperative, to fit in, to collaborate, and ultimately be destroyed by the enemy machine, but it is all done in a very English kind of self-effacing way. His agreeable surrender to chance and the Stock Exchange attacks eighteenth-century liberal ideas of progress, wealth creation, freedom of action, and a prevailing philosophy of human nature as privileged, innocent, and motivated by a benign and total selfishness.

The underlying criticism represents an amalgam of Alexander Pope's and William Blake's eighteenth-century messages that Enlightenment philosophy and industrial progress have led to social deprivation, financial collapse, public immorality, and revolution—in today's terms, that history has repeated itself in the twentieth century in terms of the industrial state, dictatorship, war, and the Bomb. As a modernist Stravinsky is determined to defend the values of "nonrepresentational" music and art, while in the role of the cicada of La Fontaine's bestiary, he also has an obligation to defend the role of the musician in civilized life (the cicada is the fiddler on the roof of the anthill of modern civilization).

Auden is so compelling an intelligence that it must appear impertinent for a mere reader to question his judgment. But question we must, because while the opinions of a great poet are incisive, they are all the same published and available as the opinions of a reader rather than a listener. A reader seemingly apt to forget that having the text in hand and being able to examine it at leisure, even going to a dictionary from time to time to check a fact or usage, is a luxury unavailable to an opera audience, listeners obliged to interpret characters and actions in order, *en passant*, and in real time.

Stravinsky has had trouble with librettists in the past, and the difficulties he is now facing are as familiar as they are profound. Few among his poet friends, apart from Paul Valéry, were willing to concede the point of Mallarmé's reply to Degas: "One does not make poetry with ideas, but with words." Words are necessary because opera is sung drama and a singer needs words to sing *with* and to have something to sing *about*. Stravinsky's irritation is directed against contemporary poets who imagine that their word is self-sufficient, who unlike the eighteenth-century poets of Handel's generation do not recognize the responsibility of music to convey meaning and implication in the delivery of a spoken text. Those for whom poetry is words on the page, imagine the text to exist in a timeless limbo. For a composer, however, the poem is a temporal process, a meaning conveyed in the dynamics of speech, less so in the words themselves, which are merely objects in flow. By way of explanation, using the famous example of W. B. Yeats's BBC recorded recitations, Stravinsky says,

> The stylistic performance problem in my music is one of articulation and rhythmic diction. Nuance depends on these. . . . Yeats pauses at the end of each line, he dwells a precise time on and in between each word—one could as easily notate his verses in musical rhythm as scan them in poetic metres. (*Conversations* 120)

In broader terms, since words are ultimately uncertain in meaning whereas actions are final and unequivocal, it follows that as human beings we are bound to live by our actions, from which arises the message of surrealism that the meaning you extract from an image is not a given but invincibly personal to the viewer. Don Giovanni is a figure of Enlightenment-era fantasy, second cousin to the Marquis de Sade, hostage to human nature, engaged in relentless moral decline, and observed by the reader with a mixture of fascination and intellectual detachment. The character Stravinsky desires for the Rake, if not quite the same as Hogarth's Rake, closer to Henry Fielding, is more sympathetic and certainly redeemable. Giovanni is a damned soul, says Stravinsky, but the Rake is a lost soul. There is a difference. Up to a point, Auden concurs:

> Don Juan . . . is not an epic hero; ideally, his external appearance is that of the man who nobody notices is there because he is so utterly commonplace. . . . [If] he is either handsome or ugly, then the woman will have feelings about him before he gets to work, and the seduction will not be absolute, i.e., a pure triumph of his will.[6]

Even to interpret Hogarth's Rake as a selfish and dissolute individual may be superficial, since the artist depicts his hero as more put upon than putting. Perhaps, suggests the composer, he is closer to Young Werther, the helpless adolescent whose story is based on Goethe's experience as a young poet inducted into high society and finding himself trapped in a situation from which he has to escape by unilateral action feigning mental breakdown—or Handel, driven to escape from the trifling duties of court composer to the Elector of Hanover, first to Italy, then to London, only to meet up with him again and be forgiven, upon the Elector's coronation as King George I of England. Auden, however, dismisses *Werther* as "a masterly and devastating portrait of a complete egotist, a spoiled brat, incapable of love because he cares for nobody and nothing but himself, and having his way at whatever cost to others" (Auden, "Werther and Novella," in *Forewords and Afterwords* 25–51).

Stravinsky's personal recollections of Diaghilev and his entourage, during and after the Great War, are painfully relevant: Debussy, wasting away from cancer; Ravel, who enlisted in World War I and was never the same afterward; poor Nijinsky, a genius, divine artist, and pure, guileless intelligence also descending into pitiful madness. One has only to read Stravinsky's clear-sighted accounts of these people in the conversation books, portraits of close associates and dear friends, to understand the powers of forgiveness he has to draw on. The composer also has to counter a prevailing perception of himself as a Voltairean lightweight and cynic. In *The Poetics of Music*, quoting G. K. Chesterton—"Try to grow straight and life will bend you"—he has already outlined, in words of remarkable beauty, a philosophy applicable to the Rake as hero: "One cannot force one's self to love; but love presupposes understanding, and in order to understand, one must exert one's self" (*Poetics* 56–57).

Composer and poet come to terms on an outline plot. They dispense with an overture. In classical opera, an overture establishes a pulse and a breath or phrase length, key indicators of temperament. Without an overture the audience is thrust unprepared into the midst of things. As it stands now, its absence, though deliberate, seems like an oversight, a genuflection perhaps to movie realism.

The opening scene in the country could be cliché pastoral, intentionally boring, possibly suggestive, like a Watteau painting; dramatically speaking, however, the country is a natural limbo from which in a few short minutes the hero, for all his profession of undying love, is due to escape for a new life in the city. A woman in love sees love as security and so wishes for life to remain the same forever, whereas a man in love is inspired, eager to get ahead, and therefore primed for change. A cynical twist would be for the young woman to be shallow and clingy and the young man already itching to escape. The Uncle is a boring figure with few redeeming or interesting features, well intentioned, adjusted to the simple life, a parsonical authority figure who lives by irritating catechisms rather than thinking for himself and in any case one who has doubts about the young man.

Auden proposes that the inheritance be from an unknown relative and not the Rake's father, and Stravinsky concedes. The effect of the change, however, is to alter the messenger (Shadow) from a morally neutral character and make him an agent for the hero's downfall, a tempter like the Devil in *The Soldier's Tale*. From a modern perspective, the hero's action in leaving a comfortable life for the excitement of the city seems just a little bit too James Dean to be believable. A convincingly headstrong character should be more than a mouthpiece.

A proposed orchestral interlude to cover the transition to city life is set aside. In scene 2, the Rake is discovered in a brothel. Pitifully, he says "I want to go home." In scene 3 his young lady, feeling abandoned, appears in traveling clothes, ready to face the dangers of the city, determined to find her man, fearing he has forgotten her. Though her guardian might have been expected to feel morally obliged to assist, even accompany her on her mission, she goes alone. Act II, scene 1, finds the hero in "digs," in limbo, with nothing to do, and bored—improbably reduced to a character in the equivalent of a reality television series. Shadow makes the preposterous suggestion that he propose marriage to a woman of formidable ugliness. It is the poet's best shot at the famous *acte gratuit* after the surrealist doctrine of taking control of destiny by submitting to the irrational, and it misses the surrealist point entirely. Says Auden, offhandedly,

> Opera in particular is an imitation of human willfulness; it is rooted in the fact that we not only have feelings but insist upon having them at whatever cost to ourselves. . . . The quality common to all great operatic roles, e.g. Don Giovanni, Norma, Lucia [di Lammermoor], Tristan, Isolde, Brünnhilde, is that each is a passionate and willful state of being.[7]

But to describe a character as a *state of being* rather than a living person identifies a crucial difference between poet and composer. The poet is concerned with definition, the composer with alteration, and a libretto that is too precise in character definition leaves no room for ambiguity or development or, rather, in a position where *every* decision, no matter how sensible, is a gratuitous act. It is *music alone* that persuades the audience that a choice is rational or emotional and in what degree. Music affects not only the character but also the audience, who do not wish to be told what to think but to be invited to work out what is going on for themselves. The attraction of Hogarth's series of engravings is that while they lend themselves to instant approbation or censure, the viewer is left uncertain whether the same impressions tell the entire story. In other words, a first impression is also a gratuitous act.

There is also a difference between an indulgence undertaken for pleasure merely "because it is possible" (famous in recent years as the Clinton defense) and a gesture undertaken indifferently but altruistically. Auden should know, since he volunteered to marry Erika Mann, daughter of the novelist Thomas Mann, such that she might obtain a British passport and be safe from Nazi persecution.[8] Stravinsky may have recalled that in 1927 Marcel Duchamp was persuaded, out of boredom, misconceived gallantry, and under pressure from his friends the Francis Picabias, to marry a docile heiress with whom he had no chance of happiness. He endured the marriage for a short while, then bowed out with as much dignity as he could muster. In the opera, a viewer is left in the dark whether the monster Baba the Turk is human or machine, fiend or chatterbox, since when the Rake tires of her, covering her face like a radio with a doily has the effect of switching off her powers of speech (though returned to full voice in the auction scene, her character redeemed through forgiving advice urging the Rake to rejoin his true love). There are models aplenty for an Ugly Duchess in Stravinsky's former life, but Baba the Turk most resembles a combination of Duchamp's *machine onaniste*, or sex machine (concocted with Julian Levy and illustrated in *The Large Glass*), and Maelzel's famous bearded Turk, a celebrated eighteenth-century android revealed as a fake operated by a concealed diminutive real person.

The bearded Turk is a necessary allusion to Mozart's Vienna, a city and culture of mechanical dolls and musical instruments on which so much of Stravinsky's music has previously drawn. In the opera, however, the mechanical element is revealed as a travesty, an infernal machine for making bread out of stones. The original script calls for a machine for extracting gold from seawater, a process that is actually feasible if totally uneconomic (it resurfaces, incongruously, in an April 1963 *Superman* comic). A machine for making bread from stones, however, is clearly an inadequate and unconvincing parody of industrial possibility from a period capable of such miracles as the Jacquard punched card weaving loom, an invention adapting music technology for weaving expensive cloth.

In act III Stravinsky reverts to his own familiar device, from *The Soldier's Tale*, of the hero in crisis gambling for his soul with Shadow, now revealed as the Devil. Unlike the earlier work, the hero wins at cards when his time is up, by magically stopping the clock, a gesture suspending a city life based on measure and mechanical time and reverting to the country life of night and day and the cycle of the seasons. Feet first, Shadow descends into the ground in the same action as Don Giovanni in Mozart's opera (a gesture seen in reverse with Lucifer's return ascent to earth, wingtips first, after *The Flood*).

Removed to the madhouse, the hero recovers his soul at the cost of his reason, mocked by those around him like the nightclub patrons in Chaplin's imaginary scenario. His faithful lover bids him adieu, and he dies alone, calling on Orpheus, Eurydice, Persephone, the chorus adding their farewells in a coda every bit as touching as the people's farewell to the blinded Oedipus. Then, before the curtain, the five principals sing Hogarth's moral: "The Devil finds work for Idle Hands to Do." So disconcerting a moral acts like a cold douche, given that nobody has been idle for a moment, and the Devil has been defeated.[9] The unstated real moral is "Love redeems all"—along with its subtext, "Music confounds even the greatest verse." By implication, the Idle Hands are the applauding Audience.

The irony is a Brechtian stroke. In having a voice, the Rake is bound to accuse himself, and in taking action, he becomes morally accountable for the choices he makes and the errors of his ways. How can a hero act badly and retain the audience's sympathy? That is the question. Mozart's Don Giovanni is a pantomime figure elevated to reality by art. Stravinsky's task for Auden—"if Auden chooses to accept it"—has been to conjure a culpable innocent out of the thin air of situation comedy, a character whose actions, however hateful, are believably forgivable. Auden and Kallman's libretto, while aesthetically admirable, appears intellectually and morally undecided, displaying the very indifference of which the composer is all too frequently accused. The most important questions are left hanging: "What does the Rake really do wrong?" and after that, "What are we supposed to condemn in the actions of those around him?"

To understand Stravinsky's intention in *The Rake*, there is no better way than to read his own writings, consider his previous works of theater and their plotlines, and set them in the context of his own experiences and the experiences of others like him, like Schoenberg and Hanns Eisler, who sought refuge in Hollywood only to find their talents rejected by the movie industry. It is sad to note how few among the composer's familiar acquaintances and guests—those, that is, whose table talk is preserved in Craft's diaries—have much of interest to say on musical matters, are ignorant or embarrassed by music, and in extreme cases, like Evelyn Waugh, cannot bring themselves even to think about it. To understand Auden's "English" view of *The Rake*, in many respects different from Hogarth's and Stravinsky's own, it is equally illuminating to read Auden's essays, published before and after *The Rake*, from which it is clear beyond doubt that collaborating with Stravinsky was a defining episode in the poet's life and one from which he never fully recovered.

To recap: In December 1947, a year into the opera, Balanchine and Nabokov are summoned from New York to Los Angeles for festive consultations, a three-day journey by train. Work on the libretto has not been going entirely smoothly. Nabokov keeps a diary.

> One entire evening was spent listening to the Toscanini records of *La Traviata*, which N.B.C. made especially for Stravinsky at his request (of Verdi's operas, Stravinsky likes *La Traviata* and *Aïda* best of all; he is less fond of *Otello* and *Falstaff*), and the Glyndebourne recordings of *Don Giovanni*. This opera is Stravinsky's special love; particularly now that he himself is busy writing an opera. (Nabokov 220)

The composer is edgy. Auden has upset him by taking on Chester Kallman as colibrettist without asking leave. He is not pleased. Nabokov reports outbursts of a "scathing, pitiless kind of humor which knows no compassion" (Nabokov 211), a strange thing to say because "compassion" is a term of understanding, not forgiveness, and Nabokov should know that Stravinsky's opinions, however terse, are invariably exactly formed expressions of "with-feeling."

Auden is hardworking but intimidated. Nabokov attributes Stravinsky's sharp opinions to a short fuse, but he misses the point that for Stravinsky to have a bad opinion of anything, he has to have conceived an attraction to it in the first place, so the composer's primary emotion is disappointment. Such sharpness makes his guests nervous, however. Nabokov and Balanchine have been summoned to the Stravinsky household in an effort to defuse tensions and help reawaken the composer's original motives and Russian habits of thought: memories of his father as the robber Giacomo in Auber's *Fra Diavolo*, of rebellious fictions of the composer's upbringing in the novels of Dostoevsky or Turgenev, as much as apt historical characters like Pisarev, the nihilist friend of Turgenev, a rebel "who wanted to enjoy life egotistically, but he suffered imprisonment and finally went mad. Such an ostentatious display of cynicism finally led him to an understanding of love."[10]

Hints of difference are scattered through Auden's published essays, early and late. On the responsibility of the poet, he is forthright: "Before Berlioz, Wagner, and Verdi in his middle years, no composer worried much about the libretto; he took what he was given and did the best he could with it," ignoring the obvious first, that the composer chooses, and second, because his music interprets (Auden, "A Marriage of True Minds," in *Forewords and Afterwords* 345–50). In a review of the (Richard) Strauss–Hofmannsthal correspondence, Auden declares that the choice of dramatic subject and its style of dramatic treatment ought to be the librettist's sole business, not the composer's. In saying that "Strauss received from Hofmannsthal a succession of libretti which, while being admirably settable, are a pleasure to read by themselves," the poet appears to imply that a composer's music is a disposable asset (Auden, "A Marriage of True Minds," 347).

Auden is surely right, however, to complain: "A librettist is always at a disadvantage because operas are reviewed, not by literary or dramatic critics, but by music critics whose taste and understanding of poetry may be very limited." The poet's contribution expresses an equal, if not the same, point of view. And he notes, "A librettist is at a further disadvantage because music is an international language and poetry a local one" (Auden, "A Marriage of True Minds," 349)—by a twist of irony precisely the argument made by Walt Disney for preferring music over dialogue as the primary narrative element in animated movies.

More critical, however, is the librettists' disagreement over the role of language in music drama: Stravinsky's assertion that words are sounds assimilated into a musical flow, against the poets' conviction, already hinted in Auden's Hofmannsthal essay, that words are ultimately supreme. Particularly revealing, among a group of essays dedicated to the composer's memory, is Auden's and Kallman's joint criticism of Donna Anna's last aria in *Don Giovanni*, up for translation into English, as

> one of the most beautiful which Mozart ever wrote, but the [original Italian] words are of an appalling banality and make Donna Anna very unsympathetic, now leading poor Don Ottavio on, now repulsing him. We felt, therefore, that we must forget the original text entirely and write something quite new. (W. H. Auden and Chester Kallman, "Translating Opera Libretti," in *The Dyer's Hand* 497)

Au contraire, mes vieux, it is not "your wish" or the wish of the audience for clarity at this moment in the drama. We do not desire to know precisely how Don Giovanni or his victim is feeling or ought to behave; we are present to witness the behavior of a character of that name as consistently motivated or not, as the case may be. What the scholar poet calls "appalling banality" may well be psychologically authentic; I don't know, not being a woman, but in Donna Anna's situation, I would not expect to be capable of acting rationally or consistently. For the poet to object to Da Ponte's "inelegant" phrasing is like Boulez objecting (as he does) to Schoenberg's employment of *sprechstimme* in *Pierrot Lunaire* as inelegant: neither view is necessarily incorrect, but the decision is not theirs to make, *it is what it is*, a problem for the audience to deal with, and nobody else. Stravinsky: "It is my conviction that that the public always shows itself more honest in its spontaneity than do those who officially set themselves up as judges of works of art" (*Poetics* 91).

The idea that the composer of *The Soldier's Tale*—or even *Renard*—does not understand moral ambiguity is ludicrous, given the moral clarity of both cautionary tales. Stravinsky has previously created what are effectively operatic cantatas, actionless dramas, on the subject of Oedipus, an innocent who is morally destroyed by the action of the gods, and Persephone, who is taken against her will and transported to the Underworld from where her release is negotiated to ensure the return of fertility to Earth, a moral tale for a Western world suffering the aftereffects of the 1914–1918 war, economic collapse, and ensuing political tensions. The soldier in *Soldier's Tale* is a survivor picked on by a malevolent and destructive Devil: the opposite of a Faust, who wants to rule the world. The female sacrificial victim in *The Rite of Spring* is an anonymous member of the tribe whose action is determined by a tribal culture in which personal identity, freedom, and happiness are meaningless (a tendency grounded in an imaginary civil ownership of language, perpetuated in linguistic philosophy and musicology, and manifested in such blatant injustices as the prosecution of Dreyfus, persecution of composers Mahler and Schoenberg in Vienna, and threats against Shostakovich in Soviet Russia for offenses against the language of music).

In the past Stravinsky has been able to make his message clear by appealing to French classical protocol and eliminating action from the drama, forcing the audience to confront the reality that "these things have happened, not through any deliberate criminal act of the persons involved, but because of critical failures of humility." But in *The Rake's Progress*, "stuff happens"—life goes on, the world is a dynamic environment, actions have consequences, and the audience is obliged to keep up. Finally, Stravinsky's setting of English is routinely criticized for offending against the natural scansion of his chosen lyrics. While not altogether true (Stravinsky's Shakespeare and his Dylan Thomas settings are impeccably phrased), the criticism ignores a rational equivalence, in speech, of the composer's arpeggiation and fragmentation of musical figures, after the broken textures of mechanical musical instruments. If a person limps, people notice it and feel for the person limping. When speech is hesitant or erratic, people listen more keenly, go with the flow, and connect with the message.

Auden's attempt at a nonsense poem, or *pribaoutka* (in the auction scene), is quirky and uncomfortable. Auden's essay "Notes on the Comic" (*The Dyer's Hand* 371–85) is a paragon of unfunniness, less funny even than T. S. Eliot's "The Music of Poetry."[11] For comparison, Chaplin's patter song in *Modern Times* initially appears to be a spontaneous invention of dadaist nonsense. But as the music is scripted, including pauses for effect, so we intuit that Charlie's character must be improvising nonsense lyrics to a song he and the band already know. In so doing the impact of the song changes from the improbable idea of Charlie and the band making it up as they go along to the entertaining fiction of an uneducated working man inventing a lyric conveying the gestures of an original text in a convincing manner but without saying anything. This carries a powerful message in code: that words are not required to make people laugh or get the point (Chaplin's rabble-rousing nonsense speeches parodying Hitler at Nuremburg are more of the same, though closer to the bone). The simple, apolitical message of nonsense poetry (which Valéry defended and Stravinsky appreciated) is the inverse of Symbolist poetry, that the sounds of words make their own sense, and in an ideal world words should be chosen for their beauty of sound, without having to worry about their meaning. Latent disagreement over the priority of language as sound over sense has made the composer uncomfortable, despite the British reputation as a breeding ground for virtuosos in nonsense Samuel Foote, Lawrence Sterne, Edward Lear, William Schwenk Gilbert (of Gilbert and Sullivan), and Lewis Carroll.

In advance of the 1951 premiere at La Scala, having consulted the English composer, an uneasy Auden "repeats his story about Benjamin Britten liking the opera very much, 'everything but the music,' a story I.S. did not find very amusing" (*Chronicle* 26). Even after the premiere, a tremendous success, Auden continues to air knowledgeable misgivings over too-obvious allusions in Stravinsky's music to Mozartian models. By contrast, over dinner in Paris in May 1952, after a performance of *Wozzeck*, Albert Camus and Stravinsky are overheard admiring Berg's exact musical sympathy for playwright Georg Büchner's revolutionary philosophy of human nature and the right to happiness, a concern hinting at unresolved differences between Stravinsky and Auden over The Rake (*Chronicle* 32–34). The European Camus understands right away that like *Wozzeck*, *The Rake's Progress* is a study of alienation: the Englishman Auden, however, appearing to regard *The Rake* rather flippantly as situation comedy with a twist, the hero a masculine Alice in Wonderland (articulate, observant, detached) to whom things are done and at whom ideas are flung so that the descent into madness registers as no more than the consequence of eating a piece of magic mushroom, after being led astray by a giant caterpillar.

Though a marvelous speaker of his own verse, Auden attaches to a younger Oxford fraternity of literary intelligence, fantasy socialists of privileged background for whom the combination of exact terminology and *being right* is a form of magic that enables the poet to deflect public scrutiny from the individual as a morally responsible person. Says Auden, "The biography of the artist . . . throws no light whatsoever on the artist's work. . . . Most genuine artists would prefer that no biography be written" ("Shakespeare's Sonnets," in *Forewords and Afterwords* 88–108). But his generation also suffers a nagging conviction that being right (having instant recourse to the right words, making the precise diagnosis) is unable to change anything. Among the English the greatest fear associated with being right is that language itself may change. The role of a poet or philosopher is thus to control the conversation by controlling the terms of discussion, even while recognizing that if there were no uncertainty, there would logically be no conversation either. In a celebrated photograph of the composer and chief librettist taken during rehearsals for *The Rake* in 1951, there is no eye contact between the two, and only the poet is looking toward the camera.

How was Stravinsky, assuming he knew them, to deal with these differences of view? Ultimately by absorbing them. A composer needs words, a poet provides words, and Auden's words and breadth of knowledge were dazzling and would survive being manhandled into the composer's feeling for intonation and rhythm, whatever the poet might think. The composer understood the persuasive force of managed imprecision. It would work to the advantage of both for an audience to be kept in a state of uncertainty over whether the words were to be believed, or the music, the composer all the while *knowing* that the music would invariably have the final say. Stravinsky knew from his youth that the secret of persuading an audience is not exact definition but contrived approximation: in instrumental terms expressed by the broken consort and ornamented, arpeggiated line of which a listener cannot say where it is or where it may be going exactly, only that it is going somewhere. If Auden's verse suggests one thing and his music another, the two do not cancel one another out but create a tension in the mind of the audience as to which to believe and which for the time being to trust (not the same thing). So Stravinsky deals with the problem by writing Auden into the play. As *Oedipus Rex* is a play in which the central character is revealed as a tragic hero who has written his own destiny, so *The Rake* is ultimately an opera in which the poet reveals himself through his defense of the words and actions of the chief character, who in Hogarth's sense is only a cipher. It is a clever if risky strategy but one enabling Stravinsky to avoid coming into conflict with a poet whose genius he truly admires. For a different reason he admired unconditionally the Welshman Dylan Thomas and Irishman William Butler Yeats, poets of oral, bardic traditions, as he had previously admired Balmont, the poet of *Zvezdoliki*.

Like John Cage, Stravinsky speaks through the forms and words of other people, of whom Mozart is one and Auden another. Neoclassicism speaks to tradition by speaking through the forms of tradition. The issue is whether the classical forms are artificial, empty convention, developed to satisfy audiences or the vanity of the feature singers, or psychologically valid, by comparison with Wagner's or Debussy's conception of drama as heightened documentary unfolding in real time. In the composer's view the artificial forms of neoclassical practice have amply proven themselves in previous works, so the question is not whether but why they work, along with how to make them work in the present case. The challenge in the present case is to make the main character Tom Rakewell sympathetic and believable, when everything about his downfall and behavior conspires against it. It is not enough to have him go mad, leaving the world as it is; his character has to be recognized and redeemed and the tables turned on the audience, just as Chaplin imagined would happen from staging the Crucifixion as a cabaret act.

The great attraction of Hogarth's series of engravings is that while they lend themselves to spontaneous approbation or censure, the viewer is left uncertain whether first impressions tell the entire story. What neither Auden nor Kallman have realized is that *The Rake's Progress* is also a parody of John Bunyan's *Pilgrim's Progress*—a parody that ends in failure and madness through redemption: like Moses reaching the Promised Land but being denied entry. In this light, Auden himself, like any artist, is also a pilgrim. Nor is the composer bound, as Auden knows, to follow the poet to the letter, quoting Rossini to the effect that the composer who marches too closely to the beat of the lyric runs the risk of creating an effect that is either incongruous or ridiculous (Schmidgall 14). This is the error known in the movie industry as "mickey-mousing," when an accompanying music—supposedly external to the action—mimics the action so perfectly that it gives the ludicrous impression of actors and extras dancing to order, instead of behaving with a semblance of free will.

9

AFTER THE FALL

The end of hostilities brought significant change to the world of modern music. Radio emerged as a force for good; the BBC was sent in to reform German radio; and American forces cultural advisors Everett Helm and Nicolas Nabokov were among those drafted into programs to purge German radio orchestras of Nazi sympathizers and organize festivals of art and music, including the Darmstadt summer courses in modern music, in an effort to rebuild morale. An important goal of the program was the rehabilitation of modernism and active promotion of cutting-edge modern art and music as cultural propaganda partly directed at Soviet bloc countries where governments continued to resist democracy and exercise a heavy hand against freedom of artistic expression.

For many European intellectuals, the trials and adjustments of postwar occupation were designed to address ideological issues of militant nationalism, cultural evolution, and identity construction radically tainted by government propaganda and the misappropriation of language. While many leading philosophers cynically sought to blame language itself, representing the collective will, for the misdemeanors of their political leaders, a number of writers and playwrights, including Eugene Ionesco, Samuel Beckett, and Raymond Queneau, found rich comic potential in exposing the inherent uncertainties of language employed as an instrument of power. Artists whose work had earlier been labeled "degenerate" and banned for a decade or more under National Socialist and Fascist regimes—art rejected as crimes against human nature—suddenly found themselves conscripted into an Allied publicity offensive in defense of freedom of speech under democracy, despite modernism continuing to be regarded with suspicion at home among their own people as an affront to fundamental principles of a common language, public order, and the collective will.

In 1946 the BBC launched the Third Programme, a domestic radio service for intellectuals whose lines of communication had been cut off for at least a decade and many of whom had been displaced. The consciously elite service reinforced an ideal perception of public service radio, at the time still a relatively young medium, as a forum of culture and intelligent debate for everyone and not just a private luxury for the well-to-do. Wartime Britain had become a refuge for exiled scholars, among them Nikolaus Pevsner, Ernst Gombrich, Egon Wellesz, Max Perutz, Erich Heller, Webern pupil Peter Stadlen, Schoenberg pupil Roberto Gerhard, Karl Popper, and others assisting the communications war effort as writers, interpreters, and cultural advisors. In 1945, overhearing a movement by Bruckner prefacing a radio broadcast from Berlin, art historian Ernst Gombrich, an exile from Vienna assisting the war effort as a foreign news monitor, identified the choice of work as a coded announcement of Hitler's death, which turned out to be the case.

Promoting music as a morale booster was taken very seriously in the years of reconstruction. The overhead drone of American cargo planes flying in with supplies during the Berlin Blockade is clearly audible in the background of a May 1949 radio recording of the Busoni Violin Concerto by the Berlin Philharmonic under Sergiu Celibidache, reissued on Membran (222121-444; a good piece, incidentally, worthy of comparison with Stravinsky's 1931 *Violin Concerto*). Among an older generation of subscribers, the provision of equal access to high culture for the masses remained controversial. Reviewing the BBC Third Programme's first year of operation, novelist Rose Macaulay welcomed the choice of an intellectually demanding production of the play *Huis Clos* (in English, *No Exit*), by Jean-Paul Sartre, commenting that the broadcast had been "a great success, one gathers, with the mass of listeners" and adding, "I hear that quite simple people, sitting listening in the provinces, say they and their maids found it most enjoyable."[1]

Throughout the war, audio companies in Britain and the United States had continued to improve the design of microphones and disc-cutting equipment for music recording, culminating in the development by Decca in England of "full frequency range recording," abbreviated to *ffrr*, high-definition audio of sharper quality than AM radio and requiring a higher-resolution disc material. This weak link in the audio chain was finally addressed in 1948 with the launch by Columbia (Stravinsky's record company) of the unbreakable vinyl microgroove long-playing record, offering silent surface audio playing at 33 1/3 revolutions per minute instead of the conventional 78. The new product, tracked with a lightweight pickup, contained upward of twenty minutes of music per side, transforming the record market. Symphonies and concert items of major length could now be conveniently and economically packaged. Composers no longer had to worry about constructing large-scale works in bite-sized four-minute chunks. The long-playing disc made *The Rake's Progress* a viable recording proposition for Columbia, as well as opening up an entire symphonic repertoire of Brahms, Mahler, Wagner, and Bruckner to the domestic market. Another radically new technology, tape recording, secretly employed as a tool of German radio propaganda in the latter years of hostilities, was seized and appropriated by the Allies as spoils of war, a technology destined to transform the commercial basis of music recording, broadcasting, the movies, and television, from the single take of traditional acetate disc recording to a movie-style cut-and-paste process, relatively easy to edit and correct for mistakes. Tape editing and program assembly converted a formerly passive studio operation into a creative playground for experiments in nonrealistic and synthetic sounds and noises, to be known as electronic music and *musique concrète* (music of concrete sounds or acoustical found objects).

As the Iron Curtain descended on Europe, the information war in the West saw advances in the peacetime commercial and intelligence applications of wartime code making and code breaking. Modern music was drawn into this research effort as a prototype of artificial language constructed according to grammatical rules. The rise of information science initiated a new and fashionable paradigm redefining human actions and choices, including language, as coded or programmed behaviors carrying hidden messages beneath the surface of conventional meanings and appearances. Intellectuals and artists of Auden's generation had used Freudian analogy rather loosely to explain the artistic subconscious as a source of creative inspiration beyond the conscious control of the individual. Similar thinking after the war was advanced elsewhere as a means of avoiding moral responsibility for criminal actions and choices. New cognitive science disciplines embarked on a concerted campaign to apply still-unproven theories and methods of wartime codebreaking to the analysis of social structures, media, marketing, and mass communication, an early and famous example being Marshall McLuhan's study of advertising, *The Mechanical Bride* (1951). Language, music, the arts, and the political process—all were considered afresh as *mechanisms* capable of being manipulated to influence the opinions and actions of target populations. Polling events such as President Truman's unexpected 1948 electoral victory were naively perceived as arcane electronic magic reading the subconscious mind of the American electorate.

To conform with the age of information processing, classical (notated) music was reevaluated as a language and the twelve-tone system of Schoenberg brought in from the cold as a prototype structuralist approach to language organization operating at a subliminal level. An early convert to presenting the arts and music as media environments was John Cage, who by the late forties was already launched on a program of inquiry into musical behavior as a conditioned response to latent stimuli in the real environment, in opposition to the conventional view of music as intentional activity whose purpose is to communicate information. Cage intuitively grasped the terms of reference of information science and cooperated with researchers at Illinois and Columbia universities, tasked to figure out where music comes from, in the process assuming a familiar role of sage or guru.

That Stravinsky took the implications of modernism, surrealism, dada, and chance operations seriously—and responded to them in his musical choices—can already be seen from the composer's adroit handling of classical metaphor and neoclassical idioms in his own musical speech, from the symbolism of the Fabergé egg representing a fragile Tsarist Russia in *Firebird*, and satire of local government in the fossilized bureaucracy of *The Nightingale*, to his adoption of despised gipsy and black American jazz idioms, along with the classically guised sociopolitical messages of *Les Noces*, *Oedipus Rex*, and *Symphony of Psalms*. A composer who describes *Oedipus Rex* as a *Merzbild*, brazenly juxtaposing ancient and modern history, is hinting that he knows what the artist Kurt Schwitters is about; equally, a composer of three major compositions—*The Soldier's Tale*, *Jeu de Cartes*, and *The Rake's Progress*, all of which turn on the fall of a card—is making a statement about the role of chance in his own musical decisionmaking. Long before Cage's *Music of Changes*, the multilayered rhythms of *The Soldier's Tale* already imagine a world of random juxtaposition similar to Messiaen's isorhythms in the *Quartet for the End of Time*, both evoking cyclical processes of theoretically indefinite extension of which the juxtaposition of cycles at any given moment of attention is implicitly arbitrary. The role assigned to the harpsichord in *The Rake's Progress*, carefully designated in the score as *cembalo*, ("optional keyboard") harks back to the menacing cimbalom of *Renard* but leaves open the possibility of its place being taken by a Bach *Lautenwerk*, or *Lyrichord*, a Mozart-era *fortepiano*, or Beethoven *Hammerklavier*, any of a range of keyboards, all tunable in theory to a disconcerting meantone or just intonation—or even bizarrely as a Cage-style prepared piano (I can hardly wait to hear pious recitatives in *The Rake's Progress* intoned against the fractured sound of Cage's *Sonatas and Interludes* as recorded by Alick Karis on Bridge [9081A] or Boris Berman on Naxos [8.559042]).[2] Cage's position in postwar modern music corresponds to the Joker in Stravinsky's musical card game, and throughout the *Conversations*, on the rare occasions that he mentions Cage by name, he does so with the respect due to a peculiarly American musical phenomenon.

* * *

> *Mass* (1944–1947) for male voice choir TrATB and double-wind quintet (*Works* 20:18–22); *Cantata* (1951–1952) for soprano, tenor, female chorus, and instrumental quintet (*Works* 20:11–17); *Septet* (1952–1953) for woodwind and string trios and piano (*Works* 12:8–10); *Three Songs from William Shakespeare* (1953) for mezzo-soprano, flute, clarinet, and viola (*Works* 15:30–32); *In Memoriam Dylan Thomas* (1954) for tenor, string quartet, and four trombones (*Works* 15:33–35).

Mass, *The Rake's Progress*, and *Cantata* form "The English Triptych" in Stravinsky's worklist. Stravinsky was determined to master the English language, the better to speak for himself, and to understand the measured English temperament that had prevailed against heated alien propaganda in the recent war. He admired the poetry of Shakespeare,

Auden, and Edward Lear and the clarity and impartiality of BBC speech, qualities with which he had already identified himself musically and philosophically in the *Poetics of Music*. In this connection, one of the odder encounters in the published Stravinsky archives is a meeting with guests the Evelyn Waughs in New York in 1949, an event duly noted in *Retrospectives*, reprinted in *Chronicle*, and mentioned in *Dialogues*. As a living example of the satirical tradition of Jonathan Swift and Alexander Pope, the English novelist belonged to an older and more truculent generation of Oxbridge literary intellectual than Auden, making him an ideal guide in principle to the character of Hogarth's Rake. The author of *Decline and Fall* and *Brideshead Revisited* depicts with surgical clarity the passage of a privileged English hero from dissolute adolescence to establishment figurehead and pious derelict in mature life. That Stravinsky prepared for *The Rake* by composing a mass is an act of piety asking to be compared with the fictional Charles Ryder's reconciliation to tradition at the end of *Brideshead Revisited*, in which the morally bruised narrator affectingly kneels in the abandoned chapel to murmur the words of a newly acquired catechism. So formal a gesture on the composer's part hints at readiness for a change of artistic faith, toward the twelve-tone system of Schoenberg.

In a scene reminiscent of W. C. Fields, Samuel Beckett, or Laurel and Hardy, Waugh and his wife appear at the hotel in full evening dress, an intimidating formality identifying the Stravinskys as enemy territory and their invitation to dinner a trap. The great Panjandrum of English Roman Catholic tradition refuses the offer of whiskey and caviar ("A gentleman does not take spirits before dining"), scolds his wife, and declines his hosts' invitation to attend the premiere of the *Mass*. Seated at table for a humble pasta meal at an Italian restaurant a short walk away, warming his Valpolicella over a candle, he unbends enough to confess that music of any kind is painful to him. His mood eases only upon realizing that his hosts are genuinely interested in him all the same and have read all of his books. An old-style English conservative, very different from the Auden generation whose youthful blend of Freudian dogma and socialist rhetoric Stravinsky finds hard to digest, Waugh in person nevertheless proves harder to talk to and decidedly less sympathetic than any one of his fictional heroes. Indeed, the author's intransigence serves only to enhance the composer's appreciation of Auden's compensating virtues of breadth of (non-English) culture and respect for music. It is an Englishness very different from the amiable cosmopolitanism that the composer is used to recalling as a guest of the Henry Wood, Eugene Goossens, Adrian Boult era of the twenties and thirties, and even further removed from the recent BBC image of composure under fire.

Insisting that his *Mass* is for church use, not for concert performance, Stravinsky reassures his religiously sensitive guests that his motive in setting the rite was not to treat it as concert entertainment but as a traditional form of worship in "very cold music, absolutely cold"—by implication, purged of all sentimental emotion (EWW 447). Perhaps a slight exaggeration, since the *Mass* is anything but frigid or unfeeling. Though sung in Latin, a remote language, in the pure tone of English choral voices crowned by boy trebles, the music is actually rich in expressive conventions and antique ornamental figurations of baroque derivation (accenting significant words or phrases, hesitations, tremors, etc.) that convey emotion just as clearly in an English ceremonial context as in old French or Italian traditions. The Hosannas are as jubilant as any Handel, the Agnus Dei serenely respectful. Of the Credo the composer insists, "I wished only to preserve the text in a special way," his way of saying that the text does not allow for subjective interpretation, no doubt to escape the charge of distorting its meaning in a bid to convert others. Of the few selected parts set to music, the Sanctus is perhaps the most controversial in marrying English aloofness with a highly inflected ornamental style closer to Middle Eastern cantillation, acknowledging the composer's lifelong affection for gipsy idioms and tearful slow movements, as noted in the *Pastorale*, the 1924 *Piano Sonata*, the *Violin Concerto*, and elsewhere.

The Rake's Progress is a number opera composed according to classical forms, set in modern English and outwardly critiquing modern values (responsible action, custom, uncertainty, and Auden's the Bourse) in loosely eighteenth-century terms. The opera's Englishness of subject matter is specific, as is the moral that where reason (words and rules) finds itself in conflict with love (empathy, music), love will prevail. *Cantata* by comparison is a sequence of stanzas and choruses to anonymous lyrics on the subject of faith and hope, written in a more hermetic style of English dating from the time of Shakespeare. What can only be described as the work's "flatness" or absence of perspective is a distinctively radiophonic feature. Whereas the sound of the *Mass* embraces height and breadth and ambience and the rite is timeless in implication, and *The Rake's Progress* is linear narrative unfolding more or less in real time and space, *Cantata* resembles a mural or *bas-relief*—a modulated surface in which time does not move; instead events are placed in an order and on the same plane with very little sense of development or spatial depth. It is as though in listening to it, one has the impression of walking past a musical object. Its relation to the listener is fixed, as with the radio or the gramophone but eliminating the qualities of animation and perspective of *Scènes de Ballet* or *Danses Concertantes*. *Cantata* outwardly shares the plagal cadences and muted palette of the slow movement of Ravel's war-weary *Piano Concerto* in G major (Naxos, 8.550753). Formally, it resembles the Mussorgsky *Pictures at an Exhibition*, a chain of events anticipating the verses and refrains of *Le marteau sans maître* by Boulez, and a reason perhaps why Stravinsky rated the latter work so highly. The name *Cantata* signifies "music to be sung" in the same way that *symphonies* implies "a sounding together" and *concerto* "a contest among instruments." The English qualities Stravinsky admires in his chosen texts, three of which are sacred, one secular, are directness, a sublime serenity, and moral integrity.

If *Cantata* were a picture, it would be Botticelli's *Primavera.* After the tragic separation of the two lovers in *The Rake's Progress*, a drama ultimately about masculine duty and the irreconcilable differences between reason and love, the new work to antique lyrics asks to be understood as a mystical (and once again, feminine) celebration of renewal and continuation of life. Significantly, the first song "The maidens came" is sung by a mezzo-soprano. Perhaps the song may have been intended for a boy treble, but even so a lyric on the life of Christ sung by a female voice in the first person is open to be read as a Marian complement to the pagan female sacrifice of *The Rite of Spring*.[3] It incorporates a striking recitative in C major to the words "Right Mighty and Famus Elizabeth," verses dedicated to Queen Elizabeth I, in 1952 no doubt inserted as a diplomatic genuflection to the future Queen of England (EWW 469).

Cantata's alternating solo soprano and tenor voices, singing from opposite pulpits like newfangled stereo speakers, and three-voice female chorus in between, deliver a constancy and immediacy of presence and evenness of tone matched to the intimacy of silent surface reproduction but less easy to deliver convincingly in a concert hall (a reason for suggesting that the work might be performed as a masque by costumed dancers in grave, courtly style, as well as sung). The instrumentation for two flutes, two oboes (II also English horn), and cello calls to mind a Monteverdian ensemble of descant recorders, shawms, tenor viol, and theorbo (bass lute), reconceived like the *Symphonies of Wind Instruments* in terms of a twentieth-century reed harmonium. Also harmonium related is the composer's use of octave doubling as a means of thickening individual lines. In a significant departure from normal custom, the composer has furnished an extensive and detailed program note in English (reprinted in full in EWW 469–71), to demonstrate his complete grasp of the language, as if to say, "From now on I will speak out for myself rather than let others speak for me"—a shot across the bows of self-appointed experts all too ready to shackle the composer to their own ready-made theories (Ansermet, Adorno, and Pierre Suvchinsky coming to mind).

Each song resembles a kind of dance within a restricted collection of notes, mostly white-note diatonic, evoking the interlaced weaving patterns of childhood nursery rhyme and folk dance. A distant echo of a wailing air raid siren is audible in both the imagery (fire, night, candlelight) and the five-note melody of "Lyke-Wake Dirge" ("This aye night") for chorus, assembled in four-note groups occupying adjacent intervals of a third—a type of figuration related in manner if not mood to the primeval Russian melodies of *The Rite of Spring*. Stravinsky's reorientation toward serialism begins here, based on the childlike idioms of Erik Satie and his own children's songs, the *Five Fingers*, *Waltz for Children* of 1918, and *Easy Pieces* for piano duo, all from the same period as the *Four Songs* recomposed for chamber ensemble in 1953–1954. For the longest and most striking canticle for tenor voice, "Tomorrow shall be my dancing day," the composer adopts a distinctive melismatic style suggesting a late medieval Spanish model that might almost have been purloined from the recently published Davison and Apel *Historical Anthology of Music*.[4] Richard Taruskin retrospectively accuses the composer of gratuitous antisemitism in the choice of an anonymous lyric telling of the betrayal and Crucifixion of Jesus, a misplaced piety overlooking the inconvenience that the lyric is what it is and its historic authenticity along with the moral challenge implied by its selection would be needlessly obscured if, as Taruskin continues to insist, the passage were to be suppressed.

Septet is Stravinsky getting down to work in a new, quasi-serial medium. The idiom combines the neobaroque style of "Dumbarton Oaks" and the carefree counterpoint of the much earlier *Octet*. Schoenberg's death in 1951 was a significant event, transferring responsibility for advocating modernism to Stravinsky, suddenly the leading survivor of his generation. A resumption of cordial relations with Pierre Suvchinsky, after more than a decade of disagreement over the merits of neoclassicism, led to a steady stream of information about the school of Messiaen, including the French composer's compositional method, the *Traité de mon langage musical* published in 1943, proposing interesting new ideas about timing, proportion, symmetrical formations, and serially compatible "modes of limited transformation." In particular Messiaen's pupil Pierre Boulez, who as early as 1948 was attracting attention as idiosyncratic analyst of the rhythmic language of *The Rite of Spring* and as outspoken critic of the Schoenberg school, creating a minor scandal in 1952 by declaring that the time of treating Schoenberg as the last word in modernism had passed and a new generation of serialists was taking over. Stravinsky's third movement Gigue—a virtuoso study of quasi-serial counterpoint in classic serial permutation—may be read in this context as a witty allusion to the relentless and long-winded contrapuntal style of Boulez's *Second Piano Sonata* (DG, 447 431-2).

Some find Stravinsky's approach to serial composition hard to categorize. Whereas for Schoenberg and Webern the unit of serial ordering is the note or interval, for Stravinsky the basic component is invariably the figure, or gesture, corresponding to the repeated note or trill identified by Manuel de Falla, or ornament of folk and baroque tradition (turn, trill, appoggiatura, etc.) from *Pastorale* to *Cantata*, which derive in turn from the distinctive inflectional signs of medieval plainchant (clivis, podatus, torculus, etc.). Assembling component figures into larger gestures has been the composer's method since the earliest compositions based on finger exercises or copied from folksong collections. For that reason it is a mistake to imagine, as Ansermet believed and others after him have persisted in alleging, that Stravinsky came to the twelve-tone method as a complete novice and *ingénu*. Of Webern's unit intervals, which the Swiss conductor, out of his depth, tried to argue were contrary to nature and "la conscience humaine," Stravinsky responded with an image combining Shakespeare and Hermann Hesse, "they are pearls"—pearls of wisdom and "pearls that were his eyes."[5] The fundamental distinction of Stravinsky's new method is in treating his basic figures of musical speech no longer as inexact terms of an exact tendency (the trill or turn as dither, the arpeggiated chord, the tremolo, etc., as elements of managed approximation of a mechanical piano roll simulation), as in *The Rite of Spring*, but now inversely as exact terms of a formal statement of potentially multiple meanings. It leads in *Septet* to the composition of dense fugue-like matrices, the purpose of which is to pack in as much information as possible, while ensuring that each thread is capable of being extricated from the mass by virtue of its distinctive shape and instrumental color—in other words, reinventing Bach counterpoint as an art of musical multiplexing for the Age of Information.

In the auction scene of *The Rake's Progress* the dialogue between Sellem and the bidding crowd is conducted in a curious speech reduced to virtually meaningless phrases: "La. Come bid! Aha! The Auk!" It appears as though the composer is seeking a fragmented nonsense speech resembling Ionesco's surreal English language primer in *The Bald Soprano* or even Raymond Queneau in *Exercices de Style* ("Ils vont se fiche des gifles! pour sûr! mais non! mais si! va h y! mords y l'oeil! fonce! cogne! mince alors!"; Queneau, "Exclamations," from *Exercices de Style* 59–60) or the plaintive "How's your mug? Better had!" spoken by Colette's English teapot in Ravel's *L'Enfant et les Sortilèges*. Quite apart from its comic potential, reducing speech to single gestures is a primary task in 1952 of computational linguistics (e.g., Noam Chomsky's "Colorless green ideas sleep furiously"), arguably as much a goal of Gertrude Stein in speech as of Anton Webern in music. The leaping, balletic intervals of "Passacaglia" and "Gigue" are therefore a kind of animated self-assembling language based on the spare, eloquent intervals of the second movement of Webern's *String Quartet* Op. 28, though infused with typically Stravinskian humor.[6] The art of composing atonally is an art of information management that avoids false connections in the form of unwanted (i.e., misleading) consonances but is open to tonal reference points as hubs of parallel coexistent functions. Instrumental timbre thus becomes a leading feature of a unit thread, like the color coding of wires in an electrical circuit. Music of this density can appear three-dimensional, like a hologram, in that the music may seem to change perspective with repeated hearings. Stravinsky uses exactly this form of words to describe the twelve-part variations for *sul ponticello* violins in the 1964 *Symphonic Variations*, which are twelve lines all of the same tone color, but the comment makes just as much sense and is easier to hear in relation to the *Septet*.

The *Three Songs from William Shakespeare* mark a new stage in Stravinsky's feeling for serial composition. The aerated texture and floating cadences of these delicious settings for mezzo-soprano, flute, clarinet, and viola (four instruments of similar range but complementary timbre, like the alto instruments of *Le Marteau* by Boulez, but more grateful) acknowledge the transparency and delicacy of Webern and his canonic imitations, without sounding anything like the Austrian master. The first of the three lyrics, "Musick to heare," makes a statement about how to listen to this new kind of singing calligramme, recalling the gestural style of the *Three Japanese Lyrics*. The subtle verse, Shakespeare's Sonnet VIII, is singled out by Auden in his "Homage to Igor Stravinsky," though curiously, nowhere in his essay does Auden refer directly to Stravinsky's setting of the poem (Auden, "Music in Shakespeare," in *The Dyer's Hand* 500–527). Despite an angular line that is sometimes hard to hear internally, the setting is exceedingly grateful and intelligible to sing. There is no fat in this music and also no added flavors. The songs are eloquent rather than ecstatic; all the same, they share the earlier songs' confident poise and demonstrate a sophisticated familiarity with English speech, the composer's turn of musical phrase perfectly complementing the poet's epigrammatic style. After Handel, Stravinsky may claim to be the best non-English composer in the English language, not only by virtue of his phrasing, but in the intelligence of his word setting, a rare quality even among native English composers. The choice of lyrics is designed to send a message to the listener about his new art, "the true concord of well-tuned sounds," a way of saying "trust me, just listen." There is a lightness and deliberate care in "Full fadom five," and high spirits in a laughing codetta, recalling Uncle Armand's gurgling bottle in *Pribaoutki*, and the birdsong of "Mazatsumi," that concludes a tongue-in-cheek setting of "When Dasies pied," Shakespeare's cautionary song about ladies tempted to stray in love in springtime. His success in *Three Shakespeare Songs* is reflected in the composer's strange and enchanting reinstrumentations of the *Two Balmont Songs* and the *Four Songs* at this time.

Stravinsky declined to use Auden and Kallman's "Delia, or Masque of Night" libretto, instead planning a second opera with Dylan Thomas on the subject of a postnuclear world obliged to reinvent language and culture. Little is stated on the record of how the poet came to the composer's attention. The subject matter of the proposed opera has an obvious relevance to the composer's adoption of a new serial language, already creating an impression as the pulverized "pointillist" avant-garde idiom of Boulez and Stockhausen, elements of which will emerge later in *The Flood*. When composer and poet first met, Dylan Thomas had published relatively little (his radio masterpiece *Under Milk Wood* did not appear on air until 1954, after the poet's death). By the end of the war he had garnished a reputation for himself as a verse speaker in classically themed BBC radio plays written and directed by Auden's friend the poet Louis MacNeice, and by 1952 Thomas's star was on the rise following a tour of the United States. Coauthor with Auden of *Letters from Iceland*, the Irish-born MacNeice had earlier been a member of the same Oxford group of young intellectuals that included Auden, Stephen Spender, and Christopher Isherwood. Stravinsky may even have considered hiring MacNeice on the strength of an acclaimed 1949 translation of Goethe's *Faust* for the BBC. Both MacNeice and Thomas combined serious alcohol addiction with powerful gifts of bardic oratory, clearly audible in the cadences and musical flow of their verse. After Thomas's sudden death Stravinsky made a movingly eloquent setting of "Do not go gentle into that good night," verses written in 1952 in memory of the poet's father. The setting is a perfect marriage of melody and poetic voice, showing a remarkable degree of sympathy considering the composer's natural tendency, as recently as *The Rake*, to impose his own Russian scansion on French or English words. Composed for tenor voice and string quartet, perhaps after the model of John Dowland, the elegy was subsequently extended by opening and closing solemn canzonas for four trombones, a gesture extending the piece's emotional range from private chapel to public ceremony, its instrumental symbolism, matching tearful strings against solemn, outgoing brass, evoking Monteverdi, Gabrieli, and Giovanni Priuli (Virgin, 7243 5 61288 2 8) as well as the Austrian school of Heinrich Biber and Johannes Schmelzer (DHM, 05472 77326 2).

Stravinsky's melodic line setting the opening words of "Do not go gentle into that good night" is strangely reminiscent of the haunting opening and closing melodies of the first movement of Bartók's 1936 *Music for Strings, Percussion, and Celesta.* Stravinsky's tenor line is raised a halftone in pitch, but the correspondence of intervallic contour and associated emotion is exact. That might not mean very much if it happened only once, but allusions to the same melodic and interval pattern are also encountered at critical moments throughout Stravinsky's late music, in *Canticum Sacrum*, *Threni*, *Movements*, and *A Sermon, Narrative, and Prayer*, through to *Abraham and Isaac*—always at the same pitch as *In Memoriam Dylan Thomas*, through to the terminal interval of *Requiem Canticles*.[7]

* * *

> *Greeting Prelude* (1955) for orchestra (*Works* 11:1); *Canticum Sacrum* (1955) for tenor and baritone solos, chorus SATB, and orchestra (*Works* 21:1–6); *Choral-Variations on the Christmas Carol "Vom Himmel Hoch" by J. S. Bach* (1956) for mixed chorus and orchestra (*Works* 20:1–6); *Agon* (1953–1957) ballet for twelve dancers (*Works* 4:11–26); *Fanfare* for three trumpets (1953; MusicMasters, 01612-67078); *Threni* (1957–1958) for six solo voices, chorus, and orchestra (*Works* 21:12–15).

Greeting Prelude, a cheerful mashup of "Happy Birthday to You" for conductor Pierre Monteux's eightieth-birthday celebrations, merits inclusion in the official worklist as an early exercise in a traditional musical form called the *canon*, an ingenious art of condensed musical autograph or *netsuke* cultivated by classical composers as a mark of skill to be written in the visitor's book of one's host. The children's round "Row, row, row your boat" and medieval "Sumer is icumen in" are relatively simple examples. Schoenberg's Op. 28 *Three Satires* for mixed choir (1925), poking fun at the composer he labeled "Der kleine Modernsky," are worked out examples of the genre, playing on the fact that a cryptic line of notes on a five-line staff can be read in a number of different ways, even upside down, to yield a substantial multipart composition (Arte Nova, 74321 27799 2). In 1971 Peter Maxwell Davies composed just such a *Canon* in memory of Stravinsky, and to be honest I have never yet been able to work it out.[8]

As an exercise in counterpoint on a commonplace theme, *Greeting Prelude* is the first of a number of nuggety canons that appear throughout the serial phase of the composer's life, in a technique that should not be too readily dismissed. Other examples include the *Epitaphium* and *Double Canon*, composed in 1959, and the *Canon on a Russian Popular Tune* of 1965. The art of canon is an art of manipulating musical code to create an enriched sign language that can be "read" frontward, backward, and even upside down—a form of encrypted wordplay connecting music from the dawn of notation to twentieth-century serial practice, by way of Bach fugue.

The *Canticum Sacrum* is the most Monteverdian of Stravinsky compositions and pays tribute to the genius and philosophical subtlety of the Venetian School in matters of time, space, and eternity ("Three Kinds of Space," in Maconie, *The Second Sense* 106–10). Following on after a number of works of close-microphone volubility, this is a measured music designed with a very specific, voluminous acoustic in mind, exploiting a range of more complex symmetries of near and far, left and right, up and down, pinched harp and timeless grand organ—an instrument rare in Stravinsky, who complained, "It does not breathe," but a logical ingredient in an instrumentation consciously organized in serial pairs and with unusual presence in the low bass register.[9] My favorite of a half-dozen selected recordings is still the Domaine Musical mono premiere recording conducted by Craft and reissued on Adès (203512), which in addition to being beautifully sung, captures the actual acoustic of the basilica of St. Mark's for which the work was composed, a complex five-domed space, stoneclad, with a long straight reverberation time.

A vibrant space calls for a declamatory music, and the dedication for tenor and baritone voices and accompanying trombones is loud and affirmative rather than meek and docile. It is followed by a summoning in-your-face noise, "Euntes in mundum," to match Messiaen on the organ at his most explosive and intimidating (the 1951 *Messe de la Pentecôte*, EMI, CZS 767400 2), or the stridency of Varèse, say *Déserts*, a work premiered with great success in 1954 (London, 289 460 208-2).

"Let us make love, and be drunk with love" is the tender message from the Song of Songs of "Surge aquilo" for an extraordinary combination of instrumental sounds. As male and female identities are merged in the song "The maidens came" for mezzo-soprano, in *Cantata*, so here a single male solo voice speaks for male and female. It is one thing to imagine sexual ecstasy in the warm, fricative texture of a trio of bass viols, resonating in harmony along with fluttering flute, twitching harp, and penetrating ejaculations of a high-pitched tenor (peaking at "*et bibite et inebriamini*"), and quite another matter to accomplish such a feat in the austere terms of Schoenberg's twelve-tone idiom—though Schoenberg himself certainly managed to do so in the "Dance of the Golden Calf" from *Moses und Aron*. This wonderful, explicit, erotically charged, and tender song is a perfect foil to Stravinsky's youthful Balmont songs, newly orchestrated for chamber ensemble. After it, a more solemn "Brevis motus cantilenae" for baritone solo and echoing choir offers a formal plea for continued faith—"Lord, I believe; help Thou mine unbelief"—faith in the composer's terms meaning to continue in the serial path. The choice of text throws some light on a frequent and presumably deliberate misquotation of St. Augustine, the composer preferring *Credo in absurdum* ("I believe in the absurd") to the conventional *Credo quia absurdum* ("I believe because it is absurd"). Since he knows Latin perfectly well, what Stravinsky appears to be saying, Cage fashion, is "No, I believe not *because* (*quia*) it is absurd" (implying conformity to an existing moral or value judgment), but rather "I [am bound to] believe *in the absurd*"—implying "because I do not presume to know for sure, and will not take anyone else's word, but desire to find out for myself," arguably a position of greater faith. (The word *absurd*, incidentally, signifies "out of tune.")

The ceremony ends with "Ille autem profecti," an exit mirror image of the earlier entrance music, a serial gesture to be compared perhaps with the ingenious descent and reverse ascent from Hades of Jean Cocteau's movie *Orphée* or the musical palindrome *Incontri for 24 instruments* by the young Luigi Nono, composed the same year. Following on from the *Three Shakespeare Songs* and *In Memoriam Dylan Thomas*, this transitional canonic idiom, part diatonic, part serial, is spare, well timed, elegantly contoured, and highly refined in color and shape. It is not surprising, given his rapidly acquired authority in the new medium, that Stravinsky eventually starts to weary just a little of the Webern-Hildegard Jone aesthetic of nature worship (the "Wie bin ich froh!" [How happy I am!] element) as just a tad *kitsch* (*Themes* 118; *Conclusions* 93).

Alongside the *Canticum Sacrum*, Stravinsky was intending to premiere a recomposition of a sacred song "Illumina Nos" by Gesualdo, for which at Robert Craft's suggestion he composed missing Sextus and Bassus parts. However, the St. Mark's authorities did not approve the performance of a work by a Neapolitan composer. In its place and for much the same musical forces, Stravinsky orchestrated J. S. Bach's *Canonic Variations on "Vom Himmel Hoch"* for unison mixed choir and instruments, a delightfully spacious and relaxed music that follows Bach in teasing the blocklike chord formation of the chorale into progressively more linear and dancelike counterpoint, the Russian composer from time to time inserting his own additional canonic voice, in Webernian dissonances, into the musical fabric like glowing jewels. Bach composed the original Variations for organ as a demonstration of skill, the skill residing precisely in his spinning blocklike vertical harmonies into scurrying linear patterns and floating webs of sound.

Agon is a suite of 12 dances, after French baroque models, grouped in threes and separated by a prelude and two interludes acting as refrains. The music was composed over an extended period of transition and incorporates diatonic and canonic exercises along with more serially integrated movements in Webernian aphoristic style. The title means "a dance contest or exhibition," and the work was commissioned by Lincoln Kirstein and George Balanchine for the New York City Ballet. Physical agility and a profound feeling for dance movement weld otherwise disparate styles into an energetic suite and inspire musical gestures and combinations of a wonderful leanness and often dazzling contrast. The humorous detail of animation and spatial projection of *Danses Concertantes* are combined with the kaleidoscopic invention of *Mavra* but without words getting in the way and slowing down the process. After ten years of composing dominated by word setting, Stravinsky returns to full-on ballet with a genuine appreciation of the greater speed and clarity of expression of dance.

A *Fanfare for Three Trumpets* survives from early sketches and is recorded by Craft, to whom the score was gifted. Along with *Canticum Sacrum* and *In Memoriam Dylan Thomas*, it shows Stravinsky developing multipart dialogue in the style of Gabrieli—giving rise to the "contest" implication of the title—but building the alternate relationship into a form of longer cadence suitable for dance. In the *Fanfare* and even more so in the opening Pas de Quatre of *Agon*, this means layering simple repeated notes, conceived as dynamic extensions of a single note (like long notes punched in a piano roll, as performed in the *Concerto for two pianos*), and building them into decorative turns and knots corresponding to question and answer. The composer then follows a procedure equivalent to (a) calling for attention, (b) greeting, (c) preparing for the first statement, (d) repeating the first statement for emphasis and adding an extension, (e) varying the extension, and so on. In other words, the musical statement is broken down into unit phrases and virtual punctuation and includes changes of emphasis and virtual error correction, a broken speech or dialogue in which each phrase may sound urgent, but collectively the sentence delivers relatively little information and at a measured, even slow pace. This gradualist development of individual lines is offset in *Agon* with great effectiveness, by sudden interruptions and alterations of musical texture, for example from trumpets and horns, suddenly to pointillist mandolin and plucked strings, then equally suddenly to high flutes and string harmonics and from classical canon to dense serial counterpoint, astonishing shifts in register, density, and color combination but linked together by a steady underlying pulse.

The suite form allows Stravinsky to experiment at will with extraordinary new sound combinations, from high flutes and low cellos in gurgling C major to xylophone and glissando strings to a solo violin cadenza with mandolin and piano reminiscent of *The Soldier's Tale* and in the Pas de Deux a more eloquent recitative, also for solo violin, in a style more reminiscent of Schoenberg. A great precision and economy of means emerges here as the composer's signature response to a newly concentrated twelve-tone idiom. In playful response to Stockhausen's *Gruppen* or a polyrhythm of Elliott Carter—or genial homage to a tapdancing Fred Astaire—in the Bransle Gay Stravinsky manages to play tricks with the audience's perception of a typical syncopation by overlaying the simplest of triple time rhythm, played by castanets, on the alternating sevens and fives of flutes and bassoons.

After the premiere of *Canticum Sacrum* Stravinsky traveled in Germany, calling on Herbert Eimert and Karlheinz Stockhausen at the electronic studios of Cologne Radio and receiving the seventy-fifth birthday gift of a brief electronic canon, *Zu Ehren von Igor Stravinsky* (In honor of Igor Stravinsky), in which a tape of Eimert's voice speaking the title dedication is passed through a Bell Labs vocoder, sliced into frequency bands, and the bands set orbiting at different speeds, eventually converging back together to allow the speaker's voice to reemerge. Vocoder technology had been used during the war to send coded messages from Winston Churchill to President Roosevelt, and the idea of exploded fragments of musical text flowing back in reverse, to reassemble as a coherent text, had already been employed by Stockhausen as a template for the chamber composition *Kontra-Punkte* (1953; Wergo, WER 6717-2). Stravinsky was impressed by Stockhausen and acquired scores and tapes, including *Kontra-Punkte* and the wind quintet *Zeitmasse*, which are an important influence on his last and most highly organized serial compositions of the sixties.

Dedicated to North German Radio, *Threni* (Threnody: Lamentations of Jeremiah) is a sacred cantata to texts from the Vulgate on the theme of suffering despair, working through prayer and repentance to renewal of faith. Since the chosen texts are recognized by Jewish as well as Roman Catholic worship, the work is open to interpretation as a rite of reconciliation with reference to the historic persecution of the Jews, as well as to the Holocaust. Set in a comparatively sober and urgent style, it is Stravinsky's most consistent serial composition to date and employs canonic refrains of a particularly mournful cadence for tenor and keyed bugle (a distant reference perhaps to the prominent roles of cantor and *shofar* in Jewish ritual).

Threni is an unfairly neglected work and led to a rift with Boulez, charged with preparing a Domaine Musical premiere with a pickup ensemble that in the composer's view was underrehearsed and not up to the standard to be expected of a major interpreter.[10] It may have something to do, perhaps, with the relatively bleak message and ecumenical sympathies of the new work, after the ebullience of *Canticum Sacrum* and witty athletics of *Agon*, recorded for Domaine Musical's Vega label by an ailing Hans Rosbaud. *Threni* marks a return to the high-speed cut-and-paste complexities of *Mavra*, unfolding at the speed of a Mack Sennett comedy. But the speed and subject matter suggest a world in fear and panic, a 1956 Invasion of Hungary world of people running in terror at the sound of crying solo voices and warning bugle, alternating with political dialogues of solemn voices in separate pulpits talking past one another.[11] *Threni* coincides in time and place with the premiere of *Differences* by Luciano Berio for chamber ensemble and tape, an ingenious but somewhat cynical reprise of Schoenberg's *Pier-*

rot Lunaire as performed by Albertine Zehme with accompanying instruments concealed behind a curtain. Here in the Berio piece, the visible live performance is gradually insinuated and overwhelmed by unseen prerecorded and electronically distorted continuations of the same music, an entertaining puzzle of "spot the performer" reinforcing a more sinister counterpropaganda implication "you can't trust what you hear on the radio." In the face of Berio's ultimately frivolous but beautifully executed student prank, *Threni* is a wake-up call, a message combining the austere musical language of the Webern cantatas (newly recorded for the Domaine Musical by Boulez) with the reawakened political conscience of *Oedipus Rex*. One has to admire Stravinsky's virtuoso combination of words of hope and reason conveyed through musical imagery of parliamentary debate and of politicians all talking at once. The work's bleak tone and subject matter are leavened by discreet but important innovations, including speaking and muttering choir and vocal noises (the choric "ssh" and "chh" sounds of letters of the Hebrew alphabet, which identify verses of De Elegia Prima and De Elegia Tertia [Aleph . . . Beth . . . Resh . . . Coph . . .]). There is an urgency in the composer's voice, a trend toward treating musical phrases as repeating elements in a tiled plane, punctuated by nuggety figures of musical speech in complicated rhythms and scurrying staccato choirs set against slower male voice cantilenas over sustained long notes in which time slows down almost to a stop. While technically not difficult to listen to, actually trying to beat time to this music is a lot harder than it looks, given Stravinsky's renewed interest in a music of multiple, seemingly independent time layers. In De Elegia Prima, for example, violins shimmer at high speed; female voices chant in eighth notes, a bugle in quarter notes, and the tenor solo in half-note or longer values (EWW 499). A particular novelty, which may have taken conductor Boulez by surprise, arises from simple-looking unaccompanied two-, three-, and four-voice counterpoints, notated exactly but on occasion Satie style, without barlines, as layered strips of music in the form of "a line going for a walk" in Paul Klee's phrase—fascinatingly difficult to compute, from "Plorans ploravit" and "Vide, Domine" canons for two tenors through to the intense double canon for four voices in De Elegia Prima and two-part polyphony of De Elegia Quinta. For exposed voices to sing independently in different rhythms, without assistance except to the cue of a conductor, is genuinely hard work, and addressed to a

Boulez or Stockhausen, both of whom at this time are composing vastly complicated scores in multiple timescales, while at the same time piously editorializing in *Die Reihe* and elsewhere about "aleatoric" theory of a music of independent time layers after the fashion of US composer Conlon Nancarrow and his *Studies for Pianola*,[12] their message is suitably terse and definitive: be careful not to assume the viability of graphic or conceptual complexities neither you nor your musicians can yet deliver.

10

LAST RITES

In 1957 the literary periodical *Encounter* published "Answers to 34 Questions" by Stravinsky and Robert Craft, the earliest appearance of what would finally be published in book form as *Conversations with Igor Stravinsky*, the first of a series of published opinions and reminiscences to be continued to the composer's death as a literary testament. The initial intention was to mark the composer's seventy-fifth birthday by publishing a dialogue to bring the message of *Autobiography* and *Poetics* up to date and perhaps to counter the slightly intimidating tone of these earlier, ghosted texts. The magazine *Encounter* was founded in 1954 with the assistance of US counterintelligence funding channeled through Nicolas Nabokov's Congress for Cultural Freedom and published under the joint UK/US editorship of Auden's friend Stephen Spender and Irving Kristol, as a kind of BBC Third Programme in print form, wideranging in intellectual scope, to feature articles by or about writers of the interest and caliber of Auden, Claude Lévi-Strauss, Samuel Beckett, Karl Popper, and Marshall McLuhan.

In publishing his views on the situation of modern music in trenchantly expressed but relaxed terms, Stravinsky may also have been concerned to counter a growing impression of the musical avant-garde as a specialist subject to be discussed only by a small Kafkaesque cabal of experts speaking a secretive, dystopian technical jargon. In speaking out as a working composer, he intends to reassure a musical readership, of the kind represented by William Glock and David Drew in Britain, Domaine Musical patrons in Paris, and supporters of contemporary music concerts in Los Angeles, that it is possible to enjoy new music and talk about it as a listening experience in simple language. An unsettling tendency to isolate, intellectualize, and polarize debate was beginning to emerge in periodicals *The Musical Quarterly*, *Die Reihe*, and Hermann Scherchen's *Gravesano Review*. At the same time, Stravinsky and Craft wished to defend the views of an older generation against the condescending and at times deliberately offensive dismissals of modernism by authorities on both sides of the fence, from the journalistic simplicities of Aaron Copland (author of the popular and misleading *What to Listen for in Music*) and major New York critics such as Paul Henry Lang (an antimodernist cultural general who, like Gilbert and Sullivan's Duke of Plaza-Toro, preferred to lead his readership from behind) to the vacuous sophistications of philosophical wordsmiths Adorno and Ansermet, weavers of elaborate arguments of no help to anyone but themselves.

Having contributed words of encouragement in support of the 1955 Webern special edition of *Die Reihe*, Stravinsky had been less than impressed at the earnest obfuscation of a majority of contributions. Discussing the letters of Webern in *Memories*, he complains,

> [Webern] contains no word of technical jargon (to Berg: "art must be simple") and no aesthetics ("I don't understand what 'classic' and 'romantic' mean").

And aiming directly at Boulez, author of the highly unreadable *Penser la Musique Aujourd'hui*, the composer adds,

> This Webern will embarrass "Webernists." They will blush for their master's "naïvety" and "provincialism." They will cover his nakedness and look the other way. (*Memories* 103–6 [UK], 97–98 [US])

* * *

Movements for piano and orchestra (1958–1959; *Works* 10:4–8); *Epitaphium* for flute, clarinet, and harp (1959; *Works* 22:3); *Double Canon* for string quartet (1959; *Works* 22:4); *A Sermon, a Narrative, and a Prayer* for alto and tenor soli, speaker, chorus, and orchestra (1960–1961; *Works* 21:8–10); *Monumentum pro Gesualdo di Venosa ad CD Annum*, three madrigals recomposed for small orchestra (1960; *Works* 19:6–8); *Anthem*, "The Dove descending" (T. S. Eliot) for choir SATB *a cappella* (*Works* 21:11).

Stravinsky's "high serial" phase is marked by a lean, virtually emaciated line and new attitude to musical time and space. By way of introduction, a listener may compare two very short works in canonic style, the *Double Canon* "Raoul Dufy in Memoriam" for string quartet and the *Epitaphium* for flute, clarinet, and harp, both works composed in 1959. The *Double Canon* is classical in conception, each of the four parts unfurling like a scroll, all on the same plane, as a layering of related intervallic shapes displaced in time and pitch in relation to one another but sharing the same time and space coordinates as a group. So this is "flat" musical patterning after the style, say, of a canzona for a consort of viols, inspired by the visual appearance of notes on the page. The *Epitaphium,* however, of precisely the same duration and similar general structure (of permutation by serial orders forward, retrograde, inversion, and retrograde inversion), alternates a flute and clarinet duo with plucked responses by harp in its low register, an unusual, muffled sonority. Here instead of a two-dimensional paper music, the oppositions are acoustical and three-dimensional: high woodwinds, sustaining instruments powered by the breath of life, alternating with low plucked strings, which are nonsustaining and quickly die away. It is as though the flute and clarinet are moving across linear time, whereas the harp notes and chords are intersecting time, cutting the thread of time, moving perpendicular to time in an acoustic sense, starting in front of the plane of the woodwinds and rapidly retreating through and into the far distance. A pictorial analogy might be Hans Holbein's painting *The Money-Changers*, the flat pictorial plane of which is diagonally intersected by a grim anamorphic shape that, viewed from an acute angle, is revealed as a skull.

This outwardly new sense of instrumental timbre as meaningful on its own plane of reality is latent in all classical music, not only modern. The troubadour with his lyre or acoustic guitar is just as aware of the imagery of mortality implied by the juxtaposition of sustaining voice and dying away plucked strings, continually demonstrating that tone of voice is imprecise but can be made to last, while string tone is stable but destined to fade, and so on. What is noteworthy about Stravinsky's conscious art of timbre composition is the way in which different qualities of attack and sustain are adopted into his serial method. Webern is an early example of the "tone color composition" composing genre, as are Messiaen's early adventures in pianistic serialism as well as John Cage's investigations in transforming piano tone by inserting objects between the strings. All play with the notion of serial (scaled) deconstruction of tone color into component parts of attack, steady state, and decay, building on Debussy-era research into the defining elements of piano performance and artistic personality, investigations in piano-roll technology undertaken by the reproducing piano industry manufacturing the same mechanical instruments to which Stravinsky devoted considerable attention during a lengthy period of his early career. So in reaffirming tonal identity transformations and relations as expressive variables in tape-recorded sound, through encounters with Varèse, along with Stockhausen's electronic studies, and French *musique concrète*, Stravinsky knew precisely what was going on and was able to draw on a wealth of his own experience in transforming live instrumental sound by pairing attack and sustain instruments in various combinations, already demonstrated in *The Nightingale*, *Les Noces*, *Mavra*, the *Capriccio* for piano, and a host of other works through to *Ebony Concerto*.

In the same way, he had long since formed clear views about the compatibility of various instruments: of bowed and plucked string sounds and strings versus woodwinds and in particular the reciprocal relationship of piano and harp. It became clear that this wealth of experience in evaluating the tone and continuity implications of different instruments could give him a considerable edge in composing serially. What Stockhausen's 1954 *Electronic Study II* clearly showed—thanks to an austerely elegant and methodically disciplined graphic score published by Universal Edition—was that changing the dynamic shape or envelope in which music of a given content is expressed can also affect its perceived acoustic character. By reversing the tape of a trumpet sound, for example, one could hear as if for the first time that the bright metallic quality of trumpet tone is confined to the first few microseconds, the "tail" sounding closer to a flute, and by time-reversing piano tone, that the percussive thud and ping of onset are followed by a long, somewhat noisy "tail" resembling the sound of an harmonium. By studying the follow-through of musical sounds more closely, new tone combinations came into view and with those new combinations, a more highly developed sense of musical sounds as objects, each harboring its own inner life, filter system, and built-in fader control.

Movements is a hugely exciting work, easy to listen to but hard to follow on the score page or to perform or conduct. The musical thinking is extremely concentrated and more intricately argued than Webern but curiously coherent to the ear. Though strictly a return to the Bach-era concerto grosso, composed after the pattern of a baroque orchestra led from the keyboard in which live instruments act the part of organ stops cued on command, Stravinsky's implied description of orchestral instruments as spinoff fragments of piano tone is also powerfully influenced by Stockhausen's *Kontra-Punkte*, a work in which a cluster of highly differentiated solo instruments circle around the piano metaphorically speaking and are eliminated one by one, audibly stretching a cloud of differently colored points of sound into lines and finally merging them into a uniform piano tone in the center. In *Movements* the piano is the grindstone, and other instruments, the sparks. The piano part seems to combine the scampering, gestural style of *Petrushka* with the permutational mathematics of Stockhausen's *Piano Pieces I–IV*, especially in the building of small groups of notes into lines and chords characterized after the mathematician Euler as beginning separately and ending together or beginning together and ending separately and so on. Initially, the music is composed largely in three-note groups, suggesting a quasi-serial running orchestration of piano, woodwinds, brass, and strings in groups of three. Certain notes appear as designated resting points or pivot points, and the whole extension of the keyboard from bottom to top is maintained in play.

There are five short "movements," separated by brief interludes. The first is binary, in two halves, the opening half being repeated (the speed of ideas is such that a listener barely has time to blink before it is all over and beginning again). It opens with a vigorous "sneeze" for flutes and trumpet, followed by a cascade of notes like the sound of a pinball machine, bouncing down to a low A flat, accented by bass viols. For listeners with perfect pitch, the A flat is a pivot note, immediately leaping up an octave to the cellos, then up another octave in pizzicato, to be caught and held by the piano. Another signal to listen out for is the interval of a fifth, initially C sharp–F sharp, first in the piano, then the violins, and repeated soon after at the same pitch by two trumpets.

Middle C ("the half-way mark") is another point of repose, at the cadence before the repeat and leading into the movement's second half.

During the first movement the piano is accompanied in turn by multiples of the same class of instrument: bowed strings, woodwinds, brass, harp plus pizzicato low strings and so on—each of distinctive composition and texture (legato, staccato, simultaneous, arpeggiated, turbulent, etc.). There is virtually no time for a listener to digest one phrase before another takes over, so even though the texture is relatively lean, the complexity of relations is aurally difficult to process. At the end of the first movement, the piano solo seems to pause and tick over like a piston engine, with coughlike interruptions by the harp.

A slower second movement introduces balalaika-like tremolos in piano, harp, and fluttertongue trumpet, offset by lyrical strings. An angular, assertive third movement recalls the click and play of snooker balls and signals a return of the F sharp–C sharp signal in open fifths, first on trumpets, then squealing on oboe and clarinet, the movement ending with a brief explosion of high-speed flutes, sounding like a tape rewind, over a humming tremolo on low clarinet. A nocturnal fourth movement is relatively easy to follow, divided in three subsections each defined by a luminous "starlight" of sustained high open-fifth string harmonies, beneath which the bright piano interacts with cooler woodwinds and a shadowy quartet of cellos.

A very loud sneezing intermission introduces the fifth and final, most complicated movement. Here the music seems to accelerate like electronic music into the stratosphere, with multiple layers appearing to speed up and slow down independently, after the style of Elliott Carter. It eventually rises to a glass ceiling of sustained cello harmonics, against which two flutes hammer with accelerating speed until it shatters into myriad fragments which tumble, then reform on a second hammering chord calling everyone to order in the manner of a suspended cadence or musical question mark. The work ends *Petrushka* style with a coda of gestures in which the piano sound is translated first into a harp, then a distant celesta, solo strings drawing the work to a close with a legato reprise of the opening tone row, gliding down to earth with a gentle thud. Of special interest among a host of alternative recordings is a startling 1984 radio recording by Sviatoslav Richter and the Moscow State Conservatoire orchestra under Yuri Nikolayevsky (Revolution, RV 10093), not only for reasons of interpretation and recorded balance, but for a wonderfully tearful string sound and overall dancelike sensibility, at times Tchaikovskian, that brings vividly to life the Russian emotional antecedence of this outwardly alien, abstract music.

While others talked their way through the late fifties and early sixties, Stravinsky, Craft, Lawrence Morton, and Goddard Lieberson of Columbia joined others in implementing programs of recording neglected new music. Such initiatives, taken up by a number of manufacturers, including Philips and DG in Europe and Time/Mainstream in New York, were only possible as a direct consequence of the long-playing record becoming available, initially in mono, then after 1956 in stereo (of inconsistent quality). Stravinsky helped by making available time allocated to recording his own complete works, to assist Craft in the preparation and recording of premiere editions of Schoenberg, Webern, and Varese, to make this music available to the public, bypassing the involuntary censorship of orchestra managements, influential critics, and broadcast media. The first complete Webern edition was an extraordinary project to take on, requiring Craft to unearth and prepare a wealth of material, a goodwill gesture for which neither Stravinsky nor his junior colleague would receive more than grudging acknowledgment, achieved in the face of continued antagonism among followers of Copland, Leonard Bernstein, and others, toward the music of Schoenberg, Berg, and Webern, and coy reluctance to recognize and support the innovations of Americans Carter and Cage, let alone interesting mavericks Henry Brant and Harry Partch. The hostility extended to Stravinsky himself, emerging in a pattern of criticism made on the record by academics, attacking the composer's opinions by questioning their authenticity, and accusing Craft of putting words in his mouth, accusations allowing detractors to avoid having to respond to the composer's criticisms. The unpleasantness continues today, needless to say, in heavyweight recent publications by a new crop of revisionist academics, the admitted purpose of which has been to discredit the composer's modernist twelve-tone aesthetic by ignoring or misreading the music in favor of the easy option of besmirching his personal character.

The politicization of musical modernism reached break point with the appearance of *Perspectives of New Music*, a new periodical of US critical opinion published under the auspices of Princeton University and a distinguished editorial advisory board including Milton Babbitt and bearing a distinguishing logo resembling a printed circuit designed by Stravinsky himself. In Europe, avant-garde loyalties were rapidly splitting into factions: Boulez's Domaine Musical severing connections with *musique concrète*, shedding Hans Werner Henze, Cage, and Xenakis from its "A" list (Xenakis signing up to Konstantin Simonovic's rival Ensemble Instrumental de Musique) and almost coming to blows with Stravinsky over the *Threni* debacle. In the musical press, fights broke out between *Die Reihe* and *Gravesano Review*, the former refusing to carry articles on *musique concrète*, audio engineering, or Xenakis, the latter ignoring Boulez and Stockhausen while publishing articles by or about Milhaud, Xenakis, and Nietzsche, along with professional papers on acoustical matters and technical innovations. *Perspectives* flexed its journalistic muscle by enticing a scientist to critique *Die Reihe* contributors and their theories, alleging gross misuse of technical terms, a risky strategy backfiring on both sides. A rare exception, Dr. Werner Meyer-Eppler, Stockhausen's associate and mentor, who in addition to impeccable scientific qualifications had good connections with the US information science community, managed to escape editorial censure and publish freely in all three periodicals.

In such a fractious climate, it is tempting to interpret the message of Stravinsky's *A Sermon, a Narrative, and a Prayer* as a plea to all involved to shake hands and make up. In three parts, the new cantata with attached melodrama on the New Testament story of the Martyrdom of St. Stephen (a somewhat more pious message than Gabriele d'Annunzio's lurid *Le Martyre de Saint Sébastien* a half-century earlier, to music by Debussy of a stoned serenity) could almost bear the subtitle "the trials of Craft by the high priests of the new conservatism." The work is dedicated to Paul Sacher, who back in the thirties had preferred Igor the Younger (Markevitch) over Igor the Elder, the latter returning the compliment, as we recall, with a commissioned "Basle" *Concerto in D* for string orchestra of unprecedented ferocity. Now with this new commission Stravinsky was able to use Sacher's patronage as a convenient mask to launch a covert attack on the new Pharisaism, starting with the "Webern cultists," extending to the high priests of *Die Reihe* and the powerful Copland/Bernstein axis who refused to acknowledge Schoenberg. For a composer ready to rebuke Britten for "bounteous literalisms" in *War Requiem* (*Themes* 13–14; an indiscretion tactfully omitted from the English edition), *Sermon, Narrative, and Prayer* is unusually rich in expressive coloring, from excitable string tremolos suggesting divine radiance, loud angular melodies to express crowd anger, and pizzicato "gnashing teeth": a comic bassoon and oboe *fugato* to parody the academicism of the men from the synagogues, to swooping crescendos to accompany the words "the Lord is a consuming fire"—a gesture exactly reprised in the *Anthem* "The Dove descending" to T. S. Eliot's verses (*Expositions* 155–58). After the stoning of Stephen, an episode staged in the style of a spaghetti Western, silence falls with a breezy woodwind shimmer suggesting a classic tumbleweed moment. It is just so obvious. In *Dialogues* Stravinsky distances himself from Berg's expressionist musical language, describing it as a musical antithesis to himself:

> What disturbs me about this great masterpiece [*Wozzeck*] and one that I love, is the level of its appeal to "ignorant" audiences, with whom one may attribute its success to: (1) the story; (2) Bible, child sentiment; (3) sex; (4) brevity; (5) dynamics, *pppp* to *ffff*; (6) muted brass [etc.]. (*Dialogues* 124)

The charitable answer to the criticism that Stravinsky is covering his own expressionist tracks in *Sermon, Narrative, and Prayer* is that the expressionist features of his work are done not to impress ignorant audiences but have a serious rationale. A more apt comparison might be Schoenberg's *A Survivor from Warsaw*, the connection being that both it and "Sermon" are story-board narratives in comic strip style, in which spoken dialogue and narrative reach a climax by bursting "out of the page" and into song. For Schoenberg, the emotional climax is when the prisoners break silence with a hymn of faith as they are led to death. In "Sermon," the text of which is "We are saved by hope," the message is rather about suddenly getting the point. The choir intones a rather elusive passage "hope that is seen is not hope," difficult to understand, then a tenor, sings, in effect, "Aha! I get it: you cannot *hope* for what you already *know*, so not knowing for certain is what it is to have faith." The epiphany moment is dramatized by the choir (to the accompaniment of tremolo strings) as a Pentecostal moment, in the transition from muttered speech to more firmly intoned speech, finally to condense on a dazzling and timeless harmony on the word "faith"—harmony shadowed by a quartet of violins to convey the effect of added reverberation.

Both the transition from speech to song and the acoustical implications of the sudden epiphany can be related to an experience of tape-reversed speech and the transition from highly reverberated to anechoic speech or song as experienced in studio recording, in circumstances where reverberation can be added at will and instrumental sounds played back to front. In this case Stravinsky appears to be imitating the effect of tape-reversed sounds, despite the words being the right way around, since in acoustic terms the transition from vague quiet murmurs to clear speech, then erupting into full-frontal song (harmony frozen in the moment, incidentally) suggests Stravinsky is drawing on a perceptual vocabulary of electronic music, specifically *Gesang der Jünglinge* by Stockhausen, possibly also on the "Pfingsoratorium" *Spiritus Intelligentiae Sanctus* by the composer's friend and serial confidant Ernst Krenek, a tape composition for prerecorded choir created at the WDR Cologne Radio electronic music studio with Stockhausen's assistance.

In retrospect, the "Narrative" is seen to follow comic-book layout and style, a narrative genre in which continuity text and dialogue telling the story are treated on multiple levels with considerable sophistication, as voiceover, caption, speech bubble, background noise, and overprinted sound effects. Stravinsky moves with ease from unrhythmicized speech to notated parlando and from there to solo song and choir. As previously in *Cantata* and *Canticum Sacrum* ("Surge, aquilo"), the gender implications of male and female voices are ignored in favor of creating the appearance of a hybrid, asexual voice of extended range, perhaps a living version of Olivier Messiaen's favored *Ondes Martenot*. A sense of deep enveloping reverberation is conveyed in the final "Prayer," a setting of words by Thomas Dekker, in which a plea for grace intoned by legato voices in serene counterpoint floats over cavernous, resonant noises in the deep bass, including three tam-tams, a novel timbre acknowledging *Chronochromie* (1959–1960) also by Messiaen (DG, 445 827-2).

* * *

Eight Instrumental Miniatures for chamber ensemble (1962; *Works* 11:21–28); *The Flood*, a musical play (dance drama) for television

(1961–1962; *Works* 18:3–9); *Abraham and Isaac*, a sacred ballad for baritone and chamber orchestra (1962–1963; *Works* 22:5); *Elegy for J.F.K.* for baritone and three clarinets (1964; *Works* 15:36); *Fanfare for a New Theatre* for two trumpets (1964; MusicMasters, 01612-67078-2).

In revisiting and orchestrating the *Five Fingers* piano pieces of 1921, Stravinsky is not just filling in time and exercising a nostalgia for childhood. The "weaving patterns" of childhood and folk music artlessly composed in his former life as a loving father are now subjected to new scrutiny as studies in instrumental possibility after the dense style of the *Septet*. The transparent originals are transformed into coruscating noises reminiscent of György Ligeti's *Atmosphères* (Teldec, 8573-88261-2) or indeed, of a speeded-up *Durations I–V* (1960–1961) by Morton Feldman, both of which register on the ear as radiophonic "sounds of delirium or dissolving consciousness" or alternatively as works broadcast from a great distance and transmitted on a slightly out-of-focus radio frequency.

Stravinsky's production in rapid succession of a triptych of cantatas on Old Testament subjects may also have something to do with moviemaker John Huston's grandiose plans for an epic production of *The Bible: In the Beginning* . . . to a screenplay by Christopher Fry, with episodes of the Creation, Noah's Flood, and Abraham and Isaac, along with *Babel*, for which Stravinsky was rumored to have been approached to provide the music. In 1966 the movie was eventually released with music by Japanese modernist Toshiro Mayuzumi and, interestingly, Ennio Morricone, composer of *A Fistful of Dollars*, the classic spaghetti Western starring Clint Eastwood. All mention of Stravinsky's association with Huston has been expunged from the official record, but even as a rumor its effect is to focus the mind wonderfully on the impact on the composer of working to Hollywood rules and would help to account for the literalisms of his developing serial language, as well as the striking (and, I think, welcome) Brechtian idiom of *The Flood*, in which librettist Craft sets Old Testament speech to one side in favor of a plain style of news television.

In its adapted form as a song-and-dance drama for television, producers were faced with the almost impossible task of overcoming the sonic limitations and poor visual resolution of the small screen—a challenge, I feel, that has still to be managed successfully. In its other life as a concert item, a different set of challenges arises of expanding the musical action to fill a concert hall and managing the flow of events so that a highly edited television montage structure, in which close-ups and camera action are designed to play defining roles, also makes dramatic sense as a continuous performance observed from an audience's long-distance perspective. Perhaps cameras onstage in the action and back-screen projections, as for a Rolling Stones concert, might provide answers.

But the music and the words are a wonderful match and a great success. Personally I am relieved that, having sought the advice of Marianne Moore, Craft as librettist has decided against preserving any of her countersuggestions, which show little understanding of the requirements of heard speech as distinct from words on the page (*Retrospectives* 227–29, *Chronicle* 296–96). *The Flood* is a serious work of great good humor, very witty musically and showing a perhaps surprising empathy and respect for the Hollywood animation industry and its craftsmen composers. One to bear in mind is MGM's Scott Bradley, virtuoso of cartoon expressionism and composer for the surreal Tex Avery: Bradley's fingerprints are detectable in *Movements*, "Narrative," and *Symphonic Variations* (the trumpet scream at [67]). Another is Warner Brothers' Carl Stalling, musical powerhouse of Bugs Bunny and Daffy Duck (Warner Bros., 9 26027-2).[1]

The opening and closing eruptions of Chaos as string tremolo "white noise" after Ligeti, out of which trumpet and trombones are hurled to fall to the ground as piano tones, are beautifully done, the "stairway to Heaven" for woodwinds and harp an ascending inversion of the descending stairs at the beginning and ending of *Orpheus*. The choral Te Deum is composed as a suitably never-ending round, and, as in his earlier *Babel*, Stravinsky conveys the words of God indirectly, here as a bass duo, against a thundering backdrop of bass drum as if to suggest electronic modulation of voices and drum, to give the impression of the Lord speaking with a voice of thunder. The Temptation in the Garden of Eden is delivered to music of a laconic and terse sinuousness, the Building of the Ark a wonderfully energetic dance alternating simple repetitive rhythms and figures of musical speech in homage to Edgar Varèse, with brilliant *fioriture* of enormous multipart complexity but at the same time great group dynamics, like the concerted movements of a flock of birds, or a shoal of sardines in a nature movie, accelerating to an electronic climax in a burst of pizzicato violins exactly matched to the click of a marimbaphone (note to Oliver Knussen: *medium* sticks!) that sounds like a sudden rewind on tape (Alas! such burbling sounds have become a thing of the past, since the arrival of digital recording).

Following an engaging Comedy for square dance caller (a sly insertion of ethnic *sprechstimme*) inviting the animals into the Ark two by two, Noah's wife—depicted after tradition as a little the worse for drink—is cajoled and persuaded to ascend the gangplank for her own safety. The Flood scene that follows is a masterpiece of plain design and crafty instrumentation suggesting, as the composer says, "not waves and wind, but time." The listener is submerged up to the neck, floating in a bottomless harmony broken by occasional gurgles, and rocked by the blast of alto trombone alternating with horn, high above which flutes and violins flutter and wheel like petrels in a storm. An extraordinary evocation of inescapable spiritual and physical limbo, a relentless and enduring presence, oscillating in expanding cycles to a maximum stretch, then, with a flurry and groan on tuba, reversing and contracting until suddenly lifting like a tornado from the surface back into the sky to a repeat flash of musical lightning. After the Flood the play structure goes into reverse, as it were, with a return of choir voices singing the Te Deum, an ominous reemergence of Lucifer as Satan, the eternal tempter, a brief reprise of Chaos, and reappearance of the Stairway to Heaven, ascending and vanishing into the light.

Commentators are divided on the success and merits of the original 1962 television production and of the work as a stand-alone concert item. We have come a long way since then. My own view is that these late works need to be taken seriously and looked at afresh by production teams, especially in respect of visual and acoustic balance and spatial realization. *The Flood* offers rich possibilities for a computer-aided (literally) immersive experience. Acoustically, the challenge is no greater in principle but also no less than the Monteverdi *Vespers* of 1610, a work of major length exploiting a great variety of delicate and powerful spatial effects and richness of musical symbolism.

Without the railroad, there would be no timetable, and without the timetable, no sense of time. The message of the Gary Cooper movie *High Noon* is not about things that happen but about waiting, not for Godot, but for the toot of an approaching train. The sense of appointment with destiny is a Stravinsky trait. In *Oedipus Rex* the king is caught unawares and the awful truth of his past suddenly revealed; in *Orpheus* the hero is undone at the last moment by acting too soon. In more recent times, Stephen faces his accusers and accepts punishment, while a wily old Noah heeds the Lord's admonition and escapes doom with his family and other animals by building an Ark. For most people the modern theme of waiting and how to deal with it is a by-product of air travel, but in dealing with boredom in a musical sense, a listener is able to develop new perceptual skills in appreciating the time sense of other cultures. In this as in many aspects of post-1950s western music, Cage is the bellwether, and his silent composition *4'33"* the benchmark, and when Stravinsky looks forward in gleeful anticipation to further silent compositions of concert-length proportions (*Themes* 18–19; *Conclusions* 29–31), he is not criticizing the silence, merely reminding readers that a benchmark is only a benchmark.

The beauty of the composer's choices is that his stories are authentic, and he treats them with the most proper respect and tact but in such a way that a listener is obliged to acknowledge a message that is not always entirely comfortable. *Abraham and Isaac* is about duty, obedience to higher authority, sacrifice, and the agony of contemplating sacrifice, experienced in real time as father and son trudge toward the appointed location in the wilderness where the sacrifice is to take place. Adding to the drama is the father's knowledge of what has to be done and the boy's ignorance of what is to befall him. All of what happens is learned through the third person of a baritone voice, since father and son do not speak or even appear, on top of which the narration is delivered in Hebrew, an authentic but to many listeners alien tongue.

The sense of observing an alien ritual of unrelieved starkness is deliberate and unflinching, like the story, leading one to suspect that Stravinsky was influenced to model this latest drama on Japanese Noh theater, which is very spare and austere, and to some degree on the Japanese-inspired miniatures of Olivier Messiaen, *Sept Haïkaï*, composed in 1962 (DG, 453 478-2), short but intense snapshots of Japanese culture from a European viewpoint. Messiaen, unlike Stravinsky, is an organist by profession, and for that reason his sense of time (of waiting for fingers to move) is very different from that of a composer for the ballet, where there is always a presumption of imbalance leading to movement.

Technically, this is a music of extraordinary sophistication in which the volatile colors of *Agon* are combined with a flexibility of time layering owing more perhaps to Elliott Carter than to Stockhausen or Berio, though all are present in some degree (Berio in the cadenza for flute at [89], more voluble than the Japanese equivalent, the shakuhachi).

> I had been watching the Kuramatengu play in Osaka one afternoon recently and had become accustomed to the Noh flute. Later, in a restaurant, I suddenly heard an ordinary flute playing ordinary (well-tempered) music. I was shocked, music apart—I think I should keep the music apart anyway—by the expressive poverty of the *tuning*. (*Memories* 121 [UK], 116 [US])

In the absence of harmony, which in any case is a largely Western phenomenon in music, a listener is bound to listen more closely to nuances of intonation (which is almost where we came in). But the same sensitivity to microtonal shifts is also a necessity in the world of electronic music, so it is not a retrograde step but rather refining the experience to combine a highly inflected and extremely relentless and demanding vocal line—demanding in the sense of "Tomorrow Shall Be My Dancing Day" of *Cantata*—with interweaving lines of unusual combinations of texturally contrasted solo instruments, temporal canons after Messiaen and Carter, punctuated by momentary flashbacks for string orchestra. I suspect that only when listening with the dispassionate attention of an audio engineer, not worrying about the narrative and its implications, is it possible to begin to appreciate the inherent humor, familiar to Darmstadt audiences, of music ritual that at the same time is a rite of endurance for its intended audiences, a hard lesson in paying attention and showing respect. At the same time, there are traps to be avoided: the tuba for example is Abraham's "voice," not a comic turn: it should sound choked and under pressure, which is the emotion of both character and narrative. Instrumental roles need to be clear and distinct, as though recorded in an anechoic environment with separate microphones and balanced by hand (in concert this means with good separation of all instruments). The defining sound of this tactile music, for me at least, is not so much the singer as the iridescent scrape of bow on string.

Elegy for J.F.K. honors the late president in a setting of a short, plain verse by Auden: "When a just man dies, sorrow and joy are one," to the plaintive, dark sound of a trio of clarinets. The lyric is deliberately detached from the terrible circumstances of the assassination, strangely calling to mind the circularity of T. S. Eliot's comforting message in *Little Gidding*, from which "The Dove descending" is sourced, in the lines "Every phrase and every sentence is an end and a beginning, Every poem an epitaph" as if to say that grief at one dying acknowledges joy at the person's having lived. I have speculated elsewhere (Maconie, "The Poetics of Milton," in *Avant Garde* 179–200) that the choice of three clarinets is both symbolic and allusive: symbolic as "ebony" instruments, hence black, hence in mourning, also in another sense because the clarinet is alto relative of the basset-horn, an instrument of Masonic symbolism and ceremonial significance since the time of Mozart and Haydn and because its dark, hollow timbre is appropriate for mourning. On yet another level, among wind instruments the clarinet timbre most closely resembles square wave electronic sound from a primitive synthesizer; well blended and performed with appropriate plainness, therefore, the three clarinets could give the impression of a Milton Babbitt–style electronic accompaniment or, failing that, of Stravinsky's favored instrument from the era of Debussy's death, the *orchestrelle* or paper-roll harmonium.

Fanfare for a New Theatre (original English spelling) dedicated "to Lincoln [Kirstein] and George [Balanchine]" is a thirty-two-second wake-up call, to be delivered virtually in a single breath, like a high-speed reprise of a two-voice counterpoint from *Threni*. A manuscript score was donated to John Cage for inclusion in a symposium, *Notations*, published in 1969, where its first page can be viewed opposite a page of working notes by Stockhausen for *Telemusik* (1966) and some distance away from a spidery example from Boulez's *Second Sonata for Piano* (1948). Its brevity and speed, considered as a modern *canzona* after Gabrieli, create interesting issues of synchronicity and perspective in a concert setting. If the two trumpets are standing on opposite sides of the platform or perform from opposite balconies (as might well be the case), it will not be easy for them to synchronize, since each player will hear the other with a delay of up to a twelfth of a second, while playing at a speed of four to six notes per second, and it will be the same for the audience as well. Second, fanfares are designed to set up a vibration, bring the acoustic of the concert hall to life, which is bound to add to the confusion in interesting ways. So this minifanfare, despite its clarity of outline on the page and on record, may well come across in real life as an impressionistic blur resembling the chattering of a high-speed (1960s) computer printer.

* * *

> *Variations* (Aldous Huxley in Memoriam) for orchestra (1963–1964; *Works* 22:6); *Introitus* (1965: T. S. Eliot in Memoriam) for male voices and ensemble (*Works* 21:7); *Canon on a Russian Popular Tune* (1965) for orchestra (MusicMasters, 01612-67177-2); *Requiem Canticles* (1965–1966) for contralto and bass soli, chorus, and orchestra (*Works* 22:7–15); *The Owl and the Pussy-cat* (1965–1966) for soprano and piano (*Works* 15:37); *Two Sacred Songs* from the *Spanisches Liederbuch* (Hugo Wolf) arranged 1968 for mezzo-soprano and chamber ensemble (DG, 4778730); *Two Sketches for a Sonata* (1966–1967) for piano (MusicMasters, 01612-67152-2).

"It really is in groups," said Stravinsky approvingly of Stockhausen's *Gruppen* for three orchestras (*Memories* 118–20 [UK], 112–14 [US]). Along with the wind quintet *Zeitmasse*, it is a score from which he took a great many ideas in orchestration and form. During the fifties the admiration was mutual: Stockhausen and Boulez both adopted the cimbalom, and Stravinsky's use of the piano in *Agon* as a bold melody sonority rather than a harmony instrument is one of several features of *Gruppen* he expressly admires. *Variations* is more than a late gesture in acknowledgment of Schoenberg's Op. 31 *Variations for Orchestra* of 1928, though the pair would make a fascinating coupling. Stravinsky distinguishes his take on "variations" as "alterations or mutations" in the sense of the German *Veränderungen*, from a "Theme and Variations" in the conventional sense. In this he is closer to the principle of the Bach *Chorale-Variations* but with the important distinction that, instead of teasing a harmonic sequence of block chords into a tissue of counterpoint, Stravinsky has attempted the reverse, to rein in and concentrate the melodic and contrapuntal possibilities of serial manipulation into a faceted or cubist interplay of block formations.

The opposition of "points" and "blocks" was first enunciated by Boulez, in relation to his *Constellation-Miroir*, from the Third Piano Sonata of 1957 (a work still incomplete at the time of writing in 2012). It is a linguistic and electronic music distinction, "points" referring to the instantaneous or onset qualities of a syllable or note and its location in pitch and time, "blocks" to the tail or residue that has extension in time. The philosopher Alfred North Whitehead said, "We live in snippets too quick for thought": he was talking about how the mind works and of the disparity between the instantaneous nature of words and photographs on the page, in relation to the multiple timescales of experience brought to bear on their interpretation and recognition in real time. In *Variations* Stravinsky is creating a new timescale of orchestral music that taps into the speed and circuitry of memory rather than unfolding in real time or at reading pace. In the same way as ballet, unencumbered by words, is quicker in telling a story than song, so this music is designed to act even faster than the physical body, indeed communicate at the speed of thought.

In 1962 the French art house moviemaker Chris Marker created a remarkable movie called *La Jetée* (the title referring, I think, to a runway at an airport). Unusually for a movie, the action unfolds in stills, like a comic or photo novel. When such a narrative is seen on the big screen, the emotional impact is huge. At a key point in the story, which is about memory and time travel, the girlfriend waking up is seen to move ever so slightly. This miniscule action, literally bringing the person to life, an Orpheus and Eurydice moment when Eurydice is retrieved from limbo, sends a heartrending message of the power of love. For Stravinsky's generation, including Picasso, the futurist painters, and Alfred North Whitehead, the equivalent mystery was how "life" is captured in a sequence of still frames and arising from that, the nature of time itself. For Stravinsky it recalled an earlier era, of Beethoven and Clementi, musical boxes and piano rolls, and the metronome of Maelzel cutting musical time into artificial chunks. The feeling is present in the introduction of Beethoven's *Symphony No. 4*: a music dividing like a developing embryo to the tick of a metronome, gradually filling out an abstract cell, long notes dividing into short, legato changing to staccato, until critical mass is suddenly reached and the music bursts into independent life. Composers involved with mechanical instruments, like Haydn and Beethoven, acquired an understanding of time and duration more absolute and very different from the one-dimensional action time of a Wagner or Richard Strauss. Perhaps the best way of describing *Variations* is as a concentrated series of flashbacks, a Stockhausen *Mo-*

mente–style narrative delivered as a potentially aleatoric, interchangeable sequence of frames corresponding to block harmonies, a story to be unravelled at leisure and at a much slower pace than its actual speed of occurrence—an experience similar to seeing a sporting event on news television replayed multiple times and in slow motion to make clear to viewers who may have blinked and missed what has actually occurred.

The serial language adopted by Stravinsky and modified by him in consultation with Ernst Krenek transforms a Schoenbergian intervallic line of possibilities into denser matrices of interval combinations determined in relation to an identifying pitch, in this case F natural or G sharp. The music "reads itself" at the speed at which chords and groups succeed one another. At the beginning one chord follows another, varying in content, instrumentation, and rhythm, as if delivering a message in Morse code. The instrumentation clusters in threes, suggesting serial derivations of twelve.

At [6] the first variation begins, a restless, roving strip of melody, constantly varying in weight, thickness, texture, and color but only one note deep, as if the earlier chords had been passed through a mangle. It begins fiercely, simmering down and accelerating away in a cloud of solo violin septuplets, chased by a second *Agon*-style flourish, this time blown away by graceful flutes gliding to a pause on keynote F.

The first of three twelve-part variations follows, for twelve solo violins playing "on the bridge" and producing a thin, wiry tone, an alteration of texture analogous to lifting the lid on a casket of sparkling jewels. In Stockhausen's *Refrain* (1959) block chords of superimposed piano, celesta, and vibraphone crumble away in similar fashion into luminous dust (Koch Schwann, 310 020 H1).[2] Like a musical box closing, the glimpse ends abruptly at the return of the flute F, and a brief variation for three flutes, oboe, and two bassoons ensues in which three-note figures are exchanged, sometimes doubling in unison, at other times going their own way (the metrics of this segment are astonishing, and it asks to be recognized as a "variation for conductor"—presumably Boulez, whose authorized recording of the work has still to appear at the time of writing). A second twelve-part variation follows, sounding closer and more resinous, transposed down in pitch to ten solo violas and two bass viols. Again the flute picks up the thread at the same note F, this time triggering a brief "quasi cadenza" flurry in free but coordinated counterpoint for woodwinds, a nod to Stockhausen's *Zeitmasse*. A sudden warning signal from trumpet and strings awakens the galloping sound of "three trombones of the Apocalypse," interrupted by guillotine-like accented chords, succeeded by a calmer texture of interchanging threadlike melodies undulating at different speeds, then reverting to sullen trombones. A brief *Agon*-like fugato for strings and piano offers a scurrying reminiscence of baroque counterpoint, rising to a second pivot note on G sharp, where once again a door opens to reveal a twelve-part mobile or collective murmur for winds, suggesting the reality crowd noises of Cage's *Variations IV*. (In each of the twelve-part variations the rhythmic content is essentially the same, differences in perception arising from transpositions in pitch range and tone quality, as if the same music were being viewed under different magnifications.) A brief coda dominated by the piano in accelerated mode compresses the music back into vertical chords, this time for strings, ending Mahler fashion on a low G sharp faded out by bass clarinet (a terminal gesture emulating the mysterious "naked clarinet note" in the Scherzo of Mahler's Fifth Symphony).[3]

The *Introitus* for T. S. Eliot is a short, solemn chorale for male voices and a predominantly percussive and bass-register ensemble in which solo viola and bass viol are employed to bring tonal definition to the whirring sounds of dual timpani, a startling foretaste of Stockhausen's combination of string quartet and individual helicopters. In this music, harp and piano vertical chords, shadowed by tam-tams, represent suspension of time, voices and strings the ongoing march of time, and muffled timpani the heartbeat of time. The instrumentation is largely flat in perspective, like an *orchestrelle*, and resembles Boulez's *Le marteau* in an ingenious serially inspired circuit of timbres leading from voices moving in time, via strings (which have pitch but no speech), to timpani (pitched percussion but no sustain) to tam-tams (unpitched percussion with sustain), to converge on harp and piano (pitch and sustain but no movement). The task for future recording engineers is to balance these several elements so that the *klangfarben* transformations of one type of sound into another are clearly executed and perceived (a problematic issue still affecting even the most recent recordings of *Le marteau*).

Stravinsky's short canons deserve greater respect. The 1965 *Canon* is a musical signature elaborating on the goodbye theme of *Firebird*, his most popular composition, newly rendered as a compact but assertive planetary system of multiple orbiting layers at different speeds and serial orders, clipped together by a staccato accent. Not only is it the composer's way of saying "My end is my beginning," but the idea of a cyclical round would also go on to inspire Boulez's *Explosante-Fixe* in memory of Stravinsky and Stockhausen's last *Klang* cycle, also of orbiting solo instrumental layers around the electronic tornado or black hole of *Cosmic Pulses.* The underlying metaphor of the canon or round is "random access memory"—a music that can be taken apart and reconstructed in an infinite variety of ways and in that sense of small size but infinite duration.

There is something final about a requiem. One might expect a requiem to be about mourning and loss, but this musical goodbye is not like that. After a decade of failing health, no doubt partly in consequence of an early smoking habit and a taste for fine lubricants, the composer was ready to sign off but not to regret. At eighty-five, he said, "The knowledge that in a half-decade at the most, but probably sooner, I will be dead, . . . has little effect on me: the possibility of death is always present, always in the cards, after all, and it is only the likelihood that has increased" (*Retrospectives* 49; *Conclusions* 111). But though sanguine about his own mortality, he is still concerned that his Canticles, as abbreviated as haiku by Messiaen (and like them also in the sense that they are not true haiku but merely long strips of music that have been cut arbitrarily to a short length), should say something, if not about death, then about time.

This is artful and, in the circumstances, courageous and affecting music but only difficult to work out for those who may not have figured out where to look or how to listen. A prelude discourses on layered time: a ticking Geiger counter of tutti strings over which a dreamlike counterpoint of solo strings condenses and floats like a cloud—on another level detaching concrete time and motion (the spiccato strings, the earthbound wheelchair) from imaginary time (an eternity of weightless thinking), a music of dozing off and waking with a jolt. Exaudi is music as attenuated as a Giacometti statue in glaring midday, glinting harp, deep shadows, a play of distant voices; I think the choir should be offstage or round the corner, like an echo choir, with only harp and violins visible (in this work Stravinsky's reconciliation with string sonority is complete). A Dies Irae with piano and timpani—kaboom! like an auto crash, five times repeated, disturbing the choir, followed by a piano and xylophone roulade winding noisily off into the distance like a loose hubcap: a miniature Tuba Mirum in which the monotone horizontal lines of twin trumpets are ensnared by bass solo voice, then hurled upward as double-octave leaping intervals for alternating bassoons, their vertical and the trumpet horizontal forming a cross.

The interlude is constructed around dense blocks of flutes, horns, and timpani, timbres recalling the inert sine tone electronic mixtures of Stockhausen's 1954 *Electronic Study II*. At intervals the flutes struggle into life, only to be hauled back to stillness.[4] A wordless dialogue of alto flute and bassoons intervenes, but again the block sound returns. Again four flutes whirr into life, like a paper kite taking the air, only to disappear. Silence and again the block chord returns. No escape. This is it. The interlude ends with a *sotto voce* dialogue of alto flute and bassoons, like medics leaving the bedside while continuing to discuss the patient. A six-voice choir, trumpet, and trombone deliver a spacious, impassioned Rex Tremendae over which throbbing, bedazzled chords on flutes and low strings attempt to draw a curtain, a juxtaposition of movement and stasis recalling the earlier prelude. A brief, sudden high C from solo trumpet admits a shaft of light at the choir's words "Salva me," a heart-wrenching moment, after which the curtain closes.

Lacrimosa reverts to the icy calm of Exaudi: the solo voice, a tremulous contralto, introducing a solitary emotion of sorrow against a musical backdrop of vast empty spaces. The Libera Me is a marvelous austere invention, Russian Orthodox in tone, recalling *Threni*, in which a solo quartet chants in repeated chords against a noisy backdrop of the remainder of the choir muttering the same text independently in a reverberant undertone. A familiar effect but unfamiliar as a composed effect, in present context yet another example of layering strict time over aleatoric or unstructured time. It might be a good idea for the singing quartet of voices to intone each phrase in a single breath. Though no phrasing or breath marks are indicated in the score, the pretext for "a single breath" as a measure of time is found in Stockhausen's *Zeitmasse* and for the soloists to sing each phrase on a single breath suggests a gradual *diminuendo* and petering out of voices during each line of text, a poetic image of loss of breath and accompanying loss of speech prefigured to some extent in the coda of *Ebony Concerto*. The postlude introduces an entirely new but musical-box familiar, compound sonority of celesta, tubular bells, and vibraphone (played without vibrato) intoning chiming chords as a group, as it were sounding the hours on cue (a sonority alluding to the crystalline sounds and suspended timing of Boulez's original version of *Le Vierge, le vivace, et le bel aujourd'hui*, as well as to Stockhausen's *Refrain*). Framing these metallic complexes, which are struck, ring, shine, and die away, are multiple flute, piano, and harp aggregations of longer sustain, the familiar symbolism of which is acoustical and exact: as harp and piano components die away naturally, the harmonies within detach and float heavenward to represent the spirit leaving the body and diffusing into the luminous radiance of high flutes.

All art is retrospective, and the same is true of studies of art: we are launched into a world of masterpieces as undergraduates, and for some of us it is a lifelong struggle to cut through time and the thicket of official jargon to get to the person, and the practice, and the method. As a schoolboy I first discovered *The Rite of Spring* as tape operator for a college drama production of *Macbeth*: "Double, double, toil and trouble" chanted in halflight to the majestic darkness of Pagan Night. At a record store, I asked if they had any Stravinsky. "I don't know," said the salesman. "What does he play?" At university as first-year students we were launched pell-mell into *Canticum Sacrum*, *Threni*, and in my second year, *Movements*, ranged alongside strange and complicated new works by Boulez, Stockhausen, and Messiaen—a repertoire I fear is still alien to a majority of listeners. For a half century since, to know this music has been the ongoing objective, in the same way as others have spent their lifetimes struggling to decode Linear B.

It is one of the ironies of retrospection that my first published article on Stravinsky's music should be a piece about his last published work, the 1968 arrangement of Two Sacred Songs, "Herr, was trägt der Boden hier" and "Wunden trägst du, mein Geliebter," chosen from the *Spanisches Liederbuch* of Hugo Wolf, works in which the presence of the Russian composer, to most listeners, is all but undetectable. The listener's task is to find him, and he is there, in the selection, in the realization that these songs are a gesture of reconciliation with the quiet, neglected (and Spanish) strain of German tradition, for so long hidden from view by the monumentality of Wagner, Bruckner, Mahler, and Richard Strauss: a domestic, modest tradition, from Mozart through Schubert and Schumann, of expressive melody and quiet devotion to themes of philosophical suffering, pain and resignation.[5] Stravinsky's settings do not encroach on the originals, other than to marry their poetic sentiment to an instrumental dialogue in which—in a reversal of the composer's normal symbolism—the voice of the supplicant is accompanied by disembodied woodwinds and the voice of Christ in response, by the tangible reality of bowed strings, the same as for John Dowland (whose *Lachrymae* for viols, we recall, are also about absence).

"Well, maestro, see you in another fifty years," said Marcel Duchamp, bidding the composer goodbye, a moment in 1967 (the two artists not having seen one another since about 1920) captured by photographer Arnold Newman in black and white. Afterward, in response to Craft's carefully planted question "Do you agree with Duchamp that an object can be transformed merely by being chosen and invested with a new thought and context?" the composer is unequivocal:

> Duchamp's objects can be, at any rate, because of the quality both of the choices and the new contexts. . . . [However,] I value some of his other achievements more highly, for instance, his demonstration that the machine-made can be better made than the handmade, and still be aesthetic. (Newman and Craft, *Bravo Stravinsky*)

Note well: "Machine-made can be better." And in a strange way, the spirit of John Cage hovers over the composer's setting of Edward Lear's *The Owl and the Pussy-cat* for mezzo-soprano and piano, a musical *billet-doux* for Vera, setting her favorite English poem, the first she learned by heart (EWW 543). It is a nonsense poem, a *pribaoutka*, to go with all the other nonsense poems the composer has dedicated in the past to those he loved. And what a treat for academics! "[The rhythm of the title] suggested a group of pitches, which I expanded into a twelve-note series. . . . The piano octaves for a syncopated canonic voice as well as a double mirror, the vocal movement being reflected between both the upper and lower notes." Ah yes, I see.

It is an Elliott Carter–style duet in which, unlike Carter, voice and piano stay together *and in the same tempo* while sounding accidentally juxtaposed. That is so clever, and the verbal nonsense the icing on the cake: imagine performing this song at an entertainment for visiting Chinese diplomats, *Nightingale* style. It could be intended to give the impression of a voice trying to engage an answering machine in conversation. Or again, the shaft of Cageian sunlight, and perfect timing, of overhearing Vera in the next room, singing quietly to herself, the irregular clink of glass and cutlery being laid on the table forming a magically coordinated and perfectly "composed" juxtaposition of completely independent rhythms.

NOTES

PREFACE

1. "Fabrizio's: Criticism and Response," *New Yorker* (5 September 1979), reprinted in *Side Effects* (London: New English Library, 1981), 129–35.

1. GHOST IN THE MACHINE

1. Surviving examples of mechanically imperfect timing are preserved on *L'Art de la Musique Mécanique Vol. 2* (Arion, 60406), track 1, which includes brief transcriptions of Paisiello, Sacchini, Cherubini, Méhul, Boieldieu, and Grétry performed on a Laprévote orgue de salon of 160 pipes dating from the first half of the nineteenth century.

2. Stravinsky may well have wished to model himself on Clementi, an acclaimed composer, successful in business, laboring under accusations of pursuing a mechanical and unfeeling style. Following a trial of skill with Mozart in Vienna in 1781 adjudicated by Emperor Franz Joseph II, out of which no clear winner emerged, Mozart furiously dismissed Clementi in letters as "a mere mechanician, strong in runs of thirds, but without a pennyworth of feeling or taste." In 1806 Clementi explained to a pupil that it was true; he had been guilty of cultivating brilliance of execution, "especially in double notes, hardly known then, and in extemporized cadenzas," but after their encounter, "striving to put more music and less mechanical show into his productions" (Edward Dannreuter, "Clementi," in *Grove II* 555–57). The word *mechanical* implies "robotic" connotations.

3. In *Scott Joplin and the Kings of Ragtime* (Retro, R2CD 40-13/1-2), recorded piano rolls of Joplin can be compared in timing and accentuation to live acoustic recordings of the same by a variety of artists on the companion CD.

4. Pierre Boulez, "Music and Invention," interview with Misha Donat, *The Listener* 83.2130 (22 March 1970): 101–3.

5. The instructional vinyl disc for medical students against which the observed comparison was made is J. Lenègre, B. Coblentz, and J. Himbert, *L'Auscultation Cardiaque* (undated, mono; Pathé, STX 109).

2. SORCERER'S APPRENTICE

1. "The conductor who impressed me most was Gustav Mahler. . . . Mahler conducted his Fifth Symphony in St Petersburg in October or November 1907" (*Expositions* 56, 58). No performance of Schoenberg is recorded, but it is not out of the question that Stravinsky would have heard, or had access to the score of, a work for string sextet by a Mahler protégé published in 1902.

2. *Musica Curiosa: Works by Leopold Mozart and Georg Druschetsky*, Capella Savaria conducted by Pál Németh (Hungaroton HCD 12874).

3. Branford Marsalis, *Romances for Saxophone* (CBS Masterworks, MK 42122).

4. Schoenberg's *Pelleas und Melisande* (1903) actually did incorporate trombone glissandi, an orchestration first and talking point among Maeterlinck followers, an interpretation to be keenly compared with Debussy's opera of the same name.

5. Rex Lawson, "On Stravinsky and the Pianola," CD booklet (MusicMasters, 01612-67138-2). These rolls are thought to have been among those heard by Stravinsky on his 1914 visit to the Aeolian Hall offices in London and "to have led to his consideration of the pianola as a solo instrument."

6. Debussy and d'Indy undoubtedly had Stravinsky in mind in a 1913 exchange of polemics in the pages of *SIM* (the monthly bulletin of the Societé International de Musique) concerning the future direction of music. "D'Indy had written disparagingly of 'cinematographic music.' . . . Whereas Debussy saw such cinematographic techniques as a renewal of form, d'Indy merely saw them as a lack of it." In a subsequent issue, Debussy responded, "There remains but one way of reviving the taste for symphonic music among our contemporaries: to apply to pure music the techniques of cinematography" (Debussy ed. Lesure 261, 298).

7. A particularly affecting plasticity of tempo is achieved by Franz Welser-Möst and the London Philharmonic on EMI (7243 5 72103 2 4).

3. RITUAL FIRE DANCE

1. "Russia was not the only country to be influenced by our people's music. Another great musical nation was to follow her example: France, represented by Claude Debussy. Although many French composers preceded him in that direction, their intentions did not go further than to make music *à l'espagnole*; and even Bizet in his admirable *Carmen*, does not seem to have set himself any other aim. . . . [Debussy] had never been to Spain, with the exception of a few hours spent in San Sebastián to attend a bullfight." Manuel de Falla, "Cante Jondo: Its origins. Its values. Its influence on European art." Anonymously published on the occasion of the first competition of cante jondo, Granada, 1922 (reprinted in de Falla 99–117).

2. Stravinsky: "I forced myself to make this *Petrushka* [Trois Mouvements] a virtuoso work, pianistic in its very essence, using the resources of the instrument and not in any way seeking to imitate an orchestra. In short, not a piece edited down for the piano, but created specially for the piano." In "Quelques confidences sur la musique" (1935; reprinted in EWW 581–85).

3. Cartoonist Gerard Hoffnung (*Hoffnung's Acoustics*) makes the point in a tribute to Falla showing the piano as a raging bull enticed into a bullring. The concept of a reproducing piano as soloist has since been realized in recordings of Gershwin's *Rhapsody in Blue* employing piano rolls of the long-dead composer as soloist (e.g., CBS, MK 42516).

4. François Lesure, "Claude Debussy after His Centenary," *Musical Quarterly* 49.3 (1965): 287–88; cited by Fernand Ouellette, *Edgar Varèse*, tr. Derek Coltman (London: Calder and Boyars, 1973), 26–27.

5. "Salomé is apparently motivated solely by lust and the desire for revenge. . . . Yet the music is full of shadows that suggest what the libretto ignores." Robert Craft, "A 'Beautiful Coloured, Musical Thing,'" *New York Review of Books*, March 18, 1976 (repr. *Current Convictions* 124–35). Craft's sympathies toward Strauss are interesting in themselves, also because of the possibility that they are colored by Stravinsky's own views.

6. On the evidence of the piano-roll edition, in which the final Sacrificial Dance is registered at a distinctly higher speed, Benjamin Zander has recorded a version for orchestra (Pickwick Masters, MCD25) at these "authentic original" tempi, a decision that, though controversial, makes dramatic and musical sense as a change of gear in response to frequent and strident "five in the time of four" trumpet signals appearing at earlier intervals throughout the ballet.

4. BEYOND TONALITY

1. In the United States, atonality came to public attention in 1912 with gramophone recordings of "Memphis Blues" by W. C. Handy, in the style of the black American lament or "holler" from the slave era, sung in a modal idiom containing ambiguous "blue notes" at the third and fifth that fall between the cracks of standard notation (Maconie, *Musicologia* 360–61).

2. Tracks by Ossman, Van Eps, and Moskowitz are included in *The Kings of Ragtime* compilation (Retro, R2CD 40-13/2).

3. "The pianos did their best to sound like an Orchestrion, a device that one might call artificial, but which I believe was justified and authentic" (C. F. Ramuz, in *Documents* 160–61).

5. IN SEARCH OF THE LONG LINE

1. Robert Craft, "Avant-Propos," booklet to *Stravinsky the Composer: Vol. 1* (MusicMasters, 01612-67078-2), 37.

2. Batten was balance engineer for a recording of *Petrushka* under Goossens and *Les Noces* in a 1934 London recording conducted by Stravinsky.

3. The list of one-act situation comedy or domestic operas includes R. Strauss, *Schlagobers* (1922); Milhaud, *Salade*, *Les Malheurs d'Orphée*, and *Le Train Bleu* (1924); Satie, *Parade* (1917), *Mercure* (1924), and *Relâche* (with René Clair, 1924); Krenek, *Sprung über den Schatten* (1924) and *Jonny Spielt Auf* (1926); Ravel, *L'Enfant et les Sortilèges* (1925); Martinu, *Revue de Cuisine* (1927); Hindemith, *Mörder, Hoffnung der Frauen* (1919), *Hin und Zurück* (1927), and *Neues vom Tage* (1929); Kurt Weill, *Mahagonny* (1927), *Der Zar lässt sich Photographieren* (1928), *Lindbergsflug* (1929), and *Dreigroschenoper* (1929); Gershwin, *An American in Paris* (1928); Walton, *Façade* (1928); Virgil Thomson, *Four Saints in 3 Acts* (1928); and Schoenberg, *Von Heute auf Morgen* (1929).

4. Part of me wonders if the voice lines should be sung in rapid sprechstimme in a cross between Debussy and Schoenberg or Berg. After listening again to the singing, however, I think that the lyric beauty of the melody writing removes that option and restores one's faith in Pergolesi.

5. "It was a most exciting experience; Schoenberg's conducting brought out the dramatic qualities of his work, making it harsher, wilder, more intense; my reading on the other hand, emphasized the music's sensuous qualities, all the sweetness, subtlety, and translucency of it" (Milhaud 119–20).

6. Stravinsky had reason to remember that year. "I can clearly recall one incident. That was Hitler's march into the [Munich] Feldherrenhalle in 1923. I was once again rehearsing in the foyer [of the National Theater] *Le Rossignol* by Stravinsky, whose music was later placed on the prohibited list by the Nazis as cultural Bolshevism. Suddenly we heard shots—and indeed, the dead and wounded were being brought into the Max Joseph Platz. . . . I had to break off the rehearsal" (Böhm 44).

7. Anonymous, "Piano Technique for Wireless," in *BBC Handbook 1929* (London: British Broadcasting Corporation, 1929), 169–70.

8. Anonymous, "Composing for Wireless," in *BBC Handbook 1929* (reproduced in full), 167.

6. THE ART OF NONEXPRESSION

1. In his later conducting career, Diaghilev's youthful protégé Igor Markevitch adopted *Divertimento* and the *Symphony of Psalms* as signature works (see *Expositions* 85).

2. Coincidentally, at about this time Schoenberg began work on his reorchestration of the Georg Matthias Monn cello concerto for Pablo Casals, another balancing act between solo string player and conductor at the keyboard.

3. In a manifesto published in the journal *Excelsior*, Stravinsky declared, "This score, as it is written and as it must remain in the musical archives of our time, forms an indissoluble whole with the tendencies repeatedly asserted in my previous works." The reference to archives implies or includes recording media (White, *A Critical Survey* 148).

4. The two-piano version of *L'Envol d'Icare* was revealingly programmed alongside Bartók's *Sonata for Two Pianos and Percussion* in a BBC Radio 3 program (19 April 1988) by Martin Jones and Richard McMahon (pianos) and percussionists James Holland, Tristan Fry, and David Johnson. In 1943 Bartók orchestrated the *Sonata* as a *Concerto for Two Pianos and Orchestra*, the same year that Markevitch recomposed *L'Envol* as *Icare* for orchestra, again eliminating the quarter-tone tuning of the original score.

5. A vinyl compilation of early stereo and full bandwidth test recordings with Stokowski and the Philadelphia Orchestra was issued by Bell Labs in 1977 (Bell Labs, BTL 7901). A brief and inconclusive extract from a Blumlein test recording of Mozart's Symphony No. 41 "Jupiter" by the London Philharmonic under Sir Thomas Beecham, recorded 19 January 1934 (matrix TT 5771), is included in the *EMI Centenary Edition* sampler (7087 6 11859 2 8; see Maconie, *The Second Sense* 303–25).

6. In 1929 a performance of *Les Noces* promoted by the League of Composers, danced by Martha Graham, choreographed by Massine, designed by Serge Soudekine, and conducted by Stokowski, was programmed alongside Monteverdi's one-act opera *Il Combattimento di Tancredi e Clorinda*, conducted by Werner Josten (Reis 90–91).

7. "German broadcasting should be made the chief instrument of political propaganda. I have always ridiculed the old idea that there is such a thing as objectivity and neutrality per se" (Eugen Hadamovsky, on his appointment as general-director of German Radio after Hitler's accession as chancellor in January 1933; Maconie, *Other Planets* 15).

8. "Tchelitchev called him a 'prancing grasshopper' and . . . Cocteau used to remark, when Stravinsky conducted, that he looked like 'an erect ant acting his part in a La Fontaine fable.' There is in effect something crickety, something insectal, about the movements of his body" (Nabokov 194).

9. Production delays, prohibitive expense, and the entry of the United States into World War II conspired against Fantasia's initial commercial success, but the movie's ultimate drawback was that the conception was aesthetically locked into the 1920s: a revival of the old-fashioned silent movie as a vehicle for Stokowski and the Philadelphia Orchestra, in color, with synchronized sound and Scriabinesque lighting effects. A remastered digital version of the optical sound track, in decodable original multichannel surround sound, was issued in 1990 as a fiftieth-anniversary souvenir on Buena Vista (UK Pickwick, DSTCD 452 D).

7. TESTAMENT OF ORPHEUS

1. *The Face of Mae West (Usable as a Surrealist Apartment*; 1934–1935), in which the actress's lips form an upholstered couch and her nose a white marble fireplace.

2. Robert Craft, "In the Mouse Trap," a review of Christopher Finch, *The Art of Walt Disney*, for the *New York Review of Books* (May 16, 1974), reprinted in *Current Convictions: Views and Reviews* (London: Secker & Warburg, 1978), 285–98.

3. "When lovely woman stoops to folly and . . . ," T. S. Eliot, *The Waste Land*, canto 3, "The Fire Sermon," ll. 253–56, in *Collected Poems 1909–1962*, 72.

4. The unusually passionate tone evokes the anguish of Dylan Thomas's "And Death shall have no dominion" (1936) and may help to explain Stravinsky's later attachment to the poet's "Do not go gentle into that good night," written in 1951, set by the composer after the poet's death in 1953.

5. "A kind of compulsion, like something unable to stop. . . . Orpheus is dead, the song is gone, but the accompaniment goes on" (Stravinsky to Nicolas Nabokov, in *Old Friends and New Music*, 203–4).

6. A compilation CD titled *The History of Pop Radio Vol. 1 1920–1927* (International Music Company, 205515-202) includes a historic 1927 Gershwin radio recording of *Rhapsody in Blue* with the Paul Whiteman Orchestra, along with Gene Austin's "The Lonesome Road" and "Lucky Lindy" in avant-garde arrangements by "Nat Shilkret & Orchestra."

7. "Our customs of speech are the outcome of a cumulative dialectic of differentiation; languages generate different social forms, these forms further divide languages" (Steiner 143).

8. Throughout his essay, the author refers to Stravinsky's most celebrated ballet as *The Rites* [*sic*] *of Spring*.

9. Stravinsky's pointedly ironic response, to dismiss fashions and schools—"the Broadway, the Appalachian, the Neo-Neanderthal (Orff)," all of whom "had come to a stalemate . . . at the end of the war in 1945" (*Memories* 123 [UK], 118 [US]).

10. "What I remember most clearly was the smoke in the recording studio. When the musicians did not blow horns they blew smoke, and of such tangibility that the atmosphere looked like Pernod clouded by water" (*Dialogues* 53).

11. Les Baxter (1922–1996), doyen of exotica, would go on to compose *Le Sacre du Sauvage* in 1951.

12. Jean Cocteau, *Cocteau on the Film: A Conversation*, recorded by André Fraigneau, trans. Vera Traill (London: Dobson, 1954), 128–29.

8. THE RAKE'S PROGRESS

1. Neither Chaplin nor Stravinsky lived to see *Monty Python's Life of Brian*, the brainchild and movie hit of a younger generation of British moralists.

2. Schoenberg's words are also a play on words: Word meaning both "The Law" in a biblical sense of authority and "word" signifying the gift of persuasion. In another parallel, the "Golden Calf" idol of Schoenberg's opera corresponds to the Bread Machine of *The Rake's Progress*: an object of false worship offered up as a panacea for the people's ills.

3. "[Diaghilev's Paris] . . . the somewhat exotic meeting place for snobs from all over Europe and the fashionable set of Paris society (as the society columnist of *Le Figaro* called it, '*ce bazar séduisant de sons et de couleurs exotiques*'—this seductive bazaar of exotic sounds and colors)" (Nabokov 71).

4. Benjamin Britten, diary entry for February 12, 1936 (cited in *Documents* 269).

5. Interlaced accounts of circumstances leading up to *The Rake* are provided by Lincoln Kirstein ("Siegfriedslage"), Nicolas Nabokov ("Excerpts from memories"), and Robert Craft ("The poet and the rake") in Spender (128–55).

6. "The two great modern erotic myths, which have no parallels in Greek literature, are the myth of Tristan and Isolde, or the World Well Lost for Love, and the countermyth of Don Juan, the seducer" (Auden, "The Greeks and Us," 1948, in *Forewords and Afterwords* 3–32). Auden's Don Juan is a compound of Don Giovanni and Byron's more amiable hero.

7. Auden, "Reflections on Music and Opera," *Partisan Review* 19 (1952), reprinted in *The Dyer's Hand* (470).

8. "When a Christian, like Augustine, talks about ethics, therefore, he begins not with the rational act or the pleasant act, but with the act gratuite [*sic*], which is neither reasonable nor physically pleasant, but a pure assertion of absolute self-autonomy" (Auden, "Augustus to Augustine," 1944, in *Forewords and Afterwords* 33–48). (Alternatively, a gratuitous act is submission to an unformulated obligation to do something rather than nothing.)

9. Both the action of stopping the clock and the singers stepping out of character at the end of the play to sing a moral directly to the audience are theatrical devices recalling Ravel's 1911 one-act opera *L'Heure Espagnole*, suggesting a perception of *The Rake* ultimately as comedy rather than tragedy.

10. Albert Camus, *L'Homme révolté* (1951); in English, *The Rebel*, trans. Anthony Bower (1953); selection republished as *The Fastidious Assassins* (London: Penguin Books, 2008), 43.

11. T. S. Eliot, "The Music of Poetry," in *Selected Prose*, ed. John Hayward (1953), reprinted (Harmondsworth: Peregrine Books, 1963), 53–64.

9. AFTER THE FALL

1. Rose Macaulay, "If I Were Head of the Third Programme," in *BBC Year Book 1947* (London: British Broadcasting Corporation, 1947), 20–28.

2. Instruments such as the cembalo and violin are also characters in the action, a point ignored by many commentators. An immaculate performance of Messiaen's *Quartet for the End of Time* by superbly coiffed and appointed players only goes to show how much more poignant and meaningful the same music is capable of sounding when performed on old instruments and a battered upright piano by players in Samuel Beckett attire, as inmates in an internment camp.

3. A listener is bound to wonder if all of Stravinsky's verse dramas should be regarded as variations on the philosophical "Dialogue between Joy and Reason" that the composer began to compose in 1924 "to an old French text" (*Documents* 217), of which a 1933 sketch for two voices and short score survives.

4. For example, "Cunctipotens genitor" from the (Spanish) School of Compostela (c. 1125), example 27b from Archibald T. Davison and Willi Apel's very useful resource *Historical Anthology of Music*.

5. Also "pearls before swine." Ansermet is quoted, "[In 1956] Stravinsky tried to persuade me to interest myself in serial music, notably in the works of Webern: 'They are pearls,' he told me. 'But my dear Igor, I am writing a book which shows that this music is contrary to the laws of hearing'" (Ansermet and Piguet *Entretiens sur la Musique*, cited in *Documents* 248).

6. The Webern String Quartet was among a very small number of twelve-tone scores Stravinsky knew. Its second movement became the subject of an important essay by Stockhausen, "Structure and Experiential Time," first published in 1955 in the music periodical *Die Reihe 2*, issued in German with a preface by Stravinsky, thereafter translated into English in 1958, revised 1959 (Universal Edition, UE 26102e), 64.

7. Robin Maconie, "Stravinsky's Final Cadence," *Tempo* 103 (1972): 18–23. Craft adds, "When [Stravinsky] knew for certain that four trombones would play in Schütz's Fili Mi Absalon, a cortège of mourning canons was added to the Thomas setting, canons for string quartet and four trombones" ("A Concert for St Mark," *The Score* [December 1956], reprinted in EWW 477). Coincidentally, the opening trombone phrase looks like a crib of a canzona by Florentio Maschera (1540–1584), a contemporary of Gabrieli, a work also reprinted (No. 175) in Davison and Apel.

8. Peter Maxwell Davies, "Canons and Epitaphs in Memoriam I.S.: Set I," *Tempo* 97 (1971).

9. Instrumental pairings match short against long, plain against ornamental, low against high, loud against soft, thin against thick, and so on, and also forward and reverse motion.

10. Robert Craft, "Stravinsky: Letters to Pierre Boulez," *Musical Times* 123.1672 (June 1982): 396–402.

11. The same topical image of talking heads on television is evoked by Cage in his 1960 four-voice lecture *Where Are We Going and What Are We Doing?* delivered at Darmstadt, in which the composer talks alongside multiple copies of himself but nobody is listening. It is a polyphony of indifference or accidental encounter specific to microphones and recording media.

12. In a 1955 contribution to *The Score*, Elliott Carter had drawn attention to an American claim, from Charles Ives through Nancarrow to himself, of

prior ownership or jus primae noctis in relation to use of complex layered tempi as a compositional device, against a similar claim by Stockhausen for the Europeans. It was left to Stravinsky, copy of Davison and Apel in hand, gently to remind both sides that metrical complexity dates from the time of Baude Cordier and is intimately related, then as now, to the development of a notational metric and associated mechanical musical instruments (*Memories* 107 [UK], 101 [US]). Elliott Carter, "The Rhythmic Basis of American Music," *The Score* 12 (1955), reprinted in Else Stone and Kurt Stone, eds., *The Writings of Elliott Carter: An American Composer Looks at Modern Music* (Bloomington: Indiana University Press, 1977), 160–66.

10. LAST RITES

1. Stalling's music for *Feed the Kitty* (1952; in *The Carl Stalling Project*, vol. 1 [Warner, 9.26027-2]) is a cheeky parody of silent movie music of the *Petrushka* era and his chase music (arranged by Milt Franklyn) for the Road Runner cartoon *There They Go Go Go* (1956), a spectacular tribute to *Petrushka* itself. Stravinsky returns the compliment in his music for "The Building of the Ark" (Maconie, *The Second Sense* 283–301).

2. The twelve-part variations have also been favorably compared to the birdsong-inspired "Epode" for eighteen solo strings, from *Chronochromie* by Messiaen.

3. David A. Pickett, "The Naked Note in the Scherzo of Mahler's Fifth Symphony" http://www.fugato.com/pickett/mahler5-3.shtml.

4. The (smallish) timpani should be allowed to ring at the beginning and damped, the sound stifled, at the ending of a phrase.

5. Robin Maconie, "Stravinsky's Last Cadence," *Tempo* 103 (1972): 18–23.

SELECTED READING

Works of immediate relevance to the life and work of Igor Stravinsky, such as correspondence, personally authored works, and major secondary sources, are annotated.

Allen, Woody. *Side Effects*. London: New English Library, 1981.

Andersen, Johannes C. *Maori Music: With Its Polynesian Background.* 1934. Christchurch, NZ: Cadsonbury, 2002.

Ansermet, Ernest, and J.-Claude Piguet. *Entretiens sur la Musique*. Neuchâtel, Switzerland: La Baconnière, 1963.

Arnheim, Rudolph. *Film as Art.* 1958. London: Faber & Faber, 1969.

Auden, W. H. *The Dyer's Hand: And Other Essays*. London: Faber & Faber, 1963.

———. *Forewords and Afterwords*. London: Faber & Faber, 1973.

Batten, Joe. *Joe Batten's Book: The Story of Sound Recording*. London: Rockliff, 1956.

Böhm, Karl. *A Life Remembered: Memoirs*. Trans. John Kehoe. London: Boyars, 1992.

Boulez, Pierre. *Penser la Musique Aujourd'hui.* Geneva: Editions Gonthier, 1963. In English, *Boulez on Music Today.* Trans. Susan Bradshaw and Richard Rodney Bennett. London: Faber and Faber, 1971.

Cage, John. *Notations*. West Glover, VT: Something Else Press, 1969.

———. *Silence: Lectures and Writings.* 1961. Cambridge, MA: MIT Press, 1966.

Carter, Elliott. *The Writings of Elliott Carter: An American Composer Looks at Modern Music.* Ed. Else Stone and Kurt Stone. Bloomington: Indiana UP, 1977.

Chaplin, Charles. *My Autobiography*. London: Bodley Head, 1964.

Chasins, Abram. *Leopold Stokowski: A Profile*. London: Hale, 1981.

Copland, Aaron. *Copland on Music*. London: Deutsch, 1961.

———. *Our New Music*. New York: McGraw-Hill, 1941.

Craft, Robert. *Current Convictions: Views and Reviews.* London: Secker & Warburg, 1978.

———. *Stravinsky: The Chronicle of a Friendship 1948–1971*. London: Gollancz, 1972. Selective but focused observations of Stravinsky in his American prime allow a reader to gauge the nature and extent of Craft's alleged influence on the composer.

———. *Stravinsky: Glimpses of a life*. London: Lime Tree, 1992.

———. *A Stravinsky Scrapbook 1940–1971*. London: Thames & Hudson, 1983. A useful collection of materials and photographs from the composer's American years.

Davison, Archibald T., and Willi Apel. *Historical Anthology of Music.* Vol. 1. 1949. Cambridge, MA: Harvard University Press, 1977.

Debussy, Claude. *Debussy on Music.* Ed. François Lesure. Trans. Richard Langham Smith. London: Secker & Warburg, 1977.
de Falla, Manuel. *On Music and Musicians.* Ed. Federico Sopeña. 1950. Trans. David Urman and J. M. Thomson. London: Boyars, 1979.
Eisenstein, Sergei. *The Film Sense.* Trans. and ed. Jay Leyda. London: Faber & Faber, 1943.
Eliot, T. S. *Collected Poems 1902–1962.* London: Faber & Faber, 1963.
Ellis, William. *An Authentic Narrative of a Voyage Performed by Captain Cook and Captain Clerke* . . . . 2 vols. London: Robinson, Sewell, and Debrett, 1783.
Goossens, Eugene. *Overtures and Beginners: A Musical Autobiography.* London: Methuen, 1951.
Hoffnung, Gerard. *Hoffnung Music Festival.* London: Dobson, Putnam, 1956.
———. *Hoffnung's Acoustics.* London: Dobson, Putnam, 1959.
Jones, Daniel. *The Pronunciation of English.* 1909. 4th ed. Cambridge: Cambridge University Press, 1956.
Kandinsky, Wassily. *Concerning the Spiritual in Art.* Trans. and intro. by M. T. H. Sadler. Originally published as *The Art of Spiritual Harmony*, 1914. New York: Dover, 1977.
Kirstein, Lincoln. *Thirty Years: Lincoln Kirstein's the New York City Ballet. Expanded to Include the Years 1973–1978.* London: A & C Black, 1979. A fascinating introduction to the New York ballet milieu in which Stravinsky flourished, along with recollections of the Diaghilev era by Kirstein and Balanchine.
Lindgren, Ernest. *The Art of the Film: An Introduction to Film Appreciation.* London: Allen & Unwin, 1948.
London, Kurt. *Film Music: A Summary of the Characteristic Features of Its History, Aesthetics, Technique; and Possible Developments.* Foreword by Constant Lambert. London: Faber & Faber, 1936.
Maconie, Robin. *Avant Garde: An American Odyssey from Gertrude Stein to Pierre Boulez.* Lanham, MD: Scarecrow Press, 2012.
———. *Musicologia: Musical Knowledge from Plato to John Cage.* Lanham, MD: Scarecrow Press, 2010.
———. *Other Planets: The Music of Karlheinz Stockhausen.* Lanham, MD: Scarecrow Press, 2005.
———. *The Second Sense: Language, Music, and Hearing.* Lanham, MD: Scarecrow Press, 2002.
McLuhan, [Herbert] Marshall. *The Mechanical Bride: Folklore of Industrial Man.* 1951. London: Routledge and Kegan Paul, 1967.
Milhaud, Darius. *Notes without Music: An Autobiography.* 1952. Trans. Donald Evans. Ed. Rollo Myers. London: Calder and Boyars, 1967. An engaging view of musical life in Paris in the Diaghilev years by a close associate and fellow composer.
Moerenhout, J. A. *Voyages aux Iles du Grand Ocean.* 2 vols. 1837. Paris: Maisonneuve, 1959.
Nabokov, Nicolas. *Old Friends and New Music.* Boston: Little, Brown, 1951. A vivid sketch of Stravinsky at the time of *The Rake's Progress* by a fellow Russian composer.
Newman, Arnold, and Robert Craft. *Bravo Stravinsky: Photographs by Arnold Newman, Text by Robert Craft.* With a foreword by Francis Steegmuller. Cleveland, OH: World, 1967. Stunning portrait photographs of the aged Stravinsky at home and still composing at the time of *Requiem Canticles* and *The Owl and the Pussy-cat.*
Ord-Hume, Arthur W. J. G. *Joseph Haydn and the Mechanical Organ.* Cardiff: University of Cardiff Press, 1982.
Orledge, Robert. *Debussy and the Theatre.* Cambridge: Cambridge University Press, 1983.
Ouellette, Fernand. *Edgar Varèse.* Trans. Derek Coltman. London: Calder and Boyars, 1973.
Queneau, Raymond. *Exercices de Style.* Paris: Gallimard, 1947.
Reis, Claire R. *Composers, Conductors, and Critics.* New York: Oxford University Press, 1955.
Sabaneev, Leonid. *Music for the Films: A Handbook for Composers and Conductors.* Trans. S. W. Pring. London: Pitman, 1935.
Sachs, Curt. *Rhythm and Tempo: A Study in Music History.* London: Dent, 1953.

Salazar, Adolfo. *Music in Our Time: Trends in Music since the Romantic Era.* Trans. Isabel Pope. London: Bodley Head, 1948. Fascinating insights into musical attitudes in Stravinsky's Paris by a pupil and protégé of Manuel de Falla.

Scherchen, Hermann. *Handbook of Conducting.* 1929. Trans. M. D. Calcocoressi. London: Oxford University Press, 1933.

Schmidgall, Gary. *Literature as Opera.* New York: Oxford University Press, 1977.

Schoenberg, Arnold. *Letters.* Ed. Erwin Stein. Tr. Eithne Wilkins and Ernst Kaiser. London: Faber & Faber, 1964.

Segalen, Victor. *Essay on Exoticism: An Aesthetics of Diversity.* Trans. Yael Rachel Schlick. Durham, NC: Duke University Press, 2002.

———. *Stèles.* Trans. Timothy Billings and Christopher Bush. Middletown, CT: Wesleyan UP, 2007.

Spender, Stephen, ed. *W. H. Auden: A Tribute.* London: Weidenfeld & Nicolson, 1975.

Steiner, George. *On Difficulty and Other Essays.* Oxford: Oxford University Press, 1978.

Stravinsky, Igor. *An Autobiography (1903–1934).* London: Gollancz, 1936. English translation of *Chroniques de ma Vie* (1935). Written with the assistance of Walter Nouvel. Reprint with corrections and an introduction by Eric Walter White (London: Calder and Boyars, 1975). New edition (London: Boyars, 1990). The scandal and notoriety of *Rite of Spring* is laid to rest in Stravinsky's unpretentious and conversational account of a restless life leading to uncertain exile, adoption of French citizenship, and conversion to a neoclassical aesthetic.

———. *Poetics of Music in the Form of Six Lessons.* Harvard University Charles Eliot Norton Lectures, 1939–1940. Trans. Arthur Knodel and Ingolf Dahl. New York: Vintage, 1956. As a new arrival in the United States, Stravinsky takes a more trenchantly critical stance toward the "enemies of modernism," among those wielding political influence in a divided Europe, in the press, the academy, and at the conductor's rostrum.

———. *Themes and Conclusions.* Rev. and exp. Robert Craft. UK edition of US *Themes and Episodes* and *Retrospectives and Conclusions.* London: Faber & Faber, 1972. Sly, witty, at times jaundiced, and for English readers slightly bowdlerized views of the current musical scene during the composer's final years.

Stravinsky, Igor, and Robert Craft. *Conversations with Igor Stravinsky.* London: Faber & Faber, 1959. The first and best "general" introduction to Stravinsky in dialogue with Robert Craft, setting the composer firmly in context of the new avant-garde of Boulez and Stockhausen and introducing the general reader to post-1950s modern developments in direct, easy-to-understand language far removed from the high aestheticism of current critical theory.

———. *Dialogues.* New and abridged edition of *Dialogues and a Diary* (1968) omitting extracts from the diary of Robert Craft republished separately in *Chronicle of a Friendship.* London: Faber & Faber, 1982. Views, vivid word portraits, emphatic endorsements, and occasional criticisms of leading composers and associated literary figures of the 1960s.

———. *Expositions and Developments.* London: Faber & Faber, 1962. The third book of the series is especially revealing of Stravinsky's early life and friendships.

———. *Memories and Commentaries.* London: Faber & Faber, 1960. US edition. New York: Doubleday, 1960. The original publication of this lively title is to be preferred to the cribbed and plaintive tone of the 1981 revised and condensed edition.

———. *Retrospectives and Conclusions.* New York: Knopf, 1969. A final collection of views and interviews in which Stravinsky reflects poignantly on declining powers and his own mortality.

———. *Themes and Episodes.* New York: Knopf, 1966. Racy, unexpurgated opinions of the world of art and contemporary music morals in the original US edition.

Stravinsky, Vera, and Robert Craft. *Igor and Vera Stravinsky: A Photograph Album, 1921 to 1971.* Photographs selected by Vera Stravinsky and Rita McCaffrey. Text from Stravinsky's interviews, 1912–1963. Captions by Robert Craft. London: Thames & Hudson, 1982. Entertaining, instructive, and revealing glimpses of the composer's domestic life and times in Hollywood.

———. *Stravinsky in Pictures and Documents*. London: Hutchinson, 1979. An essential, if disorderly, documentary resource offering fresh insights into artistic and political allegiances barely intimated in the composer's other publications.

Taruskin, Richard. *Stravinsky and the Russian Traditions: A Biography of the Works through Mavra*. 2 vols. Oxford: Oxford University Press, 1996. A heavyweight two-volume survey by a former pupil of historian Paul Henry Lang that has more of interest to say about peripheral figures such as Maximilian Steinberg, the composer's brother-in-law, than about Stravinsky's own creative processes. Discussion of the composer's neoclassical period (1924–1950) after Mavra is omitted, the study ending with a patchwork of late technical analyses purporting to identify the Russian origins of the composer's controversial serial aesthetic.

Thomas, Tony. *Music for the Movies*. New York: Barnes, 1973.

Vlad, Roman. *Stravinsky*. Trans. Frederick Fuller. 3rd ed. London: Oxford University Press, 1978.

von Langsdorff, G. H. *Voyages and Travels in Various Parts of the World, during the Years 1803, 1804, 1805, 1806, and 1807*. London: Colburn, 1813.

Watkins, Glenn. *The Gesualdo Hex: Music, Myth, and Memory*. Preface by Claudio Abbado. New York: Norton, 2010. A modestly instructive survey of the American early music renaissance that inspired Stravinsky's interest in Gesualdo and reinterpretation in *Agon* of French classical dance forms. Watkins is also illuminating on Stravinsky's sincere and explicit admiration of John Cage.

White, Eric Walter. *Stravinsky: The Composer and His Works*. 1966. 2nd ed. London: Faber & Faber, 1979. White's revised and updated edition of his earlier graceful *Survey* remains a valuable study resource for further reading, free of the polemics exhibited in more recent high-profile publications.

———. *Stravinsky: A Critical Survey*. London: Lehmann, 1947.

Yates, Peter. *Twentieth Century Music: Its Evolution from the End of the Harmonic Era into the Present Era of Sound*. London: Allen & Unwin, 1968. A sympathetic account of Stravinsky's late music from the perspective of American modernism by a colleague of Lawrence Morton and cofounder of the Los Angeles Evenings on the Roof concert series.

SELECT LISTENING

This abbreviated selection of CD titles from my reference collection is intended to draw attention to rare, meritorious, historic, and unusual items, not all of which are included in the recommended core Sony composer's edition.

Agon, Rite of Spring, Symphony in Three Movements (1994, 1995, 1993). Decca C20, 2012. Vladimir Ashkenazy and the Berlin Royal Symphony Orchestra in vital performances with sharply defined timbres and great depth of percussion.

American Classics: Genesis Suite (1945). Seven settings of the Old Testament by Schoenberg, Shilkret, Tansman, Milhaud, Castelnuovo-Tedesco, Toch, and Stravinsky, originally commissioned by Nathaniel Shilkret, conducted by Gerard Schwarz. Naxos, Milken Archive, 2004. First recording of the complete orchestral suite allowing Stravinsky's *Babel* to be heard in context of Schoenberg's *Prelude*.

American Stravinsky: The Composer, Volume 4, conducted by Robert Craft. MusicMasters, 1993. Includes *Greeting Prelude* (1955), *The Star-Spangled Banner* (1941), the original jazz version of *Scherzo à la Russe* (1944), the *Balanchine-Stravinsky Chorale* (1946), the composer's setting of a four-line stanza, and melody composed by George Balanchine for the composer's sixty-fourth birthday.

Boulez dirige Stravinsky, Debussy, Bartók, Berg. Les grands concerts inédits du Théâtre des Champs-Elysées. Concert du 18.6.1963. Disques Montaigne (1987). Rare early Boulez recordings of *Quatre Etudes pour Orchestre*, *Le Roi des Etoiles* (Zvezdoliki), *Symphonie[s] pour instruments à vent*, *Sermon, Narration et Prière* (A Sermon, Narrative, and Prayer), and *Le Sacre du Printemps* (Rite of Spring).

Canticum Sacrum, Agon, Requiem Canticles, conducted by Michael Gielen. SWR Hanssler Classic, 2008. Crisp, laid-back accounts of late Stravinsky masterpieces by the distinguished SWF German radio orchestra and conductor.

Firebird, complete, conducted by Franz Welser-Möst. EMI Classics, 1997 (1993). A superbly integrated and graded performance with an uncanny unity of tempo and pitch.

Histoire du Soldat (Suite). *The Robert Craft Collection: Music of Igor Stravinsky, Vol. 7.* Naxos, 2007 (some tracks previously issued on MusicMasters, 1991). Includes *Pastorale*, arranged by Stravinsky and Samuel Dushkin for violin and wind quartet (1924), with the unpublished *Pour Picasso* for solo clarinet (1917) and *Song of the Volga Boatmen*, arranged for wind instruments (1917).

Igor Strawinsky: Le Domaine Musical de Pierre Boulez. Adès, 1991 (reissue of Vega, 1956, and Adès, 1962, 1969). Landmark recordings of *Renard*, conducted by Pierre Boulez, *Three Pieces for String Quartet*, by the Parrenin Quartet, and *Three Japanese Lyrics*, conducted by Gilbert Amy, with premiere mono recordings from 1956 of the *Vom Himmel Hoch Choral Variations* and *Canticum Sacrum* with exemplary soloists Jean Giraudeau and Xavier De-Praz, conducted by Robert Craft and recorded in St. Mark's Basilica, Venice.

Igor Stravinsky the Composer, Volume 1, conducted by Robert Craft. MusicMasters, 1991. Includes *Oedipus Rex*, narrated by Paul Newman, *Apollo Pas de Deux* (1927–1928), and *Fanfare for Three Trumpets* (1953; from sketches for *Agon*).

The Klemperer Legacy: *Symphony in Three Movements*. EMI Classics, 2000 (recorded 1965). The aged conductor brings a fierce resolve and determination to a work of resistance composed when both were neighbors in exile in Beverly Hills.

Les Noces. Pokrovsky Ensemble, arranged and conducted by Dmitri Pokrovsky. Elektra Nonesuch, 1994. Instrumentation of *Les Noces* re-created with American expertise for Apple Macintosh synthesizer, sung in authentic peasant style with a selection of Russian village wedding songs identified with Stravinsky's composition. A vivid glimpse of the work's ethnic origins, arguably also of the composer's stated conception of a mechanically instrumentated work.

Movements for Piano and Orchestra, conducted by Yuri Nikolaevsky. Revelation, 1997 (recorded 1984). A sparkling, dancelike, and nuanced interpretation by Sviatoslav Richter of one of Stravinsky's hermetic late scores, bringing out an unexpected, hidden plaintiveness of the composer's Tchaikovskian heritage.

Movements for Piano and Orchestra: Stravinsky, Volume 11, conducted by Robert Craft. MusicMasters, 1998. Also includes a spine-tingling original setting of the Russian song *Sektanskaya* (1919) for soprano, flute, and cimbalom.

Persephone live recording (1960) with Fritz Wunderlich (tenor) and Hessische Rundfunk choirs and orchestra, conducted by Dean Dixon. Audite, 2011. Sublime performance in German of a work of special resonance for Europe in the grip of the Cold War.

Petrushka, Rite of Spring, Four Etudes, conducted by Antal Dorati (1959, 1964). Clean, airy Mercury reissue (1993) of classic Living Presence recordings using just three overhead Telefunken microphones direct to half-inch tape.

Piano Music. Victor Sangiorgio, Naxos, 2008 (reissue of Collins Classics, 1993). Includes the early *Scherzo* (1902) and *Piano Sonata in F Sharp Minor* (1903–1904).

Pianola Works. Reproducing piano editions by Pleyela and Aeolian articulated by push-up pianola at a Baldwin concert grand piano under the supervision of pianolist Rex Lawson. MusicMasters, 1994. Piano rolls of *Petrushka*, *Etude for Pianola*, and *Rite of Spring*.

Picasso et la Musique. Centre George Pompidou (Paris), 1997. Compilation of rare and historic recordings illustrative of the musical traditions of Andalusia and collaborations with Picasso, juxtaposing piano rolls by Manuel de Falla from 1913, a 1930 recording by Arthur Rubinstein of Falla's *Ritual Fire Dance*, authentic flamenco, and "Sinfonia" from Stravinsky's *Pulcinella*.

Pierre Boulez Conducts Stravinsky. A budget price six-CD collection of Boulez recordings for DG (2010), including rarities *3 Pieces for Clarinet solo*, *Concertino for String Quartet*, *Elegy for Viola Solo* (1943), *Eight Instrumental Miniatures*, *Ebony Concerto*, *Concerto in E flat "Dumbarton Oaks"* (1937–1938), the original vocalized version of *Pastorale for Voice and Four Wind Instruments* and *Two Sacred Songs*, transcribed from Hugo Wolf (1968), along with superb versions of the major ballets and symphonies and an especially poignant interpretation with the Berlin Philharmonic of the *Symphony of Psalms* from 1999.

Rite of Spring. Orchestral version to the original timing of the Pleyela piano roll edition, conducted by Benjamin Zander, with pianola version by Rex Lawson. Pickwick International, 1989. A 20 percent (5:4) increase of tempo for the climactic Danse Sacrale in the composer-supervised piano roll edition persuaded conductor Zander that it might indicate the originally intended tempo, a culmination of accent quintuplets repeatedly punctuating the musical fabric. His reinstatement of the extreme tempo with the semiprofessional Boston Philharmonic Orchestra is plausible, well executed, and highly exciting.

Rite of Spring, Petrushka. Live recordings by Israel Philharmonic Orchestra. DG, 1984. Complete takes of two great ballet scores by an aging but inspired Leonard Bernstein showing a marvelously supple and persuasive feeling for rhythm and line.

Stravinsky: 125th Anniversary Album. Naxos, 2007. Includes *The Rite of Spring* in a version incorporating Stravinsky's corrections to the score from 1947 and 1967.

Stravinsky in America. BMG-RCA Victor Red Seal compilation conducted by Michael Tilson Thomas, 1996. Includes the symphonic version of *Scherzo à la Russe*, the 1964 *Variations: Aldous Huxley in Memoriam*, *Concertino* in the 1954 arrangement for twelve instruments, and the enigmatic *Canon on a Russian Popular Tune* (1965).

Stravinsky in Moscow 1962. Live recordings (Melodiya, 1962; reissued BMG, 1996) from the composer's 1962 return visit to Russia, as chronicled by Robert Craft (*Chronicle*, 179–208), a program including *Fireworks* (1908) and *Orpheus* (1948).

Stravinsky Orchestral Miniatures. Orpheus Chamber Orchestra (1995, 1996). Brilliant Classics, 2009 (DG, 2000). Chamber works including the jazz version of *Scherzo à la Russe*, *Suites 1 and 2 for Small Orchestra*, *Fanfare for a New Theatre*, and the unpublished *Lied ohne Namen: Duet for Two Bassoons* from 1918 (EWW 604).

Stravinsky Plays Stravinsky. Masters of the Piano Roll series. Dal Segno, 2004. Digital transcription of Duo-Art piano rolls by Stravinsky of the *Piano Sonata* (1924) and two-piano reductions of the *Concerto for Piano and Wind Instruments* (1924) and the complete *Firebird*, clearly delineating the priorities and structural layering of the original scores.

Stravinsky—Prokofiev. EMI Classics compilation (1989) of EMI France mono recordings of *Divertimento* (suite from *The Fairy's Kiss*) originally recorded in 1954, *Pulcinella* (1954), an authorized sixteen-minute "short suite" of *Petrushka* (1954), together with a London Abbey Road stereo recording of *Rite of Spring* from 1959, conducted by "the second Igor," Diaghilev protégé Igor Markevitch, with ballets by Prokofiev.

Stravinsky the Composer, Vol. 7. MusicMasters, 1995. Includes the composer's arrangement of *La Marseillaise* for violin solo (1919), the Satie-esque *Waltz for Children* for piano solo (1917), the composer's aphoristic last original composition, *Two Sketches for a Sonata* (1966–1967) for piano solo, along with the composer's augmented instrumentations of Gesualdo madrigals *Monumentum pro Gesualdo ad CD Annum* of 1960.

Three Movements from "Petrushka." Maurizio Pollini, DG (1972; reissued 1995).

Works of Igor Stravinsky. Sony Classical (2007; twenty-two CDs). Recommended budget price edition of the composer's collected recordings for Columbia, conducted by Stravinsky and Robert Craft.

INDEX

ABOUT THE AUTHOR

Robin Maconie is a New Zealand–born musicologist and composer. Born in 1942, he majored in music and English literature at Victoria University of Wellington under Frederick Page and Roger Savage before traveling to Europe for postgraduate studies with Olivier Messiaen in Paris (1963–1964) and electronic composition and music theory with Bernd-Alois Zimmermann, Herbert Eimert, Karlheinz Stockhausen, Henri Pousseur, and others in Cologne (1964–1965). A specialist in the music of Stockhausen and the European avant-garde, he brings to difficult new music idioms an understanding of ideas and procedures from the history and philosophy of music technology. He is the author of *Musicologia: Musical Knowledge from Plato to John Cage* (2010) and *Avant Garde: An American Odyssey from Gertrude Stein to Pierre Boulez* (2012), where he identifies the important role played by musical concepts in the history of science, philology, and philosophy. Specialist knowledge of technical issues in information theory and applications has also enabled him to identify trends in avant-garde music and literature since 1945, including the music of Stravinsky, Boulez, Stockhausen, and John Cage, with high-priority research initiatives in cognition, communications science, linguistic theory, and artificial intelligence, and to use that information to defend the integrity of musical modernism in the past decade against a continuing backwash of high-profile academic incredulity. He returned to New Zealand in 2002 and lives in Dannevirke.